FAMOUS
BRITISH GENERALS

FAMOUS
BRITISH GENERALS

Edited by Barrett Parker

CONTRIBUTORS

The Hon. Sir John Fortescue · Major-General J. F. C. Fuller

Captain B. H. Liddell Hart · Sir George Arthur

The Rt. Hon. Winston S. Churchill · Major H. A. De Weerd

Captain Cyril Falls

LONDON
NICHOLSON & WATSON

These Essays were
first published in this form
by
Ivor Nicholson & Watson Ltd.,
26 Manchester Square,
London W.1
1951

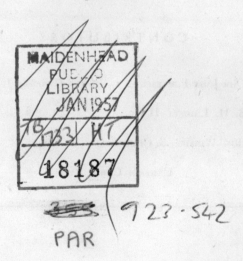
Printed and Bound in Great Britain by

LOVE AND MALCOMSON LTD., London and Redhill

To My Father

CONTENTS

LIST OF ILLUSTRATIONS

(The maps are given in the Index.   See "Maps")

FOREWORD

THE essays in this book are not intended to comprise a definitive study of British generals. They have been collected at will and at the discretion of the editor. They do presume to bring together in chronological sequence nine men who have affected the course of English history by their leadership.

It has been said that great crises produce great men to meet them. Whatever the truth of that statement may be, the fact remains that in time of war, Britain has been served by men of vision, integrity and skill in their profession. The number of fighting men whose names have found a place in the pages of her history would appear to indicate a vast number of crises. I prefer to emphasize the point that they indicate the number of able men available for service in a common cause. Furthermore, regardless of where we look in a long history we discover the enduring tradition of public service. That tradition has often proved the pricking goad to notable achievement and has established itself among the vital inheritances of the country.

It is with difficulty that anyone can select a few men to represent so large and so strong a company. He who has the temerity to undertake a selection is at once aware that his choices mean omissions. The temptation is to begin early in history and to include many. It would have been interesting and in many ways profitable to have included, for example, Richard the Lion Heart and Henry the Fifth, but it would have led to a long and ultimately a divided book and seemed unfeasible. It is generally agreed that the division between medieval and modern warfare in England came with Cromwell. Therefore, it is with Cromwell that we begin, omitting some of the most colourful and exciting periods of British arms in order to abide, in more limited scope, by the injunctions of consistency.

Lord Wavell (then General Sir Archibald Wavell) some years ago gave a series of lectures at Cambridge University on the subject of "Generals and Generalship," in which he quoted Socrates concerning the qualities needed by the good general:

"The general must know how to get his men their rations and every other kind of stores needed for war. He must have imagination to originate plans, practical sense and energy to carry them through. He must be observant, untiring, shrewd; kindly and cruel; simple and crafty; a watchman and a robber; lavish and miserly; generous and stingy; rash and conservative. All these and many other qualities, natural and acquired, he must have!"

Lord Wavell later spoke of the moral qualities needed by the good general:

"He must have 'character' which simply means that he knows what he wants and has the courage and determination to get it. He should have a genuine interest in, and a real knowledge of, humanity, the raw material of his trade; and most vital of all, he must have the fighting spirit, the will to win. You all know and recognize it in sport—the man who plays his best when things are going badly, who has the power to come back at you when apparently beaten, and who refuses to acknowledge defeat. There is one other moral quality I should stress as the mark of the really great commander as distinguished from the ordinary general. He must have the spirit of adventure, a touch of the gambler in him. As Napoleon said: 'If the art of war consisted merely in not taking risks, glory would be at the mercy of very mediocre talent.'—The general who allows himself to be bound and hampered by regulations is unlikely to win a battle."

It is left to the reader to decide whether the men described in the following pages had the qualities of the great commander as prescribed by Lord Wavell. I believe that all

had some of those qualities to a marked degree. As you will
notice, Wavell is among them.

One of the sobering facts of history is that the opportunity
to execute great generalship is often linked with the obliga-
tion to administer wise statesmanship. Crises of national
dimensions require leadership of the highest order. In the
case of each of the men whose record and achievement is
portrayed in this book, it becomes apparent that he was
not merely fighting a war or winning a battle. Upon him
in considerable measure rested the outcome of a national or
an international emergency. The robustness to withstand
the rigours of a campaign was not all that was required.
In addition was demanded the quality of character to share
the weight of national anxiety as well as the burden of a
nation's peril. Cromwell, Marlborough, Wellington,
Kitchener, Haig, Allenby, Wavell, Alexander and
Montgomery, all have been called upon to carry statesmen's
obligations on warriors' shoulders.

Some readers will possibly be saying: 'This is all well and
good, but what of the men in the eighteenth and nineteenth
centuries whose service was so conspicuous and whose
records you are omitting?' The names of Wolfe, of Gordon,
of Napier and of Roberts, together with others, have
been considered and finally set aside because it was felt
that upon no one of them did the safety of the nation in
any ultimate sense depend. It is open to fair debate whether
Allenby, Alexander and Montgomery rank in equal position
beside the others. It must be pointed out, however, that
they have borne a heavy share of exacting responsibility
and they have independently proved themselves masterful
soldiers in the field.

Perhaps a brief comment on the author of the essays on
Wavell and Montgomery is not inappropriate. They are
the only two essays in the book written by an American.
Professor H. A. De Weerd was historian of the Operations
Division of the War Department General Staff in 1945–1946.
His contributions to military journals are among the most
significant that have appeared. It should be added that six of
the essays in the present collection have been published
before and are reprinted through the courtesy of the authors

and the permission of the publishers. They are: *Cromwell* from *Six British Soldiers*, by the Hon. Sir John Fortescue, by arrangement with the publishers, Williams & Norgate, Ltd. ; *Kitchener* from the volume, *From Wellington to Wavell*, by Sir George Arthur, by arrangement with Hutchinson & Co., Ltd.; *Haig*, from *Great Contemporaries*, by the Rt. Hon. Winston S. Churchill, published by Macmillan & Co., Ltd.; *Allenby*, from *Reputations* by Captain B. H. Liddell Hart, published by John Murray; *Wavell*, from *Great Soldiers of the Two World Wars*, by H. A. De Weerd, by arrangement with W. W. Norton & Co., New York; *Montgomery*, from *Great Soldiers of the Two World Wars* by H. A. De Weerd, by arrangement with W. W. Norton & Co., New York. The essays on *Marlborough* by Major-General J. F. C. Fuller, *Wellington*, by Captain B. H. Liddell Hart and *Alexander*, by Captain Cyril Falls, have been written for this volume.

I should like to express my thanks to the Victoria and Albert Museum for permission to reproduce the portrait of the Duke of Wellington by Sir Thomas Lawrence; to the Royal Engineers Headquarters Mess, Chatham, for permission to reproduce the portrait of Earl Kitchener by Sir Arthur S. Cope; to Earl Haig for permission to reproduce the portrait of his father, the first Earl Haig, by Mr. James Guthrie; to the late Earl Wavell for permission to reproduce a portrait of himself by Mr. James Gunn; and to the Haileybury and Imperial Service College for permission to reproduce the portrait of Viscount Allenby by Sir Oswald Birley. I should like to express my particular thanks to Mr. Maurice Codner for permission to reproduce his portrait of Viscount Alexander which was exhibited at the Royal Academy in 1946, and to Mr. James Gunn for permission to reproduce his portrait of Viscount Montgomery. Both Mr. Codner and Mr. Gunn have permitted the heads and shoulders of these subjects to be reproduced without their respective backgrounds.

The task of reading and selecting was aided immeasurably by the professional knowledge of Major Marshal O'Donovan, formerly of the War Office, by the kindly cooperation of the librarians of the War Office Library, by the generous interest of Mrs. Phyllis Biscoe of the English Speaking Union, and by the precise and scholarly advice of Mr. A. K. Adams, Director of the National Portrait Gallery.

B. P.
London, March, 1951.

OLIVER CROMWELL

CROMWELL

By

The Hon. Sir John Fortescue

In the year 1642, when King and Parliament first came to
blows, the military organization of the country hardly
existed even in name. Under Elizabeth it had been imperfect,
and under the Stuarts it had sunk into utter decay. James I
avoided war as far as possible, but, when at last he came to
open breach with Spain in 1624, he could send only a
rabble to Holland to help the Dutch against the Spaniards.
Charles, more enterprising, sent out two expeditions, one
to Cadiz in 1625 and one to the Isle of Rhé in 1627. Both
failed ignominiously, the men being of the worst quality,
without training and discipline of any kind. It was in the
service of foreign states, principally in Holland and Sweden,
but also in France, Spain, Denmark, Austria and even
Russia that English and Scottish officers and regiments
maintained the fighting reputation of their race. For defence
at home not less than for aggression abroad England was,
as a military nation, impotent. The militia or trained
bands of the counties were absolutely worthless. In London
there were fifteen regiments which, though imperfectly
disciplined, were at least more or less practised in the handling of arms; and even these owed, perhaps, such efficiency
as they possessed to the voluntary enthusiasm of societies
of amateurs.

The first task of both sides then was to call an armed force
into being. At first they scrambled for the command of the

militia, which was a prize not worth the winning; but soon they settled down to raise and train such men as they could get. As usual, at the outset, plenty of volunteers were forthcoming, but, once again as usual, the ardour of these soon cooled down; and after a year both sides resorted to impressment. The Royalists had the advantage that most, though not all, of the gentry were on their side, and that these, from the mere fact of their social standing, were accustomed to handle weapons. On the other hand, every county magnate wished to raise and command a regiment all to himself, with the result that they produced a vast number of units of very unequal strength, making organization a matter of great difficulty. The same trouble arose later, notably during the American War of Independence and the war of the French Revolution, and was a source of constant vexation to the military authorities. The Parliament on their side had the City of London at their back, which ensured to them not only solid financial support, but also the services of the one body of more or less trained infantry in the Kingdom.

The art of war was at this period in a state of transition, standing somewhere midway between Crecy and Blenheim. In medieval days the mailed mounted men had at first borne down everything before them. The Swiss infantry had responded by arming themselves with long pikes and forming themselves into dense masses into which no horseman could penetrate. This was to oppose shock-action to shock-action. The English with the long-bow introduced efficient missile action, dismounting their mailed men-at-arms and forming them into solid blocks as a refuge for the archers when threatened with shock-action. Then fire-arms came in and superseded bows; and the infantry was divided into two elements, pikemen for shock-action and musketeers for missile action, the rule being at first that a regiment should contain equal numbers of both. The mailed men tried to secure themselves against the new missiles by adding to the weight of their armour, but before long gave up the attempt in despair. They availed themselves, however, of the new missile weapon by arming themselves with pistols or carbines, and, instead of trying to break in among the pikemen, halted within close range and fired at them. The pikemen met these tactics by covering themselves with armour to mid-thigh, which served fairly well for protection but was intolerably heavy to bear on the march and wore men down even on the battlefield. However, the general result was that cavalry at this time was more of a missile than a shock-arm, though the horse always continued as the most formidable engine of shock-action. On the whole, therefore, the cavalry remained the most formidable portion of an army, and orthodox opinion laid down that the proportion of horsemen to footmen should be one to two. The Royalists at first generally brought into the field an even greater proportion of horse, the country magnates having plenty of horses and of men to ride them.

With the cavalry wholly and the infantry in part committed to missile action, the great problem was how, with the existing weapons, to maintain a continuous fire. The first idea was to mass men, whether mounted or afoot, ten ranks deep, when each rank should fire in succession, file to the rear and reload. In practice it was found that men who had once filed to the rear tended to disappear from the field. Then the contrary system was tried—that the ranks should file to the front in succession—; but this again was not very satisfactory. Gustavus Adolphus went further than anyone else in reform by reducing the ten ranks to six, "doubling" these again into three, making the front rank kneel and the second and third ranks stand, and so firing a volley of all three ranks. The next refinement was division of the companies into platoons, which fired volleys in succession, first the odd-numbered, then the even-numbered platoons, so that the fire was always travelling from end to end of the line and yet there was time for the platoons to reload.

The theory of the infantry attack was that the musketeers should prepare the way by missile action for the advance of the pikes to shock-action; and sometimes it was carried out. But the missile weapons were very imperfect. They might be match-locks, wheel-locks, or flint-locks. The match-lock, which was the common arm for infantry, required a long length of smouldering match held between the finger

of the musketeer, one burning end of which match was
fixed, in action, to the cock of the musket and was brought
down to the priming by the pressure of the trigger. The whole
business of firing as well as of loading was thus both clumsy
and dangerous. Misfires were frequent, for a puff of wind
might blow the priming away; and flying sparks from one
man's match might kindle the pan of another man's musket
and discharge it prematurely with possible death to a
comrade in front. Match-locks in consequence were never
allowed near the artillery, who kept their powder in barrels
to rear of the guns. They were, of course, out of the
question for cavalry, as also were wheel-locks, which
required winding up after each discharge. Cavalry, therefore,
always carried fire-locks; but as they had a horse and a
sword, they were never disarmed and could always fall back
on shock-action. Indeed, it became the rule later—and no
doubt there were instances in the Civil War—for cavalry
to empty their pistols once, throw them in the enemy's face
and strike in with the sword. So, too, the musketeers, though
nominally a missile arm, would attack at close quarters with
the butt. The truth is that the missile action of the time,
though occasionally very effective under favourable conditions, must have been most uncertain. Very severe
grounding in the manual and firing exercise must have been
necessary to make an efficient musketeer; and, beyond that,
the drill of both cavalry and infantry was most difficult.
The men fell in, not shoulder to shoulder, but with an interval between them sufficient to admit the entry of another
man or another horse, so that the ranks might be "doubled";
and the correct judgment of this interval must have led to
much confusion.

As to the artillery there is not much to be said. The guns
were mostly so cumbrous and heavy that they generally
lagged on the march; and, their teams and drivers being
hired (as they continued to be until 1793), a gun once placed
in position, rightly or wrongly, was likely to remain where
it was until the action was over. Light pieces seem to have
been attached by ones and twos to each regiment of infantry,
like the battalion-guns of a later day, but they seldom
counted for very much. The rate of firing was slow, for the

powder (as already mentioned) was carried in barrels and was introduced into the gun with an iron ladle; and if a gunner forgot the important duty of covering the open barrel with a sheepskin before each round was fired, there was the practical certainty of an explosion.

As to war at large, it had by no means lost its medieval character of a game of profit for those of the military profession, a game attended indeed with great risks but offering also great prizes in the way of plunder and ransom. Pillage and wanton destruction were still an essential part of it; and the dearth of roads—excepting the paved roads left by the Romans—made transport a matter of extreme difficulty. Armies consequently lived, as a rule, on the country; and, no matter what rules and regulations are laid down, what rations are fixed and what requisitions are made, an army that lives on the country can hardly be maintained in proper discipline. Napoleon tried the experiment for twenty years and failed.

*   *   *   *   *

Such briefly was the state of military organization in England and such the current practice of war in Western Europe. Two parties were going to work anxiously and busily to raise rival armies. Both had officers who had served and learned their business under great captains abroad. Of the Swedish school of Gustavus Adolphus, the Royalists had Jacob Astley, and the Parliament Crawford Ramsay and many other Scots; of the Dutch school of Maurice of Nassau, there were Goring on the King's side, Philip Skippon and Balfour on the Parliament's. Two more Royalists, Ralph Hopton and Gage, had borne arms under the Kings of Bohemia and Spain. Which of these was to make an English Army, and that a victorious English Army? Not one. The work was to be done by a little country squire of the Eastern Counties, son of a younger son of a good family, a big-limbed, coarse-featured, harsh-voiced man with little regard to his personal appearance, named Oliver Cromwell. He had been his own master ever since he had come of age, having lost his father at the age of eighteen, and had lived quietly, looking to his fields and herds and transacting county business for twenty-two years since then, only going up to London for the Parliamentary Sessions of 1628 and 1629 as member for Huntingdon, and in 1640 again as member for Cambridge. At the age of forty-three he was to discover his vocation as a soldier, an example without a parallel in our history until Thomas Graham, in 1793, made the like discovery at the age of forty-six.

His first military business was to raise a troop of horse—troop No. 67 of Lord Essex's army—sixty men strong, with which he went into action at Edgehill on October 21, 1642. This was a confused, indecisive business, which need not detain us, save for Cromwell's famous conversation with John Hampden when it was over. "Your troops," said Oliver, "are most of them decayed serving-men and tapsters; their troops are gentlemen's sons and persons of quality. Do you think the spirits of such base and mean fellows will ever be able to encounter gentlemen who have courage, honour and resolution in them? You must get men of a spirit that is likely to go as far as gentlemen will go, or you will be beaten still." Hampden said that it was a good notion but impracticable. Cromwell thought differently.

By the spring of 1643 he was a Colonel, no longer commanding one troop, but many, raising and to be raised. His recruits were the sons of Puritan yeomen and farmers of the Eastern Counties, men of education and of substance, who brought their own horses with them to the muster. The quarrel that divided King and Parliament was as much religious as political, so much so that it was difficult to disentangle the religion from the politics. Cromwell, himself something of a religious fanatic, was careful to enlist steady men of good character and to exact from them a high standard of moral conduct. In his view duty—obedience to God's orders—was the first step to discipline—obedience to man's orders. A good man could not be a bad soldier nor a bad soldier a good man. In war, as Napoleon said, moral force is to physical as four to one, and it was moral force that Cromwell strove above all to inspire into his troops—the indefinable sense of superiority which gives victory to fighting men. Swearing, drinking, impiety, plundering were all alike sternly repressed; and the inclusion of plundering in this list shows that Cromwell had broken away from old military traditions. There was nothing quite new in this. The Huguenot Commander La Noue in the sixteenth century trained his own regiment upon exactly the same lines; and it is possible that his military treatise, which was translated into English, had fallen into Cromwell's hands. But the idea of combining military with moral discipline recurs constantly through history. Some of the Spanish guerilla-bands raised during the Peninsular War were as sternly ruled by their leaders as ever were the Ironsides by Cromwell.

The qualifications laid down by him for officers were the same as for the men. "If you choose honest godly men to be Captains of Horse, honest men will follow them. . . . I had rather have a plain russet-coated Captain who knows what he fights for and loves what he knows, than that which you call a gentleman and is nothing else. I honour a gentleman that is so indeed." In fact, what Cromwell asked for in all ranks was, in his own phrase, men who made some conscience of what they did; but he did not underrate the value of those who, besides answering to this requirement, enjoyed through social position the habit of command.

For the rest the military spirit latent in this country squire seems to have blazed out from the moment that he had men to command. Where and how he learned his drill, whether from books or from some veteran of foreign wars, and how he trained his corporals and his men, we can only guess. According to the practice of the time, a Colonel had a troop of his own, and Cromwell evidently took great pride in it. "I have a lovely company; you would respect them if you did know them." And from scattered indications it should seem he was vigilant and swift in all minor matters within his district. He had evidently good information as to the opinions and doings of all powerful neighbours, characteristic of a man who was later to possess the most efficient secret service in Europe. Good intelligence, prompt decision, immediate action—we see signs of all this in him from the first—and it is thus that a commander wins confidence.

His troops were soon tested in the field. In May, 1643, they defeated a force of twice their number at Grantham.

Two months later they rendered a more signal service. The King had formulated a good plan of campaign, which was so successfully carried out, up to a point, that there lay nothing between his northern army, under Lord Newcastle, and London except Cromwell's force. Advancing with cavalry and infantry, Cromwell met Newcastle's vanguard of horse and defeated successively this, its support and its reserve, by skilful manœuvring, and then found himself face to face with Newcastle's main body. His infantry at once ran away, but the horse, though weary after a long day's fighting, stood fast, and Cromwell drew them off by alternate bodies without the loss of a man. The time thus gained was the salvation of London; but the remarkable point is that Cromwell knew by instinct how to conduct a retreat when pressed by a very superior force, for there is nothing about withdrawal by alternate bodies in the contemporary text-books. That his men, after the flight of the infantry, should have behaved so staunchly speaks eloquently for their discipline.

We must pass over Winceby fight, where Cromwell's troopers went into action singing psalms and charged home, although their leader had his horse shot under him and came very near his death; and we must come to Marston Moor, on July 2, 1644. There Cromwell commanded the left wing of horse, being opposed to Rupert himself. Having taught his men to rally as well as to charge, he completely defeated the opposing horse, and, though the Parliamentary right wing had been routed and most of its centre dispersed, was able to turn the fight into a victory.

The whole issue of the war had been hitherto so doubtful, and the discontent excited in the country by undisciplined hosts living upon it was so great, that the Parliament now resolved to form a permanent, disciplined, regularly paid army and make an end of matters. The idea was not wholly Cromwell's. It was Sir William Waller who gave the Parliamentary leaders to understand that it must be done; but it was Cromwell who had shown how it could be done.

So the remnants of three so-called armies were taken as a nucleus round which to form what was called the New Model. Fresh recruits were impressed, and a regular army was organized of twelve regiments of foot, each of ten companies of one hundred and twenty men apiece, eleven regiments of horse, each with six troops of one hundred men apiece, one regiment of dragoons (mounted infantry) with ten companies of one hundred men apiece; while two more regiments of infantry with two companies of fire-locks were attached to the train of artillery. The whole amounted to about twenty-four thousand men. Cromwell's regiment of horse ranked as the Sixth but his services were too urgently required, to watch the country round the King's headquarters at Oxford, for him to join the New Model during its training at Windsor. It was not until the eve of Naseby that he reached it, with the rank of second in command to Sir Thomas Fairfax, having six hundred troopers at his back. In the battle of the following day, June 14, 1645, Cromwell commanded the right wing of horse and was chiefly responsible for the victory. Probably the Parliamentary leaders, though there was already much jealousy and dread of him, counted upon him to direct all military matters, for, after the action, he wrote a dispatch to the Speaker of the House of Commons commending not only the men but also his superior officer, Fairfax, which seems rather a curious proceeding. However, as the New Model pursued its victorious march to the west, Cromwell was once again charged by Fairfax to inform the Speaker of the storm of Bristol, whence it would appear that Cromwell was virtually the commander-in-chief. A little later he was detached to direct the siege of Basing House, where Lord Winchester had for three years defied the utmost efforts of the Parliamentary forces. Cromwell, bringing up heavy cannon, made short work of Basing House, which was stormed and sacked from roof to cellar. He then rejoined Fairfax in the west; and in April, 1646, the work of the army being practically done, he returned to London to receive the thanks of Parliament. A few months later the Royalists were utterly quelled, and the first civil war was over.

By that time the New Model, thanks to plenty of hanging and other sharp punishment in the course of fifteen months' service in the field, had been hammered into a really efficient instrument. It had served its purpose; it was very expensive;

and the country was anxious to be relieved of the burden. The Parliament, with the usual and inevitable jealousy of politicians towards soldiers, was specially eager to disband it, but they were not equally eager to discharge the arrears of pay due to it—some £330,000. They tried by every kind of discreditable shift to get rid of the men without getting rid of the money, and were so foolish as to alienate the officers also by negligence and insult. Cromwell for long did his utmost, at the risk of forfeiting the confidence of the soldiers, to uphold the authority of Parliament, and at one time he even contemplated carrying his sword, with any men who would follow him, to the wars in Germany. The army showed prolonged patience, but at last broke into open mutiny, and Cromwell and Fairfax, despairing of obtaining justice for them by other means, placed themselves at their head and, marching to London, forcibly purged the House of Commons of the hostile majority. No man wanted a military revolution less than Cromwell, but it was forced upon him by the politicians.

In 1648 the war broke out anew with Royalist risings in Kent and Wales, which kept Fairfax and Cromwell busily employed; and meanwhile the King having thrown himself into the arms of the Scots, a Scottish army on July 8, crossed the border and occupied Carlisle. On July 11, Cromwell having received the surrender of Pembroke, which he had for three weeks been besieging, marched north to meet the invasion. A small Parliamentary force under Colonel Lambert, lay about Barnard Castle in Durham, and Cromwell, having no guns, but hoping to find some in the north, set out to join Lambert, sending the bulk of his cavalry in advance. The march was a miserable one. The rain was continuous, the roads were almost impassable, and most of the infantry were both shoeless and stockingless. The Scots meanwhile in a very leisurely fashion trailed southward through Lancashire; and Lambert, seeing his left turned, fell back upon Knaresborough, where, on August 13, Cromwell, having received artillery from Hull, came up with him. Even then Cromwell's numbers were well under nine thousand men, whereas the Scots were reckoned at twenty thousand. Their main body was then

at Preston, with a body of some four thousand English under
Sir Marmaduke Langdale a few miles to north-east to serve
as a flank-guard, and their cavalry strung out to southward
as far as Wigan. Cromwell decided to strike swiftly and at
once. Leaving his artillery behind for the sake of greater
speed, he marched westward, and, after three arduous days
spent in traversing a wild and difficult country, arrived on
the evening of the 16th at Stonyhurst, a few miles to north-
east of Preston. He decided to attack the enemy on the north
side of the Ribble rather than cross the river to head back
the Scottish vanguard; and on the 17th he fell furiously
upon Langdale. This detachment made a stubborn fight
but was overpowered by superior numbers, and Cromwell,
pressing on, cut off a portion of the Scots before they could
cross the river. The enemy meanwhile was streaming southward upon Wigan, and Cromwell, leaving four thousand
men to hold Preston, followed hard at their heels, hunting
them on until dusk of the 17th. On the two succeeding
days the chase was pressed beyond Warrington, some
thirty miles from the battlefield, when Cromwell made
over the pursuit to Lambert, his men and horses being
utterly exhausted. "The Scots are so tired and in such
confusion," he wrote, "that if my horse could but trot after
them we should take them all, but we are so weary we can
scarce be able to do more than walk after them. . . . My
horse are miserably beaten out and we have ten thousand
prisoners." The Scots, utterly worn out and discouraged,
surrendered on the 22nd, and Cromwell turned about and
marched northward to make an end of Royalism in
Scotland.

How his army was fed during this march from Wales to
Yorkshire and back to Warrington we have unfortunately
nothing to show us, but that the business was done with
decency and order we may be sure. "Want of shoes and
stockings," wrote one of his officers from Leicester while on
the march from Pembroke to Knaresborough, "gives
discouragement to our soldiers, having received no pay these
many months to buy them, nor can we procure any unless
we plunder, which was never heard of by any under the
Lieutenant-General's conduct nor will be, though they march

barefoot, which many have done since our advance from Wales." So too when he crossed the Scottish marches Cromwell issued an order that any officer or man guilty of taking or demanding money, goods or victuals or "abusing the people in any sort" should be tried by a Council of War and punished according to the articles of war, "which punishment is death." A complaint of pillage by a party of horse on the border brought an instant answer from Cromwell that he had ordered the offenders back into England, and had ascertained that they were not troops which had been "under our discipline and government. I have been as diligent as I can to find out the men who have done the wrong and I am still in the discovery thereof, and I trust there shall be nothing wanting on my part that may testify how we abhor such things. . . . . For the remaining regiments, which are of our old forces, we may engage for them their officers will keep them from doing any such things . . . ." In the matter of victuals "they shall be so far from being their own carvers as that they shall submit to have provisions ordered and proportioned by the consent and with the direction of the gentlemen and committees of the country."

In October, Cromwell, being able to report that all of the enemy's forces in Scotland were disbanded, began his return march southward, and meanwhile a strong feeling had risen up in the army in the south that it was hopeless to try to come to terms with the King, since no form of words would bind him, and that he should be brought to trial. By the end of November, Cromwell was of the same mind with them. In January, 1649, the King was tried and executed, and the Government of England passed to a Council of State of which both Fairfax, the nominal Commander-in-Chief of the army, and Cromwell were members. The first and most urgent business before them was Ireland which, since the rebellion of 1641, and the massacre of Protestants by Catholics, had been in utter confusion and was now a stronghold of Royalism. There had been much strife between the Catholic and Royalist parties, but these were in 1649 combined under the Duke of Ormonde, who had in all over forty thousand men in arms. Two places only held out for the Parliament, Dublin and Londonderry, and both of them were under siege.

In April, Cromwell accepted the command in Ireland; and fourteen regiments of foot and as many of horse were chosen by lot to go with him. The officers were well content; but agitators had been at work among the men preaching the doctrines of equality and the like which later became current during the French Revolution. There were dangerous mutinies both in London and in the country, which Cromwell took the leading share in repressing, moving swiftly and striking sharply. A cornet and two corporals were shot against the wall of Burford churchyard, the bullet-holes in the masonry to this day showing where they stood. Then, order having been restored, Cromwell in August embarked at Milford Haven with the title of Lord-Lieutenant and full civil and military powers.

He had sent before him two regiments of foot and one of horse to Dublin, which enabled the Commandant to make a successful sortie and raise the siege, and on August 15, he reached Dublin himself, completing the disembarkation of his whole force four days later. His first acts were to take in hand the garrison of Dublin, which was in a bad state of discipline, to purge out of it a number of bad officers, and to publish a proclamation prohibiting all pillage and ill-treatment of the inhabitants, and promising protection and due payment to all persons who would bring in provisions. He then set apart five thousand men to hold Dublin, which left him eighteen thousand, including two thousand horse, for his field army. By the 30th all was ready and he began his Irish campaign.

It promised to be a difficult task. For once all parties in Ireland were combined, and combined against him. Eight years of anarchy had caused a famine, and he could look for neither food nor fuel. He was obliged to supply his troops with everything from England and to draw all that he needed from a fleet, under Admiral Ayscough, which accompanied him and which had to look not only to the army but to a Royalist fleet under Prince Rupert on the Irish coast. He was, therefore, necessarily tied to the sea, and, whether he moved to north or south, there were rivers whose passage, guarded by strong places, must be forced before he could advance to any distance. The north claimed first attention owing to the peril of Londonderry; and in that direction the Irish occupied the line of the Boyne, Ormonde with a strong force holding Trim on the upper waters, with some of his best troops at Drogheda by the sea.

Marching northward along the coast, Cromwell came before Drogheda on September 3, the fleet having sailed in company with him, and prepared to attack the south town. It is somewhat singular that he thought it necessary in his dispatch to apologise for not investing both sides of the place, upon the ground that there would have been such a want of "correspondency" between the two parts of the army thus divided as to offer the enemy a chance of beating them in detail. A week was spent in raising two batteries; a summons was sent to the garrison and answered with defiance; the guns maintained fire for twenty-four hours, and on the morning of September 11, a column of seven or eight hundred men delivered the assault. They were beaten back with heavy loss, whereupon Cromwell rallied them and led them forward himself. After a stiff fight he bore down all resistance. No quarter was given. "Being in the heat of action," wrote Cromwell, "I forbade them to spare any that were in arms in the town; and I think that night they put to the sword about two thousand men." Scattered parties in isolated posts held out until next day. "Their officers were knocked on the head, and every tenth man of the soldiers killed. . . . I am persuaded that this is a judgment of God upon these barbarous wretches who have imbrued their hands in so much innocent blood, and that it will tend to prevent the effusion for the future." According to the reigning customs of war there was nothing that called for apology. A garrison which rejected a summons could not complain if it were cut off to a man by a successful assault. Moreover, the attack upon Drogheda itself was a hazardous enterprise, with a hostile army hanging about Cromwell's left rear at Trim. All this may be admitted as an excuse for severity. But there was much more than killing of combatants at Drogheda. There was indiscriminate slaughter of friars and even of women, there was burning of buildings in which desperate men had taken refuge, and there was plunder. It may be truly said that such incidents may be matched in the stories of a hundred assaults, and that when the blood of men is up they pass out of control. But Cromwell's army did not break loose, like that of Wellington at Badajoz. It was turned loose by its Commander, and was completely out of hand for thirty-six hours; and the consequences, as shall presently be seen, were very serious. The terror inspired by the storm of Drogheda was certainly very great, but the loathing which it left behind it was even greater and was not lessened by Cromwell's attribution of his men's behaviour to the Spirit of God.

After the fall of Drogheda the other strongholds held by the Irish on the Boyne were evacuated, as also were Dundalk, Carlingford and Newry; and Cromwell, leaving Colonel Venables with a detached force to deal with Ulster, returned with his main body to Dublin. Though victorious, he was still anxious, for his force was already greatly diminished by the need for occupying captured posts, and was suffering also from sickness. "We keep the field much," he wrote, "our tents sheltering us from the wet and cold. But yet the country sickness overtakes many; and therefore we desire recruits and some fresh regiments of foot may be sent to us. For it's easily conceived by what the garrisons already drink up what our Field-army will come to if God shall give more garrisons into our hands." Tents, it may be added, were a novelty in the Parliamentary armies. Even with them Cromwell was in difficulties before his campaign lasted a month. Without them he could hardly have proceeded with it at all.

He now set himself without loss of time to take in hand the south of Ireland. Ayscough, detaching a squadron to watch Rupert's fleet at Kinsale, made for the entrance to Wexford Haven, while the army marched along the coast upon Wexford itself. Every strong place was abandoned at its approach, and Ormonde, who lay at Kilkenny, not more than fifty miles away, with twenty thousand men, durst not face it in the field nor even strive to impede its advance. On October 1, Cromwell came before Wexford and summoned it. The Commandant played with him for many days with negotiations, and at last Cromwell, having chosen the Castle which commanded the town as his point of attack, opened a cannonade upon it on October 11, and soon received its surrender. The defenders of the town no sooner saw the redcoats at the top of the Castle than they quitted the walls; and thereupon, apparently with one mind, the remainder of Cromwell's troops, in his own words, "ran violently upon the town with their ladders" and stormed it. There was little resistance, but there was massacre and there was wholesale pillage. Some two thousand of the defenders fell, and not twenty of the assailants. It is plain from the wording of Cromwell's dispatch that the whole proceeding was not only unsanctioned by him but altogether against his wishes, and that he was not only disgusted but ashamed. He punished no one, however, and excused his army in his own peculiar way. "We intended better to this place than so great a ruin, hoping the town might be of more use to you and to your army, yet God would not have it so," and therewith he proceeded to recite certain atrocities committed by Catholics upon Protestants in the rebellion of 1641 and to assure his masters that though "the soldiers had got very good booty in this place" he had secured some valuable captures for the use of the State. It is possible that exaggerated stories of the rebellion had inflamed the soldiers' minds against all Irish, and that fanaticism bade them exterminate all Papists; but the true motive for this spontaneous assault was pillage, and the ready yielding to this motive was the result of the storm of Drogheda. Cromwell might charge the fault upon his Maker, but really it was his own. He knew it and, to do him justice, was deeply chagrined.

Striking inland from Wexford, after providing it with a garrison, Cromwell on the 17th came before New Ross, which at first rejected his summons but surrendered after the firing of a few shots. There he halted for several days while throwing a bridge over the river Barrow; and, receiving the voluntary surrender of Cork and Youghal, he made Cork the naval base for the fleet. Throughout this time the inhabitants came in with provisions which were faithfully paid for, and thus the army was better supplied than the

Irish armies had ever been. None the less, there was much sickness owing to the hardships of a winter campaign. "I scarce know one officer of forty among us that hath not been sick," wrote Cromwell at this time, and he was himself so ill that he could not in person take charge of the next operations which resulted in the capture of Carrick-on-Suir. Waterford refused to surrender, and in December he marched to Cork to give his men rest in winter-quarters.

In February, 1650, he started again with two weak columns to clear Tipperary, Limerick and Kilkenny, and secure the communications between Cork and Wexford to east and with Dublin to north-east. By the third week in March he was before Kilkenny, the Irish headquarters, which after a short defence, surrendered with the honours of war. Then returning to Carrick-on-Suir, he marched to lay siege to Clonmel. Here there were two thousand foot, all Ulstermen, who repelled Cromwell's assault after four hours of stiff fighting on May 9, but evacuated the place in the night and suffered heavily from Cromwell's pursuit next morning. This was the stoutest enemy encountered by him in Ireland, and the last. Waterford was still untaken, but there was urgent danger in England which called for his immediate presence; and, making over the command to Ireton, he embarked at the end of May for Bristol. Practically he had reconquered Ireland in eight months with a small and continually shrinking army, overcoming every kind of difficulty with quiet resolution and, it must be repeated, in spite of the slaughter of Drogheda and Wexford, enjoying greater confidence among the inhabitants than Ormonde and the Irish commanders. He has left a name which is eternally abhorred in Ireland, bearing in reality the whole burden of a hatred which should rightly be shared by many before him whose names are forgotten.

The new danger in England arose from the rallying of the Scots to the legitimate King, Charles II. It was certain that they would invade England in the King's name. Cromwell was for attacking them before they could cross the border. Fairfax demurred and resigned his commission; and on June 26, Cromwell started for the north as Captain-General and Commander-in-Chief. On July 19, Cromwell mustered

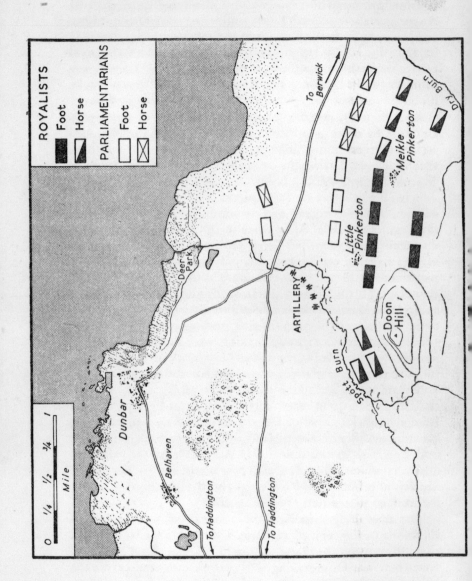

sixteen thousand men, one-third of them cavalry, at Berwick,
and on the 22nd he crossed the Tweed and advanced up
the east coast, drawing his supplies from ships that sailed
parallel with them by sea. On July 28, he reached Musselburgh and came in sight of the Scottish army, some twenty-
five thousand strong, entrenched between Leith and
Edinburgh. For a month Cromwell tried to entice David
Leslie the Scottish commander, out of his position to meet
him in the open field. Leslie was too shrewd to be tempted,
and Cromwell found himself in difficulties. The weather
was rough and rainy, making difficult the landing of provisions at Musselburgh; dysentery broke out; supplies
began to fail; and Cromwell was fain to fall back to his
ships in the safe haven of Dunbar. Leslie pressed him closely
during his retreat; the discipline of the English began to give
way; and they reached Dunbar on September 1, "a poor,
shattered, hungry, discouraged army." Leslie having
driven it into the peninsular of Dunbar, sent a detachment
to cut off its retreat by occupying a defile on the road to
Berwick; and Cromwell was fairly caught. His strength was
now reduced to eleven thousand men, whereas the Scots
were still over twenty thousand. Leslie lay the line of his
retreat to the Tweed and had only to await a favourable
moment to attack his enemy when trying to embark, or
while struggling in the defile in the effort to retreat.

Leslie, however, was not an independent commander,
but subject to the orders of an Aulic Council called the
Committee of Estates. At their bidding he came down from
his impregnable but exposed situation on the hills to the
lower ground beneath, where he could more conveniently
obtain supplies and stand within closer striking distance of
his enemy. He drew up his army in the orthodox fashion—
infantry in the centre, cavalry on either flank—astride the
road to Berwick, facing north. In his front was a burn which
along the whole length of his array ran in an impassable
channel fifty feet deep, but at the extremity of his right ran
down an easy slope to the sea and for about half a mile
offered no obstacle. Here, having great superiority of cavalry,
he judged that he could pass over with a great mass of horse
and assail the English who lay on the other side of the burn.

All through the day of September 2, Cromwell watched
Leslie keenly as he took up his ground, until at four in the
afternoon the disposition of the Scottish army was complete.
Then turning to Lambert he said that he thought that the
enemy gave him an opportunity. Lambert answered that
the same idea had occurred to him. George Monk, who was
present with his own regiment—the regiment which is now
called the Coldstream Guards—was called into consultation
and heartily agreed. The details of the dispositions were
left to Lambert, and the time of the attack was fixed for
four o'clock on the morrow morning.

The fact was that Leslie had drawn up his troops faultily.
The ground on which he stood formed, roughly speaking, a
right-angled triangle. The burn before his front was one
side, the sea at right angles to it on his right the base, and
a great mass of steep hills the hypotenuse. Had he kept the
whole of his infantry on his left, towards the apex of the
triangle, and the whole of his cavalry on his right, where
there was plenty of room for it to manœuvre, all would have
been well; but carelessness or pedantry had led him to
place half of his cavalry on his left, where it was penned in
tight between the impassable burn and the hills. Cromwell
reasoned that if he massed his artillery with part of his
infantry on his own side of the burn to check any movement
of Leslie's centre and left, and, crossing the water with the
bulk of his force, fell with them upon Leslie's right flank, he
could drive the horse of Leslie's right wing back upon the
centre, and the centre again upon the left, until all were
huddled together in the narrow space at the apex of the
triangle and so destroyed.

At four o'clock on the morning of September 3, Lambert
with five regiments of horse crossed the burn at the highest
possible point to engage Leslie's right in front, while
Cromwell in person with three regiments of foot and his
own regiment of horse passed the stream lower down to
make the turning movement which was to strike upon
Leslie's flank. Though taken by surprise, Leslie's right wing
of horse and his centre changed front to their right. Lambert's
attack was checked, and Monk, who had passed round
Lambert's rear with three battalions to engage Leslie's

infantry, could make no progress. Both Lambert and Monk were for the time forced back until Cromwell, coming up, relieved the pressure upon Monk with two battalions and directed the third to move wide round the flank of the Scottish infantry. Shaken by this counterstroke, the Scottish foot gave ground. Monk's brigade rallied; Lambert's horse advanced again to the attack ; and just at the right moment Cromwell threw his remaining battalion upon the flank of the Scottish centre, and his own regiment of horse upon that of Leslie's right wing of cavalry. "They run, I profess, they run," said Cromwell, as he saw the Scots recoil; and as he spoke the sun leaped up over the sea. "Now let God arise and let His enemies be scattered," he cried, as the Scots, some of them still fighting desperately, crowded helpless into the narrow angle between the impassable burn and the sea. The Scottish horse fled away as best they could with the English in pursuit till Cromwell ordered a rally, and while the broken ranks were reforming, he sang, loudly:

O give ye praise unto the Lord
All nations that be,

and the chorus swelled louder and louder behind him as the troopers fell into their places. Then they trotted away to the chase, nor paused until they had reached Haddington. Three thousand Scots had fallen in the field; ten thousand more, with all their guns, baggage and two hundred colours, were captured. Leslie's army had ceased to exist.

On the next day Lambert entered Edinburgh with six regiments of horse, occupied the city and the port of Leith without resistance and blockaded the Castle, while Cromwell pushed on to Stirling. Here Leslie had collected five thousand men and entrenched himself too strongly to be driven out with the troops that Cromwell could spare. Cromwell, therefore, returned to Edinburgh, where he presently received the surrender of the Castle; and the operations for that year came to an end. In the spring he was disabled for weeks by fever and ague, but in June the army was assembled on the Pentland Hills ready to deal with a new Royal Army that was assembled in an impregnable position at Stirling. Knowing that he could not lure Leslie from this position, he

turned it by transporting his troops across the Firth of
Forth, and moved against Perth to cut off his supplies. As
he anticipated, King Charles marched south from Stirling
to the invasion of England, and he hurried away from
Perth to the pursuit, having already matured his plans in
advance. General Harrison, pursuant to orders long since
received, had marched at once from Edinburgh with three
thousand horse for the English border; Lambert, with three
thousand more horse, was now dispatched to hang upon the
enemy's rear; a letter was written to the House of Commons
bidding the House be of good heart; the trained bands were
summoned from London and called out in Yorkshire and
Lancashire; such a concentration was in progress as had
never been seen in England.

Charles marched by the west coast, hoping to pick up
recruits. Cromwell, who had moved from Perth to Edinburgh in two days, started after forty-eight hours' halt on
August 6, and pursued his way south with his ten thousand
men in two parallel columns. They marched at the rate of
twenty miles a day in their shirt-sleeves, their arms and
coats being carried by the country people. Charles, meanwhile, had been overtaken at Warrington by Harrison and
Lambert, who, though joined by some Yorkshire militia, did
not attempt to do more than delay him, but fell back south-
eastward towards the route of Cromwell. On August 23,
Charles reached Worcester; and Cromwell moving by
Pontefract, Mansfield and Nottingham, entered Coventry
on the 25th. Here Harrison and Lambert joined him, and
turning south-eastward to Evesham, he there picked up
General Fleetwood with the troops from London, and on
the 28th drew near Worcester. He was now between the
Scots army and London in very superior force, and Colonel
Whalley, who had followed them with a force from Lancashire, held Bewdley Bridge on the Severn, cutting off their
retreat to the north-west. The net was closing fast round
Charles Stuart.

Some days were necessary to collect boats for the bridging
of the Teme, to enable Fleetwood to move upon Worcester
from the south-west, and of the Severn, so as to secure
communication between him on the right bank and

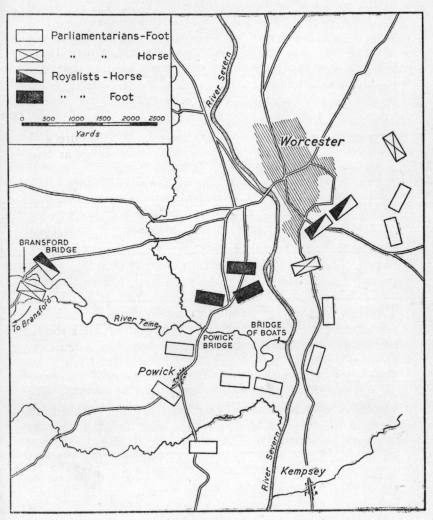

BATTLE OF WORCESTER

Cromwell on the left. On the afternoon of September 3, Fleetwood opened his attack with the support of Cromwell. The Scots then made a sortie from Worcester against the troops which remained on the left bank, and Cromwell recrossed the river to support them. Both then closed upon the Scots, twenty-eight thousand against sixteen thousand, and, though the Scots fought desperately, drove them through the streets of Worcester and at the northern extremity made an end of them. Not two thousand of the sixteen thousand escaped, and the Scottish war was finally ended at a blow. Worcester was the first example of the enveloping movement which was to be made famous by the battle of Sedan.

This was Cromwell's last campaign, though not the end of his military career. Since 1645 the Standing Army had grown steadily and now amounted to thirty regiments of foot, eighteen of horse and one of dragoons, or close upon fifty thousand men; and in 1652 Cromwell was appointed Commander-in-Chief—the first in our history—not only of it but of all the forces in the three kingdoms. He chiefly had made that army, perhaps the most remarkable army that the world has ever seen, showing first how a single troop should be trained, then a regiment, then many regiments, and next how they should be wielded against an enemy. Enough has been said to show how he contrived to inspire it with moral force; but it would be a mistake to think that he was a mere fanatic who gathered other fanatics about him. Equally is it a fallacy to imagine that the New Model was an army of saints. There were preachers to be found in it, as also there were in Wellington's army in the Peninsula; but the rank and file, with the possible exception of the cavalry, were quite commonplace individuals who responded best to commonplace methods of discipline, such as the lash and the halter. One regiment of the New Model mutinied when the Colonel opened his command with a sermon, and Parliament had the good sense to prohibit the preaching of laymen in the army. Nor must it be thought that piety was to be found only on the Parliamentary side, for there was no lack of chaplains or of godly men among the Royalists. As a matter of fact, moreover, religious fanaticism, closely allied with political fanaticism, among some of his officers gave Cromwell endless trouble during the years of the Protectorate. He himself took a broad view of the qualifications of an officer and expressed it plainly. "Sir, the State in choosing men for its service takes no notice of their opinions. If they be willing faithfully to serve it, that satisfies."

Meanwhile the power of his personality had lasting influence in keeping up the standard of moral force in the army. His power as Commander-in-Chief was indeed immense. He issued all commissions, regulated all promotions and decreed all dismissals. The arbitrary use of this last power was, indeed, a grievance with officers, who complained of the uncertainty of their tenure and standing. But none the less the army of those days offered a good career to a young man. There was no difficulty about rising to a commission from the ranks; and, after the battle of Worcester, voluntary recruits came forward so readily that there was no occasion for impressment. This is clear proof that the army trusted the man at its head not only as a victorious leader in the field, but as one who judged uprightly, and governed righteously, and, if severe against bad soldiers, recognized always the merit of the good. In brief, the army had a high tone. When it was disbanded the old soldiers were conspicuous for orderly, sober and diligent lives. And that high tone was set by its chief.

As to the man himself, as apart from the soldier, it is extremely difficult to form a judgment. In the first place his mind widened greatly as responsibility and high command increased his knowledge of the world. The government of men, always an unclean business, left its mark upon him, and his religious jargon, which had begun with sincerity, ended as mere cant. But with his enormous power as sole ruler of the most formidable fighting machine in Europe, he took the right view of his duties—that the first thing was to keep the peace at home and the next to make England respected abroad. His design to take all of her dominions in the New World from Spain was an ignominious failure; but the Dutch war, in which some of his best regiments helped to man the fleet, and one of his best

generals, George Monk, held high command, was a success
of which we feel the benefit to this day. Never was England
so much dreaded as in the days of the Protectorate; for she
had an army without a peer and a man at its head of ruthless
will who had never been beaten.

For the rest, he has left a stronger mark upon the present
army than is probably recognized. It is from the New Model
that we take our organization of regiments, with cadres of
fixed strength, a fixed establishment for artillery and
transport, the historic scarlet uniform and sundry administrative details—in fact, the essentials of a standing army.
It is from Cromwell that we derive the origin of our military
discipline and especially the great tradition that an army
marching through a country must take nothing without
payment. In a word, Cromwell set the standard for the
British Army that was to come after him as truly as the
"Old Contemptibles" set the standard for the levies that
replaced them after they had been destroyed. And these
are no small services from a country-squire who began his
military career at forty-three and died, worn out by many
campaigns and the cares of government, at fifty-nine.

Burke styled him "one of the great bad men"; but he
was a great good soldier.

THE DUKE OF MARLBOROUGH

Reproduced from an
engraving by
John Smith after a
painting by
Sir Godfrey Kneller

MARLBOROUGH

By

MAJOR-GENERAL J. F. C. FULLER

JOHN CHURCHILL, son of Sir Winston Churchill, of Ash, near Axminster, in Devonshire, was born on June 6, 1650, and on September 24, 1667, he was gazetted an ensign in the King's Regiment of Foot Guards, now the Grenadier Guards. Between this date and August 8, 1701, when William III appointed him Ambassador Extraordinary to the United Provinces and Captain-General of the Confederate Armies, he saw much service both on land and sea. First at Tangier, in 1668; next under the Duke of York and Marshal Turenne, between the years 1672 and 1674; also in the Monmouth Rebellion, in 1685, and in Ireland, in 1690. These several experiences stood him in good stead. Not only did they bring him into touch with the realities of war, but they enabled him to plumb the French character and take the measure of several of the adversaries he was destined to meet and beat in the War of the Spanish Succession.

Briefly, the origins of this war were as follows: On November 1, 1700, Charles II of Spain dying childless, by his will nominated Philip of Anjou, son of the Dauphin of France, as his successor. Thereupon Louis XIV recognized him as King of Spain, and shortly after occupied the Dutch Barrier fortresses. As this was an act of war, the old Grand Alliance (England, the Empire and Holland) of 1689 was revived. Next, on September 17, 1701, James II died, and, in defiance of the Treaty of Ryswick, Louis recognized his son as King of England. At once William III prepared for war, but unfortunately, on March 8, 1702, he was thrown from his horse and died of his injuries.

As Captain-General of the Confederate Armies, the situation which faced Marlborough could hardly have been worse. France stood supreme; England was now ruled by a woman of no marked ability; the United Provinces were wrapped in dismal selfishness, and the Empire was in its normal state of decrepitude.

Though nearly ten years of intricate warfare lay ahead of him, instead of examining them as a whole, I intend to restrict my observations to his four great battles, Blenheim, Ramillies, Oudenarde and Malplaquet, and his forcing of the lines of 1711, and lastly summarize his generalship. The first of these battles I shall consider in detail, as it is generally accepted as his masterpiece, and the remaining three in outline only. Before doing so, however, and in order to establish a background to them, I will briefly describe the changes which took place in the art of war during the second half of the seventeenth century.

Throughout this period, road communications remaining primitive, the size of armies was governed by supply, and, as cavalry was still the decisive arm, strategy was largely dependent on forage. Water transport and grass were, therefore, all-important, as also the establishment of magazines which, in their turn, led to the predominance of siege warfare over field battles, and the general acceptance that the defence is more important than the attack. This led to the avoidance of battles by what may be called the strategy of evasion, or of exhaustion, which consisted in manœuvring rather than in fighting, in order to weary an adversary out. Battles were between generals more so than armies, and among the former the great Turenne was a past-master in these operations. Also it is of interest to note that his most famous opponent, Montecucculi, laid it down that, "the secret of success is to have a solid body so firm and impenetrable that wherever it is or wherever it may go, it shall bring the enemy to a standstill like a mobile bastion, and shall be self-defensive."

From this defensive type of warfare Marlborough broke away, returning to the offensive strategy of Gustavus and the violent tactics of Condé and Cromwell. He did so because he was imaginative enough to understand the meaning of the military changes of his day. Since 1648 there had been two supremely important ones—the universal adoption of the flint-lock musket (*fusil*) and the substitution of the bayonet for the pike. Besides fusiliers, in 1667 grenadiers were introduced. Therefore, between 1650 and 1700 there were four kinds of infantry—pikemen, musketeers, fusiliers and grenadiers. By 1703 these four categories were reduced to one main type—fusiliers armed with flint-lock and socket bayonet.

This reduction in the number of weapons led to a simplification in formation and tactics; the firing-line of four and sometimes three ranks replacing the heavy column and six-rank line. Battalions, normally 800 strong, were organized in right and left wings, each divided into divisions, platoons and sections. A platoon in the English service was fifty strong, and in the French one-hundred. Firing, which hitherto had been by successive ranks, was now normally delivered by divisions or platoons at close range—thirty to fifty paces—and under cover of the smoke of the discharge the assault was driven home with the bayonet.

Marlborough; more so than his contemporaries, realized that these changes favoured the attack; consequently, both his strategy and tactics were offensive. By persistent infantry attacks he pinned his enemy down, and then broke him up by the shock action of his cavalry. As we are told by General Kane: "He would allow the horse but three charges of powder and ball to each man for a campaign, and that only for guarding their horses when at grass, and not to be made use of in action."

These were the tactics which he applied during the War of the Spanish Succession.

The first two campaigns he fought, those of 1702 and 1703, were abortive, not on account of his lack of skill, but because the pusillanimity of the Dutch States General thwarted him at every turn. So desperate did the situation become that he threatened to relinquish his command. On October 12,

1703, he wrote a strongly-worded letter to Gueldermalsen, the Chief Field Deputy, and then returned to England to think out his plan for the following year.

Judging that in the forthcoming campaign the French, faced as they were by the main Imperialist army on the middle Rhine, would attempt to destroy it before reinforcing their troops in northern France, Marlborough decided on the following plan : while the Dutch protected the Low Countries, he should first bewilder the French centre, which stretched from the Channel to Switzerland, and secondly, strike at the French wings in Baden and Spain. To effect the first of these last-mentioned operations, he decided to wage his main campaign on the Upper Danube, and to effect the second to invade Spain by way of Portugal, while Admiral Rooke attacked Toulon from the sea, and Victor Amadeus, Duke of Savoy, attacked it from the land. Once Toulon was occupied, Rooke was to sail to Messina, and there persuade the Austrian party to declare for the Allies. By these operations Marlborough hoped to contain four French armies, and so prevent their dispatch to the French centre and right.

Arriving at Maastricht, on May 10, 1704, Marlborough found the general situation to be as follows:

Facing him was Marshal Villeroi, who lay within the lines of Mehaigne (Antwerp–Diest–Namur), with Count de Coignes and 10,000 men watching the Moselle. Round Vienna the Imperialist army, 30,000 strong, was encamped, watched from Ulm by the Elector of Bavaria and Marshal Marsin and their 45,000 men. In April, 10,000 reinforcements had crossed the Black Forest to join Marsin, and were in no way impeded by the Emperor's ally, Louis of Baden, and his 30,000 men at Stollhofen, whereas Eugene, who was in the neighbourhood, having but 10,000 under his command, was too weak to do so. To cover these reinforcements and to protect the French line of communications with Bavaria, Marshal Tallard with an army 30,000 strong, lay at Strassburg and Kehl.

Though this distribution of forces was a formidable one, Marlborough's main difficulty remained the Dutch. To disembarrass himself from their control, before leaving

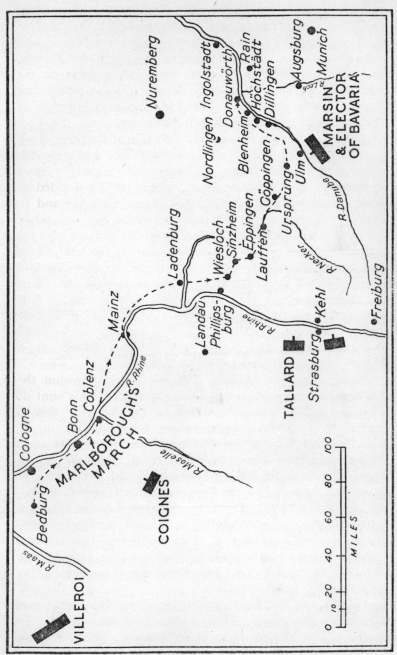

MARLBOROUGH'S ADVANCE TO BLENHEIM

England he had arranged that all troops in English pay should come under his direct command. This was fortunate, for when he informed the Dutch deputies that the forthcoming campaign would be on the Moselle, they at once began to obstruct. Thereupon he handed over the defence of the United Provinces to D'Auverquerque and 70,000 men, and ordered his own army to concentrate at Bedburg—twenty miles west of Cologne—on May 16. It consisted of ninety squadrons and fifty-one battalions, of which nineteen and fourteen respectively were British. On the 18th, he reviewed his troops, and two days later the army set out for Bonn. There he learnt that Villeroi had crossed the Meuse and was menacing Huy, and that Marsin had been reinforced.

At Coblenz, to the consternation of all, instead of marching up the Moselle, the army headed for Mainz, and, on June 7, from Wiesloch, instead of moving on Phillipsburg, the order was given to turn left and march on Sinzheim. No longer able to keep his intentions secret, Marlborough informed the States General of his true destination, and Tallard, then at Landau, waiting to confront his enemy once he had crossed the Rhine at Phillipsburg, was thrown into consternation. On the 10th, Prince Eugene and Louis of Baden joined Marlborough, and at Gingen, on the 27th, it was decided that, whereas the latter would work in conjunction with the Duke, the former with 30,000 men was to command on the Rhine and prevent Villeroi and Tallard from reinforcing Marsin and the Elector of Bavaria, then entrenched around Dillingen.

Pushing on, Marlborough reached Donauwörth on July 2, and in spite of a long march he at once stormed and carried the Schellenberg, a fortified hill which dominated the town. Thus he gained an all-important bridge over the Danube and opened the road to Munich. On hearing of this defeat, the Elector entrenched himself at Augsburg, and Marsin appealed to Tallard for assistance. Raising the siege of Villingen, Tallard marched on Ulm. Whereupon Eugene, to mystify his enemy, carried his army into the Swabian hills and then headed for Donauwörth.

Learning of Tallard's advance, it now became of utmost importance for Marlborough to bring the Elector to battle, and to compel him to fight he set about devastating Bavaria. Though in this he was unsuccessful, he compelled his enemy to split up his army in order to protect his estates. Next, to disembarrass himself of Louis of Baden, whom he did not trust, he persuaded him to lay siege to Ingoldstadt. Lastly, he wrote to Eugene to hasten his march.

On August 10, Tallard, having linked up with Marsin, set out to cross the Danube at Dillingen, and the next day, from his camp at Münster—two hours march from Donauwörth—Eugene wrote to Marlborough, saying:

"The enemy have marched . . . the whole army is passing the Danube . . . I am, therefore, marching the infantry and part of the cavalry this night to a camp I have marked out before Donauworth. Everything, milord, consists in speed and that you put yourself forward in movement to join me to-morrow, without which I fear it will be too late."

At once Marlborough set out to support Eugene.

Meanwhile, Tallard moved to Höchstädt, where, on learning that Marlborough was joining Eugene, he decided that, as Louis of Baden was absent, Marlborough would fall back on Nördlingen. Thereupon the Elector, who was in nominal command, urged an advance. But as Tallard doubted the wisdom of this, a half-measure was agreed upon. It was to advance three miles downstream to a position a little west of the village of Blenheim, which move, it was considered, would compel Marlborough and Eugene to retire, as it was against the rules of war to deliver a frontal attack upon a numerically superior force holding a strong position. "That night" (August 12), Count de Mérode-Westerloo writes, "spirits were at their highest in the Franco-Bavarian camp, for no one doubted that Marlborough and Eugene would be forced to withdraw."

The Franco-Bavarian camp was pitched on the top of a gentle rise about a mile west of a shallow, marshy brook called the Nebel. Its right rested on Blenheim, close to the Danube, where Tallard established his headquarters. Through the village ran a boggy stream—the Maulweyer—and about one-and-a-half miles up the Nebel, on its left bank, stood the village of Unterglau, and a mile-and-a-half further up that of Oberglau, where Marsin pitched his

headquarters. A mile-and-a-half further west lay the village
of Lutzingen in broken country. Here were the Elector's
headquarters. These four villages may be likened to bastions
protecting the camp with the Nebel as its moat. What
the strengths of the opposing armies were is not exactly
known. Mr. Churchill places the Allies at 56,000 and the
Franco-Bavarians at 60,000.

While the Franco-Bavarian camps were wrapped in sleep,
at 2 o'clock on the morning of the 13th, Marlborough and
Eugene set out in eight columns, and advancing westwards
crossed the Kessel stream an hour later. On the Reichen
stream, a halt was made in order to call in the outposts.
These were formed into a ninth column and were placed
under command of Lord Cutts, known to his men as
"Salamander." Next the advance was continued to Schwen-
nigen, where another halt took place, Marlborough and
Eugene riding forward to the high ground north of Wolpertstetten to reconnoitre the enemy's position. It was now
6 o'clock, and an hour later, the mist rising, the enemy
took alarm and fired two cannon.

Though the surprise was complete, the two Marshals and
the Elector were so obsessed by the idea that their enemy
could do nothing other than retire, that at first they judged
his advance to be but a covering operation to protect the
withdrawal of the main body. Then, as the columns came
steadily on, Tallard realized the truth, whereupon he ordered
the drums to beat and the trumpets to sound, and pande-
monium swept the Franco-Bavarian camps.

His plan was to fight in line where the armies stood, his
on the right and Marsin and the Elector's in the centre and
on the left; the left and centre to dispute the crossings of
the Nebel, and the right to be held 1,000 yards back from
the stream. His idea was to let his enemy's left cross the
Nebel and be caught between the fires of Blenheim and
Oberglau, when he could be counter-attacked by the
French cavalry and driven back into the swamps.

Tallard's distribution was as follows: (1) To Blenheim he
allotted nine battalions as garrison, with seven in support
and eleven in reserve in rear of the village; (2) between
Blenheim and Oberglau he drew up forty-four squadrons in

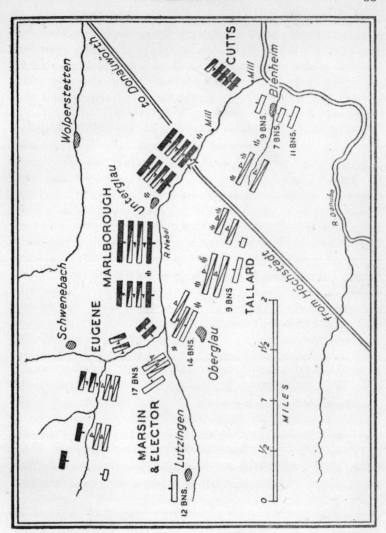

THE BATTLE OF BLENHEIM

two lines, supported by nine battalions and four squadrons of dismounted dragoons; (3) on their left he posted thirty-two squadrons of Marsin's cavalry with fourteen battalions in Oberglau; (4) on their left thirty-two squadrons and seventeen battalions of Marsin's; (5) and on their left, under the Elector, fifty-one squadrons, with twelve battalions in Lutzingen.

From their reconnaissance Marlborough and Eugene saw that the enemy's right was stronger than his left. Suspecting, therefore, that Tallard would least expect an attack on his right, it was decided that while Eugene vigorously attacked the enemy's left in order to distract the Franco-Bavarian command, Marlborough should deliver the decisive blow against his right.

As Tallard's front was extended between the villages of Blenheim and Oberglau, Marlborough saw that, if their garrisons were not contained, the risk to his advance would be great. Therefore he decided to attack them in such strength that they would be too busy defending themselves to take in flank the central advance he intended to thrust between them. Should he be able to occupy these villages, the front would be cleared; if not, then by containing them the teeth of their garrisons would be drawn. Not knowing whether he would be able to cross the Nebel unmolested, he drew up his order of battle in four lines. The first of seventeen battalions to secure the right bank; the second and third respectively of thirty-six and thirty-five squadrons for the main assault, and the fourth of eleven battalions to hold the ground beyond the Nebel and cover the withdrawal of the cavalry should the assault fail. On the left of this distribution he drew up Cutts's column to assault Blenheim. Lastly, he ordered his engineers to build five bridges across the stream and repair the existing one as it had been broken.

Eugene set out, and while his columns were toiling over the hilly and wooded ground west of Wolpertstetten, Cutts cleared the left bank of the Nebel immediately east of Blenheim; drove the French out of some water mills, and occupied the right bank. There he posted his men in a bottom close to the village, where "with wonderful resolution" for several hours they "stood the fire of six pieces of cannon." For four hours the artillery duel was kept up, and during it, in order to sustain the morale of his troops, the Duke ordered the chaplains to conduct a service. Also, in full view of the French gunners, he cantered down the line, and while doing so a round-shot struck the ground beneath his horse, and to the horror of those watching him, for a moment he was lost to sight in a cloud of dust.

A wonderfully brave man, he was more perturbed by not hearing from Eugene than by the dangers of the field, and it now being 11 o'clock, he sent galloper after galloper to the right to ascertain the cause. About this time the situation is vividly described by Taylor as follows:

> "The sun shone brilliantly on acres of yellow grain, slashed with long, glittering lines of scarlet, blue and steel. The music of both armies rose and fell in challenging pæans. And always the cannon boomed across the marshy stream, and men and horses were cut down, now singly, and now in swathes, and the dismal procession of wounded trailing slowly to the rear. The heat became intense, for it was now high noon. The day was half spent, and already the casualties of the allies amounted to 2,000 when an aide-de-camp of Eugene's came racing from the distant right. The moment had arrived."

It was now 12.30 o'clock, and Marlborough, turning to his generals, said: "Gentlemen, to your posts." Fifteen minutes later Cutts ordered his leading brigade, commanded by General Rowe, to assault Blenheim, and under the cover of this attack the columns on the right began to move towards the bridges over the Nebel.

Giving the order that not a man was to fire until with his sword he had struck the palisade of Blenheim, Rowe advanced to within thirty paces of it, when a withering volley swept a third of his men down. Nevertheless, his brigade pressed on through the smoke, and so uncertain seemed the contest that the Marquis de Cléambault, commanding the troops in Blenheim, called up not only his seven supporting, but also his eleven reserve battalions. Thus 12,000 more men were jammed into the village, and so tightly were they packed that many were unable to move. Of this incident Parker writes:

> ". . . we mowed them down with our platoons . . . and it was not possible for them to rush out upon us . . . without running upon the very points of our Bayonets. This great body of Troops therefore was of no further use to *Tallard*, being obliged to keep on the defensive."

Nevertheless, the assault failed and so did a second, and as it was beaten back, the French Gendarmerie, the finest cavalry of France, moved forward on both flanks of Blenheim. On the southern they were speedily driven back, and on the northern were met by Colonel Palms, who with five squadrons scattered eight by simultaneously attacking them

in front and on both flanks. A third assault on the village
was in preparation, when Marlborough called it off, for he
saw that his object had been gained: the French were fixed,
and his leading infantry were now over the Nebel, the
cavalry following.

When the battle was rolling around Blenheim, the Prince
of Holstein-Beck, at the head of ten battalions advanced on
Oberglau to be severely repulsed by the Marquis de Blainville, commanding its garrison. Driven back to the Nebel,
Holstein-Beck's defeat uncovered the right of Marlborough's
centre; whereupon Marsin drew up a large force of cavalry
in rear of Oberglau, preparatory to charging down upon it.

Realizing the danger, Marlborough despatched an A.D.C.
to Eugene requesting him to detach Fugger's cavalry brigade
to fill the gap. Though Eugene was hard pressed at the time,
he at once complied, and as Marsin's horsemen charged
towards the Nebel, Fugger fell upon their left flank and
drove them back. Holstein-Beck, having thus been saved,
he once again advanced, and this time drove de Blainville's
infantry back into Oberglau, where he "kept those within it
so besieged," that, as John Campbell writes, "the Allies could
now march before it and attack the enemy with great liberty."

It was now 3 o'clock, and though the two French bastions
of Blenheim and Oberglau had been deprived of offensive
power, Eugene was making little headway, and if the Allies
could not advance, they would soon be compelled to retire,
which, in face of the as yet intact French cavalry, was to
risk a rout. Marlborough, however, knew that, so long as
Eugene held on, victory was his, because the garrisons of
Blenheim and Oberglau were now neutralized, in fact these
villages were actually under siege, and in between them
yawned the gateway to Tallard's doom.

By 4 o'clock, the whole of Marlborough's centre having
crossed the marshes, the order of attack was changed, the
cavalry forming up in two lines in front, with two lines of
infantry, supporting them. Marlborough now had at his
disposal an overwhelmingly superior force at the decisive
point, for against Tallard's fifty to sixty squadrons and nine
battalions he marshalled ninety and twenty-three respectively. Waiting until half-past four, when he learnt that

Eugene was working round Lutzingen, he set the whole of his centre in motion.

Seeing his enemy advancing, and gauging his intention, Tallard called up his nine reserve battalions and drew them up to the south of Oberglau to impede Marlborough's cavalry. At once the Duke moved forward three Hanoverian battalions and some cannon, and a desperate fight took place which resulted in the Hanoverians being driven back and the whole of Marlborough's cavalry recoiling. This was Tallard's last fleeting chance, but his horsemen stood still.

At five-thirty, the Duke instructed his cannon to pour grape on the nine battalions which still stood in his way, and under cover of their fire he ordered a general advance. "With trumpets blaring, and kettle-drums crashing and standards tossing proudly above the plumage and the steel, the two long lines, perfectly timed from end to end, swung into a trot, that quickened ever as they closed upon the French." Thereupon panic seized the enemy horse. It did not wait to receive the shock. Firing their carbines and pistols, the French troopers, including the famous Maison du Roi, swung their horses about and galloped from the field. Some made for Höchstädt and others for the Danube, where thirty squadrons plunged over its steep bank near Sondenheim into the marshes and river below. Meanwhile, the nine heroic battalions were cut down to a man. "I rode through them next morning," wrote Parker, "as they lay dead, in Rank and File."

The Franco-Bavarian armies were now rent asunder, and in vain did Tallard appeal to Marsin, for at this moment Eugene was storming round the village of Lutzingen. This appeal only pressed home the sense of the general danger, and the result was that Marsin and the Elector ordered an immediate retreat. It was now 7 o'clock, and the Duke, drawing rein, hastily scribbled on the back of a tavern bill the following pencil note to his wife:

"I have not time to say more but to beg you will give my duty to the Queen, and let her know her army has had a glorious victory. Monsieur Tallard and two other Generals are in my coach and I am following the rest. The bearer, my aide-de-camp, Colonel Parke, will give her an account of what has passed. I shall do it in a day or two by another more at large."

Within ten days this message was handed to the Duchess in Windsor.

While the pursuit was taken up, Marlborough turned his attention to Blenheim. There twenty-seven battalions were still being held by Cutts's brigade now reinforced by Lord Orkney. Cléambault had however escaped, and when trying to cross the Danube was drowned. Left leaderless, at 9 o'clock his men surrendered and the battle ended.

What were its costs? The Allies lost 4,500 killed and 7,500 wounded; their enemy, according to Millner, 38,609 in killed, wounded, drowned and prisoners. That there was no sustained pursuit of Marsin and the Elector was due to lack of fresh reserves, to nightfall and the fact that the Allies were encumbered by 15,000 prisoners and immense booty.

Such was Marlborough's most skilfully fought and most decisive battle. Writing to his "dearest soul" on August 14, he called it "as great a victory as has ever been known." So it was, because Blenheim put an end to the grand design of Louis XIV. It decided the fate of Europe, for as Mr. Churchill has said: "it changed the political axis of the world." Had Marlborough been defeated, the Elector of Bavaria would have replaced the house of Habsburg on the Imperial throne; Munich would have ousted Vienna, and the Empire would have become a satrapy of France. Instead, the Elector was chased from his dominions, which were annexed to Austria. As important, at one stroke Blenheim cancelled the designs of the house of Stuart; for had France established a hegemony over the entire west and centre of Europe, there can be little doubt that, single-handed, England would have had to fight her on account of the Pretender's claims.

Nevertheless, the war continued, in the Netherlands, on the Rhine, in Italy, and in Spain, for another eight years, during which many battles were fought and many sieges undertaken, and among the former, so far as Marlborough was directly concerned, are Ramillies, Oudenarde and Malplaquet. Tactically, all three are different: Ramillies, like Blenheim, was a battle of manœuvre; Oudenarde, an encounter battle, and Malplaquet a deliberate attack on a strongly entrenched army.

The first of these battles was fought between Marlborough
and Villeroi, on May 23, 1706, their armies numbering
some 60,000 men each. From left to right, which was from
north to south, Villeroi drew up his order of battle as
follows: His left wing, consisting of his best infantry and a
portion of his cavalry, he extended between the villages of
Autre Eglise and Offuz, in front of which trickled a small
marshy brook, the Little Gheete. In his centre he marshalled
his main force of infantry and rather more cavalry from
Offuz to the village of Ramillies, which was strongly

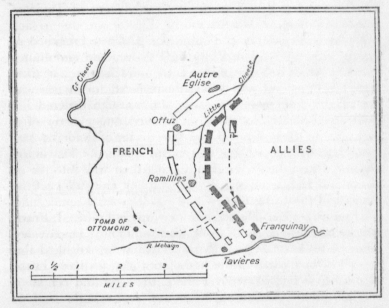

garrisoned. On its right, the right wing, mainly cavalry,
was extended to the swampy left bank of the head-waters
of the river Mehaign, on which stood the villages of
Tavières and Franquinay, both held by infantry.

When Marlborough came up with his enemy and the
morning mist cleared, seeing that Villeroi's battle front was
concave in form, he at once decided to turn this to his
advantage. His plan was, first to deliver a powerful attack
against Villeroi's left, and then, having led him to believe
that a decision was to be sought there, to reinforce his left
wing cavalry with his right wing cavalry. This he could do

more speedily than his opponent, because, as his front was convex and Villeroi's concave, he could move along the chord of an arc, whereas Villeroi could only move round the outside of the arc he was holding.

Marlborough, therefore, drew up his army in the following order: On his right, facing Autre Eglise and Offuz, he posted a strong force of infantry and cavalry under Lord Orkney. His centre, mainly infantry, he drew up opposite Ramillies, and on his left, under Count D'Auverquerque, he marshalled the main force of his cavalry supported by Dutch infantry, whose special task was to occupy the villages of Tavières and Franquinay.

About 2 o'clock in the afternoon Orkney launched a violent attack on Autre Eglise and Offuz, and simultaneously the Allied infantry of the centre and left moved against Ramillies, Tavières and Franquinay. Next, no sooner was the French front engaged than Marlborough ordered his right wing cavalry to move unobserved under cover of a slight rise in the ground to join the cavalry of the left wing. Lastly, when this march was being made, he instructed Orkney, whose men were then forcing their way into Autre Eglise and Offuz, to break off his attack and fall back to the east of the Little Gheete.

Meanwhile, the Dutch infantry having cleared Franquinay and Tavières, D'Auverquerque moved his cavalry forward, broke through Villeroi's right wing, engaged the French cavalry north of the Mehaign and was driven back. Marlborough's right wing cavalry then coming up gave D'Auverquerque such a superiority of force that the bulk of the French horsemen was pushed back towards the Tomb of Ottomond, a funeral mound a little short of two miles south-west of Ramillies.

As the French centre was now outflanked and threatened in rear, Villeroi withdrew from Ramillies, and, pivoting on Autre Eglise, he swung his centre and left northwards. For a space order was maintained, then the French broke into rout, streams of fugitives fleeing west and north pursued by the Allied cavalry. In all Villeroi lost 15,000 men in killed, wounded and prisoners, whereas Marlborough's losses were about a third of this figure. The pursuit which followed was

almost as remarkable as Napoleon's after Jena. Within a
fortnight of the victory nearly every stronghold in Brabant
opened its gates: thus the French lost the Netherlands.

Louis XIV wanted peace, but as he insisted upon maintaining his hold on Milan and the two Sicilies, the war
continued, to bring with it Marlborough's third great
victory, that of Oudenarde in 1708.

Shortly before this battle was fought, the Duke was at
Gembloux, watching the French and awaiting the arrival
of Eugene's army, when, on July 5, a rising of the citizens
of Bruges and Ghent enabled the French, under the Dukes
of Burgundy and Vendôme, to steal a march on their enemy
by occupying those cities and in consequence threaten
Marlborough's communications with England.

On learning of this and not waiting for Eugene's army,
Marlborough at once concentrated his 60,000 men at
Assche, a small town lying half-way between Brussels and
Alost on the Ghent road. Meanwhile, to secure their own
communications before operating against those of their
enemy, Burgundy and Vendôme decided to occupy Oudenarde and Menin, both garrisoned by the Allies. To accomplish this, on July 7, they set out at the head of an army
some 70,000 strong, to occupy Lessines, in order to secure
the crossing of the Dender before turning westwards on
Oudenarde. Advancing by leisurely marches, on nearing
Lessines they were dumbfounded to find that it was in
enemy hands.

What had happened was this: Receiving the news of the
fall of Ghent on the 8th, Marlborough, rightly judging that
the two Dukes would next move on Oudenarde, had at
2 o'clock the following morning set out by forced march
for Lessines, his advanced guard under Cadogan arriving
there a little before the French. Completely surprised by
this rapid move, Burgundy and Vendôme turned about and
at no great speed made for Gavre, below Oudenarde, with
the intention of holding the Scheldt. Once again they were
surprised, for Cadogan, by another forced march reached
that river before they did; threw several pontoon bridges
over it immediately below Oudenarde, and at 10.30 a.m.
on the 11th, began to cross.

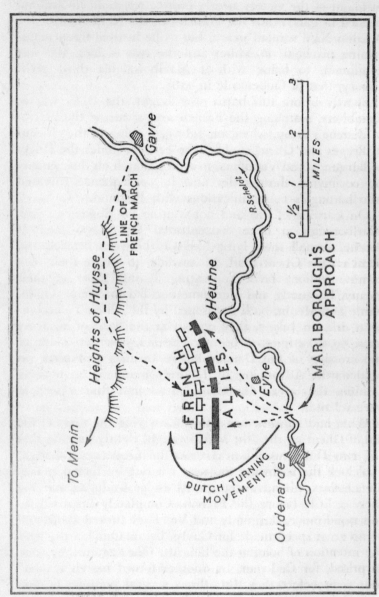

THE BATTLE OF OUDENARDE

When Vendôme, from the Heights of Huysse—to the west of Gavre—saw what was in progress, his intention was to move south and drive Cadogan back over the Scheldt before Marlborough's main body caught up. In this, however, he was frustrated by Burgundy, who being a royal prince was in nominal command. The upshot was that, as Marlborough's crossing was unimpeded, it was soon found too risky to carry out a flank march in face of it, and that, therefore, there was no choice but to accept battle.

Vendôme was for attacking Marlborough's right, and Burgundy for attacking his centre. This argument was concluded by Burgundy prematurely launching the French centre against Marlborough's, and as but half of the Allied troops had deployed, his attack succeeded in driving Marlborough's centre back. About 6 p.m. the position was, however, stabilized, and, as fresh forces came up, Marlborough pushed them out to the left in order to overlap the French right. At length, the sun having now set, on the arrival of D'Auverquerque's column, Marlborough took command of it in person, and moving round the French right, he placed the whole French line in a critical position. "We drove the enemy," writes Millner, "from ditch to ditch, from hedge to hedge, and from out of one scrub to another in great hurry, confusion and disorder." Had it not been for the fall of night the French would have been annihilated; for as Marlborough wrote to his wife: "If we had been so happy to have had two hours more of daylight, I believe we should have made an end of this war."

Though Oudenarde was not, like Blenheim and Ramillies, a decisive battle, it was, indeed, a very great victory. The French lost 17,000 men to the Allies' 3,000. Vendôme fell back on Ghent, and Marlborough marched on Lille, besieged it and accepted its surrender on December 8.

Once again Louis sought for peace, but the terms the Allies demanded were so humiliating that not only he, but all France rejected them; consequently the war continued, and on June 27, 1709, the Allies lay siege to Tournai. Not until September 3, did its citadel capitulate, when Marlborough secretly moved over the river Haine and lay siege to Mons. At once Marshal Villars counter-marched and occupied a position south-west of Mons in the wooded country about the village of Malplaquet. Thereupon Marlborough raised the siege, and at the head of some 100,000 men set out to bring Villars and his 80,000 to battle.

At first his intention, as at Oudenarde, was to attack as rapidly as his columns came up, but on approaching the French position it was found to be so strong that a council of war decided against it. The upshot was that two whole days were lost, and during them Villars strongly entrenched his positions.

There can be no question that the battle of Malplaquet, which was fought on September 11, was the worst conceived of all Marlborough's battles. The attack was purely frontal and made against two entrenched woods linked together by a strongly fortified gap. Though it led to a tactical victory, the French withdrew from the field in perfect order. For the Allies it was a political defeat, because the losses they sustained—about a fifth of their force—filled the Allied statesmen with consternation. Triumphantly, Villars wrote to Louis: "If God gives us another defeat like this, your Majesty's enemies will be destroyed." This was sound judgment, because Malplaquet broke the Allied endurance, also it gave the French time wherein to build the "Ne Plus Ultra" Lines, the breaking of which, in 1711, was, after Blenheim, Marlborough's greatest exploit.

These lines extended from the sea along the river Canche to its headwaters at Rozière; thence across the twelve miles of (entrenched) watershed which separates them from the sources of the river Scarpe at Montenescourt. From there the lines were continued to Arras, and from east of Arras along the marshes of the Sensée to Bouchain on the Scheldt. Seven to eight miles west of Bouchain, a causeway, linking Douai and Cambrai, crossed the marshes through two villages, Aubigny au Bac on the northern bank of the Sensée and Aubencheul au Bac on the southern. Three miles west of the first of these villages lay the village of Arleux on the Vitry road. At the time it was held by a French garrison. Such was the tactical board upon which Marlborough played his last famous war game.

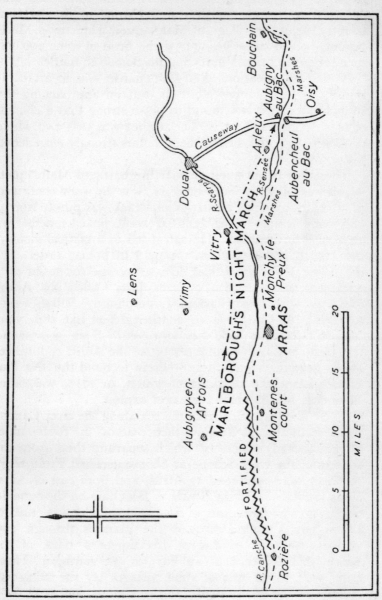

THE "NE PLUS ULTRA" LINES

On May 1, 1711, the Allies advanced from the Lille area to south of Douai, to face Villars, whose army lay between Bouchain and Monchy le Preux. There they remained until June 13, when they moved westwards to the plain of Lens. Marlborough's plan was as follows: By means of a feint attack draw Villars westwards; next counter-march and force a crossing of the causeway; lastly, capture Bouchain and open the Paris road.

Appreciating that so long as Arleux was held by the French, a crossing was impossible, on July 6, he took that village and posted a force under General Hompesch near Douai to guard it. Three days later the French surprised Hompesch and as this placed Arleux in danger, Marlborough strengthened its garrison and then moved his army north-west of Arras, which automatically drew Villars westwards. While on the move, hearing that Arleux had been attacked, Marlborough dispatched Cadogan to relieve it, but he arrived too late and Arleux was lost. Thereupon Villars razed its fortifications and abandoned it. Whether through-out Marlborough intended that this should happen, or whether the loss of Arleux was a genuine loss to him, has never been settled. Nevertheless, so far as his plan was concerned, Arleux razed was nearly as good as Arleux held.

The next incident also played into his hand. Villars detached a raiding force into Brabant. Taking advantage of this, Marlborough sent his artillery and a large reinforce-ment to Hompesch, as if he intended to follow up this raid. Next he sent all his wagons and pontoons two marches east-wards of his camp, and lastly, set about repairing the roads in front of him, as if he were preparing to move on Villars' army.

On August 1, he began to move forward, and on the 4th he carried out a minute reconnaissance of the French lines running across the watershed between Rozière and Monte-nescourt. At 9 o'clock that evening all tents were struck, and the army set out on a nineteen mile march for Vitry. It arrived there between 4 o'clock and 5 o'clock on the morning of the 5th, to find pontoon bridges already laid over the Scarpe. Meanwhile, that same night, Hompesch and Cadogan had moved south and without opposition had occupied the causeway, and by 3 o'clock had spread out to Oisy.

From Vitry another forced march of ten miles was made, Marlborough's van crossing the causeway during the morning and his rearguard by 4 o'clock in the afternoon. The infantry had thus been on their feet for nineteen hours, and had covered in all from thirty to thirty-four miles, much of it under a broiling summer sun. Not a few died on the march and nearly half fell out on the road.

Thus was Villars completely outwitted, for though he had learnt of Marlborough's move by 11 p.m. on the 4th, he was unable to catch him up. As his lines were now pierced at their vital point, he fell back on Cambrai. Marlborough lay siege to Bouchain, which, however, resisted him until September 14, when both sides took up winter quarters. Thus ended Marlborough's last campaign, for in January, 1712, he was dismissed "from all his employments," and the year following the war was concluded by the Treaty of Utrecht. Therefore, all that remains now for me to do is to attempt to appreciate his generalship.

First, it must be remembered that the operations I have discussed are but major incidents in a war which embraced the greater part of Western Europe, and that in this war Marlborough was never given a free hand. Not only was he more often than not impeded by his allies, but also at times by his friends, for though he could see the war as a whole, frequently their eyes were riveted on some purely local situation. In 1705, his first idea was to carry part of his army into northern Italy, but though this project was welcomed by Eugene, it was too startling for the other allies. After Oudenarde, he planned to mask Lille and invade France; this time Eugene objected. Yet, as Captain C. T. Atkinson writes: "This was what Wellington and Blücher did after Waterloo, and it shows Marlborough at his greatest. None of his contemporaries could have freed himself so completely from the trammels of the conventional strategy of his day . . . or could have realized so clearly the limitations of fortresses." Nevertheless, as a grand strategist what stands to his greatest credit is his ability to relate sea to land warfare. More so than any other British general he understood the full meaning of Sir Walter Raleigh's famous saying: "A fleet could easily without putting itself out of breath outrun the soldiers that coast it."

In 1690 he set before Queen Mary's Council a project for a combined operation against Cork and Kinsale. In 1702 he was responsible for the sending of an expedition to Cadiz. In 1704, as we have seen, he based his strategy as much on the Mediterranean as the Danube, and in that year Rooke seized and held Gibraltar. In 1708, largely at his insistence, Minorca passed into British hands. In 1713, that England, as Admiral Mahan says became *"the* sea power instead of one of the sea powers," was mainly due to Marlborough, and as Sir Julian Corbett writes: "To the unsurpassed richness of his military renown we must add the greatest achievement that British naval strategy can show."

In the field, though his decisions were always rapid, they were nevertheless invariably flexible, for they were based not only on probabilities but also on possibilities, and therefore were open to alternative actions. They were never rigid as were those of so many of the French generals. And though, regarding them, Marlborough could keep his own counsel, as he notably did in 1711, he never shunned advice and always listened attentively to others. His self-reliance was outstanding. "He was peculiarly happy in an invincible calmness of temper and serenity of mind," writes Parker, "and had a surprising readiness of thought, even in the heat of battle." Also Lediard says: "In the days of battle he gave his orders with all the clearness and composedness imaginable, leading on his troops without the least hurry or perturbation, and rallying those troops that were disordered without those harsh and severe reproaches which rather damp than animate the soldier's courage."

Few generals in history could better fathom their enemy's plans than Marlborough. First, because of the excellence of his secret service, which in its day was unrivalled; secondly, because he either personally knew or had minutely studied his opponents, and lastly because he had a wonderful tactical eye and never failed to see things for himself if it were possible to do so. Conversely, two reasons why he was never defeated were that his own plans were kept secret and were always worked out with meticulous care. In this he compares with Napoleon who once said: "If I appear to be always ready to reply to everything, it is because, before undertaking anything, I have meditated for a long time— I have foreseen what might happen. It is not a spirit which suddenly reveals to me what I have to say or do in a circumstance unexpected by others: it is reflexion, meditation."

Once having upset his enemy's plan, and to upset it was his constant aim, he never gave him time to recover. If it were humanly possible, he never failed to bring his enemy to battle, and when he could not, he, nevertheless, forced him to change his plan. Further, he knew how to accept risks which were unheard of in his day, such as fighting the unpremeditated battle of Oudenarde in piecemeal fashion and with his back to a river. Though frequently outnumbered, he generally succeeded in concentrating a superiority of force at the decisive point. At Blenheim he created that point by neutralizing Tallard's infantry, and at Ramillies he exploited it by a cunning use of the ground.

It is notable that in the ten campaigns he fought during the War of the Spanish Succession, no single action was a defensive one. His strategy was as offensive as were his tactics, and both were based on surprise and speed of movement. First, he attacked his enemy morally, consistently mystifying him, secondly, physically, and as consistently misleading him. In 1711, Parker writes that Villars was "so baffled and confounded that he knew not what to do against an adversary so vastly superior to him," and Kane says that "Villars not offering the least attempt to disturb our passing shows what a terror the Duke of Marlborough struck into France who were but the other day the bullies of all Europe."

In the field he proved himself a master of combined tactics, for he handled all three arms with equal skill, and as an organizer and an administrator of armies he was as outstanding as he was as a strategist and tactician. The Blenheim march, though not unduly rapid, under cover of surprise was organized to spare his men all possible fatigue, because it was essential for him to carry the greatest number he could to the Danube. Whereas, in the marches before

Oudenarde and in 1711, numbers being secondary to surprise, the utmost speed is to be seen. Of the advance on Blenheim, Parker writes:

"We frequently marched three, sometimes four days, successively, and halted a day. We generally began our march about three in the morning, proceeded about four leagues, or four and a half each day, and reached our ground about nine. As we marched through the Countries of our Allies, Commissaries were appointed to furnish us with all manner of necessaries for man and horse; these were brought to the ground before we arrived, and the soldiers had nothing to do but to pitch their tents, boil their kettles, and lie down to rest. Surely never was such a march carried on with more order and regularity and with less fatigue both to man and horse."

Whether on the march, on the field of battle or in the siege lines, no general, until the coming of Napoleon, knew better how to inspire his men and get not only the most but the best out of them. Lediard informs us that he "secured the affections of his soldiers by his good nature, his care for their provisions and vigilance not to expose them to unnecessary dangers," and that "The poor soldiers who were, too many of them, the refuse and dregs of the nation, became after one or two campaigns by the care of their officers and by good order and discipline, tractable, civil, orderly, sensible and clean and had an air and a spirit above the vulgar." "Each and every soldier," writes Millner, "under his Grace's command, being animated by his graceful presence and inviting example, did in like manner, with heroical spirits and undaunted courage, unanimously fully imitate the steps of the same leader."

Such, then, was "Corporal John", as his men affectionately called him. And it is remarkable that a hundred years later even a greater than he, was called by his men "Le petit caporal." The one was the forerunner of the other, as well as heir of Gustavus; for by breaking down the formalities of late seventeenth century warfare and fitting the ways of the great Swede, as well as those of Condé and Cromwell, to the new weapons of his day, Marlborough opened the road for Frederick and Napoleon, and, therefore, may truly be said to be the initiator of modern warfare.

WELLINGTON

By

CAPTAIN B. H. LIDDELL HART

FEW men in history have played so big a part in the world while keeping so apart from it as did Arthur Wellesley, Duke of Wellington. That detachment was his most distinguishing characteristic. Heredity, personal environment and social heritage can all be traced as factors in its formation.

His father died when he was twelve, and in absorption with music had neglected the family estates. His mother was beautiful but cold. She showed him little affection, and seeing no sign of promise in him, often spoke scornfully of him. He grew up in Ireland, where a great gulf separated the Anglo-Irish upper classes from the rest of the people. All these factors tended to foster a sense of aloofness.

His grandfather, Richard Colley, came of a Gloucestershire family which had settled in Ireland in or about the sixteenth century, but had changed his name to Wesley on succeeding to the estates of his cousin, Garrett Wesley. In 1746, he was made an Irish peer, and took the title of Baron Mornington. In 1760 his son and successor was raised two steps in the peerage by George III's favour; he took the titles of Earl of Mornington and Viscount Wellesley. The latter title emphasized a reputed descent on the female side from the ancient Somersetshire family of de Wellesleigh. The new earl's pleasure was increased by the arrival in the same year of his first son, Richard, destined to become Governor-General of India in 1798. In that year the recently adopted family name of Wesley was itself changed once again into the more aristocratic form of Wellesley.

Arthur, the fifth son and sixth child, was born on an uncertain date about the end of April, 1789. Like so many men who have risen to fame, he was delicate in his youth. Lack of robustness tended to produce shyness, and his mother deemed him a dunce. Following in his brilliant eldest brother's footsteps, he was sent to Eton, but was idle at class-work and cared little for games—another dual sign of high ultimate promise. On his father's death, his mother thought it would be a justifiable economy to take him away from Eton. She put him in a *pension* at Brussels, where he received private tuition and enjoyed playing on the fiddle. In later years he grew ashamed of his musical accomplishment and burnt his instrument. Soldiers are apt to be shy about such unsoldierly pursuits. But even at the time, his mother was not impressed by this evidence of interests which had proved so expensive to the family in his father's case. She decided that her "awkward son" was fit to be "food for powder and nothing more." Consigning him to the "fool's profession," she sent him, at sixteen, to a French military academy at Angers. Here again, handicapped by poor health, he did not shine in any of the normal subjects—riding, fencing or bookwork—but he at least learned to stay on a horse and became fluent in French.

After a year at Angers he went home, and Richard made some effort on his behalf to secure him a commission—writing to the Viceroy of Ireland: "He is here at this moment and perfectly idle. It is a matter of indifference to me what commission he gets provided he gets it soon." Richard's indifference was explained by the view, which he expressed to a friend, that his younger brother was "the biggest ass in Europe." In March, 1787, Arthur became ensign in the 73rd Foot, a regiment which was then serving in India, but he never got nearer to it than the depot, as within a few months he was appointed aide-de-camp to the Lord-Lieutenant of Ireland. He remained in that social staff post for over five years. Meanwhile he made successive changes of regiment—six in five years—covering both horse and foot. While such changes were usual in those days, his were unusually frequent, and had the effect of enabling him to gain steps in promotion without paying for them, until 1793, when Richard lent him the money to purchase a majority in the 33rd Foot. This showed a sense of manœuvre.

As an aide-de-camp at the Viceregal court, Arthur Wesley was slow to shine, and it was perhaps in an effort to overcome his shyness that he gained some notoriety for practical jokes. But he also began to take more practical interest in the military spheres than was expected in holders of such social appointments. He went so far as to have a soldier weighed with and without his kit, in order to gauge the extent of the marching load. Richard's action in making him a member of the Irish Parliament, for his own private borough of Trim, may also have been encouraged by new signs of seriousness; in any case, Richard was subsequently moved to express satisfaction at Arthur's performance and his judgment.

Arthur then proposed to Catherine Pakenham, but her father, Lord Longford, saw serious drawbacks to the suitor's private income of merely £125 a year, and the marriage had to be deferred. That spurred Arthur to apply himself harder to his military career. Opportunity had now increased through the outbreak of war with revolutionary France. He sailed with the 33rd Foot, as a major, to join the ill-trained and ill-equipped force which had gone to the Low Countries under the Duke of York. By September he was a lieutenant-colonel commanding his regiment. He gained some distinction, in a gloomy campaign, by his handling of a rearguard which helped to cover the later stages of the gradual British retreat from Dunkirk through Belgium and Holland to Bremen. From there the army was evacuated to England. As a guide for the future, Arthur Wesley had at least learned, as he remarked later: "what one ought not to do, and that is always something." The campaign had demonstrated, above all, the importance of competent commanders and an adequate supply system.

After returning home, he applied for a civil post under the Revenue or Treasury, seeing no prospect in his soldiering career in view of "the manner in which military offices are now filled." Such a civil post would also have enabled him to marry. But his application did not succeed—he was fated to become the most successful soldier of his time. Then his regiment was ordered to the West Indies, but the ship in which it travelled was driven back by storms, and he there missed the chance of taking part in an expedition from which the survivors were few. The 33rd was now sent to India. On the long voyage he devoted several hours a day to study, having given up both cards and his fiddle.

He landed at Calcutta early in 1797, shortly before his twenty-eighth birthday. That same year, as a colonel by brevet, he was given command of the Bengal contingent of a small expedition against the Philippines. He pungently criticised the high command and the general arrangements, while labouring to put his own part in better order. The expedition was recalled after reaching Penang, but he had at least gone far enough to grasp, and point out, the strategic importance of the Malay peninsula. On his return, he turned his attention to the civil and economic side of the Bengal administration, and with remarkable swiftness, drafted a memorandum on the subject. The state of British India had shocked him.

At this moment Richard was made Governor-General of India. From the time of his arrival in 1798, he leaned on his younger brother's advice, and came increasingly under the influence of his more resolute character. How much he had changed his opinion of the latter is shown by a remark he made to a friend at this time: "Arthur is a much cleverer fellow than I am, you may depend upon it."

Arthur Wellesley—the name was changed this year— urged steps to remove the menace presented by Tipu, Sultan of Mysore, who was being incited by the French to oust the British from India. But he also saw the importance of diplomacy to neutralize other powerful princes, and possible allies of Tipu.

After pacts had been secured, both with the Nizam of Hyderabad and the head of the Mahratta Confederacy, the invasion of Mysore was launched early in 1799. It was carried out under the command of General Harris, a rather

indolent and weak-willed soldier, who was glad to find an
energetic junior who would do most of his work for him,
and was the more ready to make good use of Colonel
Wellesley because he was the Governor-General's brother.
He gave Wellesley command of the Nizam's contingent of
about 16,000 men. General Baird, an abler soldier than
Harris, was the principal executive commander, and
expressed prompt resentment of what he considered the
favouritism shown to such a young and comparatively
inexperienced officer. He found fuel for his fire when, on
arrival before Seringapatam, Wellesley suffered repulse
in a night attack which he had been ordered to make on an
outlying position. Baird's indignation waxed fiercer when,
after he himself had played the main role in storming
Seringapatam, Wellesley was placed in charge of the
administration to consolidate the victory. The flames of
that controversy have subsequently spread through the
pages of history. But Wellesley justified his appointment by
the way that he restored order through a combination of
force and tact.

As a start, he checked the outburst of looting in which
the conquering troops had indulged—enforcing disciplined
behaviour by some drastic hangings and floggings. Subsequently he quelled a dangerous guerrilla movement against
the new order, countering the tip-and-run tactics of these
guerrillas by organizing an even more mobile campaign
against them. At the outset he created an efficient transport
service, to supply his own columns; at the finish he pinned
down the main body of the guerrillas and smashed it with a
cavalry charge, which he led in person. Then he was able
to turn to the task of resettlement, which he achieved with
remarkably little friction. While he was quick to see through
the wiles of the native chiefs and officials he maintained a
rule of good faith in his dealings with them that impressed
them greatly and paved the way to a personal ascendency—
which helped to clear his path and safeguard his rear in the
next campaign.

This period of administrative work was valuable training
for him, and he applied himself particularly to problems
of health, both among the troops and among the people. A

personal sidelight is provided by a letter in which he remarked: "I know but one receipt for good health in this
country; that is to live moderately, to drink little or no wine,
to use exercise, to keep the mind employed, and, if possible,
to keep in good humour with the world. The last is most
difficult, for there is scarcely a good-tempered man in
India." He found it the more easy to be abstemious since
he had so indifferent a palate that he did not notice if
butter was rancid or wine was sour. Energy, curiosity, and
ambition drove him to exercise both mind and body all the
time. But he had a harder struggle to control his temper,
particularly after catching the "Malabar itch." The combination of ambition, a passion for efficiency, and a young
man's natural contempt for easy-going seniors, did not help
him to maintain good humour. Sometimes these exaspera-
tions overcame his sense of detachment.

At the end of 1802, a quarrel among the Mahratta
princes led their nominal head to ask British help in regaining
his capital, Poona, from which he had been driven by
Holkar of Indore. While an army was being assembled,
Wellesley was sent on with an advanced force. Hearing that
the bulk of Holkar's forces had withdrawn, Wellesley made
a dash for Poona with his cavalry, and occupied it. This
exploit and his presence on the spot helped him to keep the
chief command in subsequent operations, despite the protests of Baird; who returned too late from Egypt, where he
had arrived too late to take part in the defeat of the French.

At Poona, Wellesley was 600 miles north of his base at
Seringapatam. So in preparation for a forward move—to
subdue two of the other Mahratta princes who were threatening trouble—he organized a depot near Bombay within
close reach of Poona. When the Bombay Government failed
to provide sufficient transport there to maintain his supplies,
he made a sudden spring on the enemy's fort of Ahmednagar
and turned this into an advanced base, before pushing on
north. The Bombay Government had also failed to deliver
the pontoons it had promised, so he got his troops to make
wickerwork boats, on which they crossed the flooded
Godavari river. His army comprised 16,000 men, of whom
a third were untrained and only a tenth were Europeans.

After a long march he came unexpectedly upon the whole Mahratta army 50,000 strong, posted in a formidable position between two rivers. Although it was his principle never to attack the enemy in a position of their choosing, he felt that the risks of a retreat at this stage would be still greater—especially in forfeiting the moral ascendency that he had established. For hours the battle hovered precariously in the balance. His left wing made good progress but his right wing gave way. Instead of retiring his left wing at this crisis he pushed on and wheeled in. In face of such indomitable determination, the nerve of the enemy leaders cracked, and they abandoned the field. In this battle of Assaye, victory largely came through Wellesley's cool direction of the fight, his knack of appearing just where his presence was needed, and the calming effect of his cool air. He had two horses killed under him.

After subduing the Mahratta territories in the Deccan, Wellesley pushed on north again. He came upon the Mahratta army at Argaum, and though it was again much larger than his own, he promptly attacked. There was once again a bad start, as three of his leading Sepoy battalions broke in panic, but once he had restored order the enemy soon gave way, and the battle ended in a rout. Commenting on the quick change in the scales he wrote—"I am convinced that, if I had not been near to rally the Sepoys and restore the battle, we should have lost the day." His self-confidence was visibly growing and with it came an increasing audacity, justified by results. Following up his victory, he found that the Mahratta forces had taken refuge in the mountain fortress of Gawilghur, but although this position was very formidable, he stormed it without difficulty—on December 15, 1803.

That marked the end of his campaign, and of his serious fighting career in India. In the peace negotiations he threw his influence into the scales in favour of moderate terms to the defeated side. But peace soon palled on him. His letters became full of grumbles at the delay in rewarding his services, and while describing himself as "not very ambitious," he began to look towards the war in Europe as a field of greater opportunity. His discontent fretted him

into a fever, and early in 1805 he obtained leave to go back
to England to recuperate. Just before starting, he heard
that he had been made a Knight of the Bath by the King,
but remained lastingly sore at the ingratitude of the East
India Company's authorities.

More important for his future than any reward they
could give, was the reputation he had made by his victories.
He had also secured his financial future by accumulating
a small fortune of somewhere near £40,000, mainly from
prize-money—it could have been much bigger if his
integrity had been less. In this connection it is recorded
that the Nizam of Hyderabad once offered him £70,000
for a piece of information. Wellesley answered "Can you
keep a secret?" Interpreting this as a promising sign, the
Nizam quickly said, "Yes"—only to be cut short by
Wellesley's riposte, "And so can I." His standards were
higher than Marlborough's. It would have been easier still
for him to squeeze a large profit out of the territory he had
administered, but he had set an unusual standard of scrupu-
lousness in this respect, while enforcing it by drastic penalties
on any subordinates who tried to exploit the opportunities
of plunder.

Most valuable of all the assets he took back from India
were the military lessons he had learned in improvisation
and adaptability, in the sphere of supply as well as in the
field of tactics. In later years, when asked how he had
succeeded in beating Napoleon's Marshals one after the
other, he replied: "They planned their campaigns just as
you might make a splendid set of harness. It looks very
well, and answers very well, until it gets broken; and then
you are done for. Now I made my campaigns of ropes. If
anything went wrong, I tied a knot—and went on." He
made his meaning clearer on another occasion when, asked
the reason for his success, he explained it as due "entirely
to the application of good sense to the circumstances of the
moment." His repugnance to over-elaborate preconceived
plans ensured his conduct of operations a vital flexibility.
But as time went on he developed the defect of his virtues,
and became inclined to depend too much on last-hour
improvisation. Thus he was apt to find himself without the

necessary tools, and thereby ran avoidable risks. Such complications were often increased by his habit of self-reliant secrecy, which tended to leave his subordinates too much in the dark about his intentions.

The voyage home was good for his health, which, on balance, had improved in India, thanks to his abstemiousness and the way that for three years he had been on field service, hardly ever sleeping in a house. His equanimity was also restored, and he made a specially good impression on Pitt, who remarked: "I never met any military officer with whom it was so satisfactory to converse. He states every difficulty before he undertakes any service, but none after he has undertaken it."

Napoleon had just abandoned his idea of invading England, and marched off from Boulogne to the Danube. Pitt thereupon despatched an expeditionary force to the continent, via the Weser, and Wellesley went in command of the leading brigade. But before it arrived, Napoleon had decisively defeated the Austrians and Russians, whereupon continental opposition temporarily collapsed, so that the British force had to return home, and Wellesley found himself relegated to the routine training of his brigade at Hastings.

This was not enough to content him, and in the spring of 1806 he went into Parliament as member for Rye. He also set out on a matrimonial venture. Hearing that Catherine Pakenham was still eager to marry him, he felt that honour required him to renew his proposal, even though he had almost forgotten her in the more active interests of his military career. On going over to Ireland, it was rather a shock to him to find that she had turned extremely religious, on Low Church lines, while her looks had also declined. He murmured to one of his brothers in dismay, "She's grown damned ugly, by Jove!" But he stuck to his purpose with the same resolution he had shown at Assaye, and they were duly married in April. Two sons were born to them before he set out on his campaigns again two years later. But when he returned to her after Waterloo, he found himself increasingly irritated by her narrowness of outlook, lack of physical grace, and, not least, her habitual unpunctuality.

Above all, her romantic emotionalism jarred on him, and the way she oscillated between worship and fear of him. In brief, he came to see her as a gushing sentimental fool—a combination of the tendencies he most disliked.

He escaped by accepting the political post of Chief Secretary for Ireland. He was there for barely a year, and during that time had a break, when he accompanied the force that was sent to seize the Danish fleet lest it might fall into Napoleon's hands. Wellesley commanded the detachment that landed first, to cover the disembarkation and then the siege of Copenhagen.

He did not have long to wait for a more active military opportunity. Napoleon retorted to Britain's forestalling breach of Denmark's neutrality by obtaining Spain's consent to a move through her territory with the aim of seizing the Portuguese fleet in compensation. Junot's army reached Lisbon just too late to catch it before it sailed to Brazil. Napoleon then decided to compel the closing of all European ports to British trade, and, as a step towards this, to occupy Spain. He seized its capital and principal fortresses by stratagem, and placed his brother Joseph on the throne. The Spanish people, to his surprise, replied by a mass rising in arms, and an appeal for Britain's help. When the news of the revolt reached England, Wellesley wrote a memorandum advocating that a force comprising all troops immediately available should be despatched to the Spanish peninsula to seize any opening. His advice was adopted, and he was given command of the force. A larger one was to follow.

Wellesley landed in Mondego Bay—on August 1, 1808—and thence moved south on Lisbon. His force amounted to 15,000 men. He met a French detachment a third of that size holding the hills at Roliça, and it fought so stubbornly that he only succeeded in forcing it to retreat after his troops had been repulsed four times. This experience impressed on him that he could not storm French positions in his Indian manner, while his next experience showed him that he could profit greatly by tempting the French to pursue their passion for the offensive, and drawing them into a defensive fire-trap of his design. This became the favoured and frequent pattern of his subsequent battles.

After Roliça, hearing that the first contingent of 5,000 reinforcements from England was off the coast, he moved down to Vimeiro to cover the disembarkation, taking up a position on a steep ridge divided by a gorge. He was about to resume the march when a senior general, Sir Harry Burrard, arrived by sea and cautiously vetoed the advance. Next morning, Junot's army suddenly appeared and launched an instant assault on Wellesley's position, concentrating on the eastern half of the ridge, which was less strongly held. But Wellesley was quick to switch reinforcements thither, and the dense French columns of attack were shattered by the fire, from front and flank, of the British troops—deployed in line to develop their maximum firepower. By noon, the French were retreating in confusion. Wellesley was eager to seize the chance of annihilating Junot's army, but Burrard, with his habitual caution, again intervened to forbid pursuit.

Next day saw the arrival of a still more senior, and more cautious general—Sir Hew Dalrymple. When Wellesley presented him with a plan for intercepting Junot's retreat to Lisbon, he nervously decided to postpone the move. A few hours later an envoy from Junot arrived with proposals for the evacuation of Portugal by the French, provided that they were allowed to depart unmolested. With characteristic realism, Wellesley—seeing that the opportunity of capturing Junot's army had faded, and appreciating the value of securing Lisbon without loss—advised that the offer should be accepted, and himself signed the preliminary agreement.

This Convention of Cintra, however, raised a storm of indignation at home, where political and public opinion insisted that unconditional surrender should have been obtained. The storm burst on Wellesley's head, and nearly drowned his military prospects, while it actually damped the King's intention of creating him Viscount Vimeiro for his victory. Even Castlereagh, the Minister of War, who believed in him, felt that it was unwise to take him to a Levee while he was under this cloud. Along with Dalrymple and Burrard, he was brought before a Court of Enquiry. This exonerated them all, but the two seniors were never employed again. Wellesley himself was allotted no part in the next campaign, when the command of the army in the Peninsula was given to Sir John Moore, who made a daring move from Portugal towards the Pyrenees, threatening the enemy's communications, in the effort to divert Napoleon from the destruction of Spanish resistance. But Napoleon, having scattered the Spanish armies to the winds, turned on Moore, and pursued him to Corunna, where the British army was forced to re-embark in order to save itself from annihilation.

Moore's death in the final battle proved to be Wellesley's good fortune, creating the opportunity for him to redeem his reputation. For the British public and Government were loth to submit to this compulsory evacuation from Europe, and, being sobered by the reverse, became more disposed to forgive Wellesley's unpopular reasonableness in 1808. Moreover, the Cabinet had received secret word that Austria was planning to challenge Napoleon in the spring, and felt the necessity of helping her as well as of saving Portugal. Thus they became more ready to accept Castlereagh's view that Wellesley was the only general on the horizon who had promise of retrieving the situation there. Castlereagh's advocacy, however, was aided by Wellesley's expression of opinion that if the Portuguese army and militia were reinforced by 20,000 British troops, the French would need 100,000 to conquer Portugal, a quantity they could not spare if the Spanish still continued to resist. Expressed in a different way, this might mean that 20,000 British would suffice to cause the "distraction" of nearly 100,000 French.

As an aid to Austria the expedition was to prove of no avail, but as a strain on Napoleon and an advantage to England it bore fruit tenfold. For by distracting Napoleon's attention and drawing upon itself his forces, it gave the national uprising in Spain time and space to gather strength, and the value of the interruption was increased by Austria's complementary if short-lived renewal of war. This British germ was to hinder the French attempts to cure the "Spanish ulcer," enabling the wound to fester and the poison to spread through the Napoleonic system. The French regularly beat any regular Spanish forces, but the thoroughness of these defeats was of the greatest benefit—to the defeated. For it ensured that the efforts of the Spanish were more and more thrown into guerrilla warfare. An intangible web of guerrilla bands replaced a vulnerable military target, and enterprising and unconventional guerrilla leaders conducted operations instead of hide-bound Spanish generals. The worst misfortune for Spain, and hence for England, was the temporary success of attempts to form fresh regular forces. Fortunately, they were soon beaten, and as the French dispersed them, so, coincidently, did they disperse their own good fortune. The poison spread again instead of coming to a head.

A total of 26,000 men was allotted to the new venture in the Spanish peninsula, and, after another hard tussle in the Cabinet, Castlereagh secured Wellesley's appointment to the command. In April, 1809, he arrived at Lisbon. Partly as a result of the Spanish insurrection, partly as a sequel to Moore's thrust at Burgos and retreat to Corunna, the French were widely scattered over the peninsula. Ney was vainly trying to subdue Galicia in the extreme north-western corner. South of him, but in the north of Portugal, Soult lay at Oporto, with his army itself dispersed in detachments. Victor lay round Merida facing the southern route into Portugal, by way of Badajoz. Better still for Wellesley's prospects, the French Marshals were out of touch with each other—and usually at loggerheads later when they were in contact.

Profiting by his central position, his unexpected appearance, and the enemy's dispersion, Wellesley moved north against Soult. Although he failed to cut off Soult's most southerly detachments as he had planned, he surprised Soult himself before the latter could assemble his force, upsetting his dispositions by a crossing higher up the Douro. This feat was achieved by Wellesley's opportunism in seizing four unguarded barges on the far bank and using them to ferry his army across in driblets. He followed up this audacious move by heading Soult off his natural line of retreat. Thus the French resistance was liquidated without it ever having had the chance to coagulate, and at the end of Soult's enforced retreat, through the bleak mountains northward into Galicia, his army had suffered loss and exhaustion out of all proportion to the fighting. In high confidence Wellesley wrote after the fall of Oporto, "The ball is now at my foot and I hope I shall have the strength enough to give it a good kick."

Wellesley's second operation, however, was neither so profitable nor so well-conceived in its adjustment of end and means. After Soult's defeat, Victor had been recalled from Merida to Talavera, where he could cover the direct approach to Madrid. A month later Wellesley decided to march by this route on Madrid, pushing into the heart of Spain—and into the lion's jaws. For he was offering a target on which all the French armies in Spain could concentrate by the easiest routes. Moreover, by thus rallying on their central pivot they had the chance of knitting together the communications between them—when they were scattered, the length of these communications was almost their greatest source of weakness.

Wellesley advanced with 23,000 men, added to as many Spanish under the feeble Cuesta, while Victor in falling back had brought himself within close reach of support from two other French forces near Madrid. The armies of Soult, Ney, and Martin had drifted towards Madrid from the north. In these circumstances, Wellesley's move became too bold to be good. Moreover, hampered by Cuesta's irresolution and his own supply difficulties, he did not succeed in striking at Victor before the latter was reinforced by Joseph Bonaparte from Madrid, bringing the total French force on the spot to nearly 50,000 men. In face of this menace, Wellesley was quick to choose, and fall back on one of his typical defensive positions—on a ridge at Talavera. The completion of his dispositions was upset by a panic among the Spanish troops, and the French attack next day was hard to withstand, but in the end the defensive method scored a further success, and the French retired after suffering heavy loss.

Wellesley would now have advanced again if Cuesta had not refused. This time Cuesta's objection was fortunate for Wellesley, since Soult was descending on his rear. Cut off from the route by which he had come, Wellesley escaped by slipping south of the Tagus. But only after a costly, demoralizing and exhausting retreat did he regain the shelter of the Portuguese frontier. Want of food paralysed the French pursuit. This closed the campaign of 1809 and taught Wellesley the worthlessness of Spanish regular forces—a lesson he might have learned from Moore's experience.

In reward for his defensive victory at Talavera, he was made a Viscount—he chose the titles of Viscount Wellington and Baron Douro—as well as Captain-General of the Spanish Army. But his general conduct of the campaign came in for much public criticism, often sharpened by political party spite. The Common Council of London even made a petition to the King for the removal of a Commander "with equal rashness and ostentation, nothing but a useless valour." To make things worse, a split in the Cabinet was produced by Canning's criticism of Castlereagh's responsibility for the Walcheren and Spanish reverses. After fighting a duel, both had to leave office, and the Government fell. With the loss of Castlereagh's support, Wellington's future looked precarious. But the new Cabinet proved favourable, for in it his brother Richard became Foreign Minister, while another brother, Henry, was made Ambassador in Spain. That assured him of good backing both at home and on the spot. He needed it in the following year.

For in 1810, with Austria now driven to peace, Napoleon was free to concentrate his attention on Spain and Portugal until 1812. These two years were the critical period of the Peninsular War, and the inability of the French to accomplish their purpose, is of far greater historical significance than their subsequent defeats, and Wellington's victories, in 1812 and 1813. The foundation of the British success was Wellington's shrewd calculation of the economic factor—the limited French means of subsistence—and his creation of the lines of Torres Vedras.

In the prologue he was aided by the Spanish regular forces in their customary way. They embarked on a winter campaign and were so thoroughly crushed and dispersed that the French, deprived of any target, were induced to stretch themselves more widely still over Spain, invading the rich province of Andalusia in the south.

Napoleon now took control, if from a distance, and by the end of February, 1810, had concentrated nearly 300,000 men in Spain, with more to come. Of these, 65,000 were assigned to Masséna for the task of driving the British out of Portugal. If the number was large, overweighing Wellington, its small proportion to the whole is illuminating evidence of the greater strain of the guerrilla war in Spain. Wellington, by the inclusion and British training of the Portuguese, had made up his total to 50,000. But he was far from optimistic about the prospects, even in his efforts to stiffen the Government's resolution. He warned them that the struggle would be long, that it "must necessarily be defensive on our part," and that "after all, I may fail." He was not prepared to say anything more encouraging than the admonishment that the Government "will betray the honour and interests of the country if they do not continue their efforts in the Peninsula, which, in my opinion, are by no means hopeless."

While satisfied with his own defensive plan, he was worried about the means with which he had to carry it out. He vented his dissatisfaction in bitter complaints about his lack of money, supplies and transport, as well as in pungent criticism of his troops, regimental officers and generals. He painted both their character and their competence in very dark colours. For his generals he had an intellectual contempt. For a large proportion of his officers he had a hard-worker's natural scorn of people more pleasure-loving than himself. For the looting habits of his "infamous" troops he had a self-controlled and orderly man's innate disgust; "they forget everything when they can get plunder and wine." In brief, he loathed inefficiency.

Masséna's invasion came by the northern route, past the fortress of Ciudad Rodrigo, and thus gave Wellington the longest time and space for his strategy to take effect. His precautions in stripping the country of provisions formed a brake on Masséna's advance. Half-way back to Lisbon, Wellington made a stand on the ridge of Bussaco. As usual he posted his line on the reverse slope, out of sight, and also made a lateral road there by which he could move reserves swiftly to any threatened spot. Masséna delivered a rushed assault in the desire to overwhelm him, and was repulsed with a loss nearly four times Wellington's.

Then Wellington fell back to the lines of Torres Vedras, which he had constructed across the mountainous peninsula formed by the Tagus and the sea, to cover Lisbon. They comprised three successive positions—the outermost thirty miles long—buttressed by 150 redoubts together with numerous earthworks, and mounting about 600 guns. On October 14, four months and barely 200 miles from his start, Masséna came within sight of the lines, a sight which struck him with the full shock of surprise. Unable to force them, he hung on for a month until compelled by starvation to retreat to Santarem, thirty miles back on the Tagus. Wellington, shrewdly, made no attempt to press his retreat or bring on a battle, but set himself to confine Masséna within the smallest possible area so that he might have the greatest possible difficulty in feeding his men.

Wellington maintained this strategy resolutely, despite public criticism at home and the more direct risk caused by Soult's advance in the south by Badajoz, as a diversion to relieve the constriction of Masséna. And he withstood every effort of Masséna to draw him into attack. He was both justified and rewarded, for at last in March, 1811, Masséna had to go; and when the starving wreckage of that French army recrossed the frontier, it had lost 25,000 men, of whom only 2,000 had fallen in action.

Henceforth Wellington's greatest influence came through his threats rather than his blows, for whenever he threatened a point the French were forced to draw off troops thither and so give the guerrillas greater scope in other districts. Wellington, however, was not content with threats. Following up Masséna's retreat on Salamanca, he used his army to cover the blockade of the frontier fortress of Almeida in the north, while he directed Beresford to invest Badajoz in the south. Thereby he divided his own force, but fortune favoured his course.

Masséna, having rallied and slightly reinforced his army,

came back to the rescue of Almeida; and at Fuentes d'Oñoro, Wellington, although overweighted and seriously imperilled, managed to beat off the attack. Here his front was too wide for his strength, and he knew that he had courted undue risks—as shown in his comment: "If Boney had been there we should have been beat." But he was saved by the inherent advantage of the defensive, coupled with the too directly offensive spirit of the French. He himself had a narrow escape when some of the French cavalry came within twenty yards of him before he outrode them. Masséna retreated after this repulse, and in penalty was superseded by Marmont—to Wellington's relief, for he considered Masséna the ablest of his many opponents. Wellington then closed in more tightly on Almeida. But the garrison managed to slip away owing to oversights among his subordinates— which provoked him to declare: "There is nothing so stupid as a gallant British officer . . . . I am obliged to be everywhere, and if absent from any operation something goes wrong." His rebukes were so biting that one of the victims shot himself.

His point was emphasized the following week in the south, near Badajoz, when Beresford marched out to meet Soult's relieving force. He took up the position which Wellington had chosen for him at Albuera, but occupied it wrongly, and then mishandled the fight. He had actually ordered a retreat when the day was saved by the stubbornness of his juniors and the troops, though at excessive cost. So Soult retreated instead, and yet another success was scored for the defensive method.

Wellington now concentrated on the siege of Badajoz, though without a siege-train, until he had to raise the siege as a result of the unfettered move southwards of Marmont's army to joint Soult. The two now planned a united advance on Wellington. Fortunately, fusion brought friction, and Soult, alarmed by the fresh blaze-up of guerrilla war in Andalusia, returned thither with part of his army, leaving Marmont in control. Thanks to Marmont's extreme caution, in face of Wellington, the campaign of 1811 petered out quietly.

The most critical period had been tided over, and now

wider events came to Britain's help. For Napoleon was preparing his invasion of Russia. Thither his attention and his strength were henceforth turned. This development and

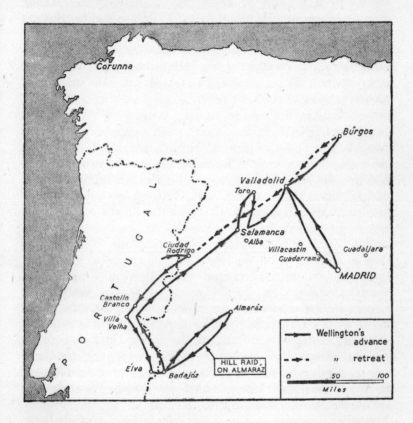

the trying guerrilla situation caused a change of plan in Spain, where the main French line of effort was altered in an attempt to subdue Valencia and Andalusia thoroughly before concentrating afresh against Portugal. Compared with 1810, the French troops were reduced by 70,000, and of those who remained no less than 90,000—from Tarragona on the Mediterranean coast to Oviedo on the Atlantic coast—were employed in practically no other duty than of securing the communications with France against the guerrillas. While the strategic mobility of the French was cramped by the Spanish guerrillas as well as by their practice of living on the countryside, Wellington had developed his own by improving his system of supply— organizing a network of depots or magazines, replenished by river or sea, so that he could keep in constant movement.

Thus given freer scope and weakened opposition, Wellington sprang suddenly on the fortress of Ciudad Rodrigo and stormed it in January, 1812, while a detachment under Hill stood guard over his strategic flank and rear. At the critical moment of the attack he found himself without scaling ladders, but met the need by the inspired improvisation of breaking up the ammunition wagons to make ladders on the spot. Craufurd, his ablest but most quarrelsome general, was mortally wounded in the assault, and sent for Wellington to express his death-bed regrets for all the friction that had occurred. Wellington's dry comment on this moving episode was—"Craufurd talked to me as they do in a novel."

Marmont was staggered by the swift completion of this coup before he could move to intervene. He was helpless to retake the fortress because his siege-train had been captured there, and helpless also to follow Wellington across the food-stripped country between them. Under cover of this hunger-screen, Wellington slipped south and stormed Badajoz in turn, though at a far greater cost and by a narrow margin of time. For all his dislike of sentiment, he burst into tears when he saw in the breach the pile of his soldiers' corpses. It was an extravagant offensive effort, in which he lost 5,000 men compared to a handful of the French defenders, and success was only gained by an escalade at an unexpected point after the assaults at the main breach had failed. In compensation for their sacrifice, the "infuriated soldiery, like a pack of hell-hounds," sacked the city with appalling brutality. Wellington, despite furious efforts, could not restore order for three days.

The strategic fruits were valuable, however, for he had now captured both the main gateways into Spain. At Badajoz he had captured the French pontoon-train. As he promptly followed up this gain by destroying the French bridge of boats across the Tagus at Almaráz, he achieved

a definite separation of the two armies of Marmont and
Soult, whose nearest way of communication was now by
the bridge at Toledo, over 300 miles from the mouth of the
Tagus. Apart from this, Soult was tied fast to Andalusia
by want of supplies and a surfeit of guerrillas.

Wellington, now able to operate secure from interference,
concentrated two-thirds of his strength for an advance on
Marmont at Salamanca. But the directness of his approach
propelled Marmont back towards his source of reinforcement. The balance of numbers thus restored, Marmont
manœuvred against Wellington's communications, with
all the more advantage because he had none of his own to
worry about.

Wellington met this threat by counter-marches to head
off the French, while looking for a favourable opening to
strike. For, with an army now tuned up by training and
experience, he felt able to develop his defensive battle-
tactics into a defensive-offensive form. Sometimes the two
armies raced alongside each other in parallel columns, only
a few hundred yards apart. The French troops could still
outmarch the British, which gave Marmont a superiority
in offensive manœuvre, but Wellington counted on the
inherent superiority that the riposte enjoys over the thrust.

Marmont gave him no opening, however, and then came
news that Joseph was on his way to join Marmont with
large reinforcements. Wellington decided that he would
have to fall back towards Portugal, and in preparation for
this retreat ordered his baggage column to start down the
road from Salamanca to Ciudad Rodrigo. Seeing the
dust, Marmont jumped to the conclusion that Wellington's
army was on the march, and sent two divisions of his left
wing to intercept the retreat while he attacked direct.

That slip was Wellington's opportunity. "By God, that
will do," he exclaimed. He quickly turned his army about
and wheeled it down to a concealed position on the flank
of the road that the French left wing was taking. "Watch
the French through your glasses," he said to one of his
staff, "I'm going to take a rest; when they reach that
copse, near the gap in the hills, wake me." He lay down
and covered himself with his cloak, and immediately dozed

off—to be refreshed by the time the battle started. When the
French left wing was far enough separated from the main
body he launched his counterstroke, against the head and
flank of the column. He followed this up with a whirlwind
charge of cavalry which swept that wing into flight.
Wellington, after watching it, for once lost his restraint,
exclaiming "By God, I never saw anything so beautiful in
my life." The panic spread to the rest of the French army,
whose own attack had been repulsed, and the rout became
general. The French loss was three times that of the British,
amounting to a third of their army. The bulk of it might
have been cut off at the River Tormes in their rear if the
Spanish garrison of a post commanding the ford at Alba de
Tormes had not evacuated this bottleneck.

Wellington has been blamed for not following up the
defeated French, but having lost the immediate chance of
annihilating them, it is unlikely that he could have regained
it before they reached the shelter of Burgos, and at that
moment such a move would have exposed him to the risk
that Joseph from Madrid might have descended at any
moment on his rear and communications.

Instead, he decided to make a move on Madrid for its
moral and political effect. His entry into the capital was a
symbol and a tonic to the Spanish, while Joseph made a
fugitive exit. But the defect of this coup was that Wellington's
stay could only be brief if the French gathered in force—
and nothing was more likely to make their armies, scattered
on the circumference, rally on the centre than the loss of
Madrid. Wellington cut his stay short without compulsion
and marched on Burgos. But the French system of "living
on the country" deprived such a stroke at their communications with France of anything like a normal influence on
their situation. Moreover, he had no adequate siege-train and
his piecemeal assaults proved ineffective—the memory of
Badajoz tended to make him chary of a lavish effort.
Thereby he frittered away more time than he could afford.
For his very success at, and after, the battle of Salamanca
had induced the French to abandon their tasks and territory
in Spain in order to concentrate from all quarters upon
him. In relation to their armies he was more dangerously

placed than Moore before him, but he fell back just in time
—and "got clear in a handsome manner from the worst
scrape I ever was in."

Once Hill's detachment joined him he felt secure enough
to offer battle to the united French armies at Salamanca
on November 11. But they did not feel that their numerical
advantage, 90,000 to 68,000, was sufficient to accept the
challenge on a battlefield chosen by Wellington—particularly at that ominous place. So Wellington continued
the retreat to his base at Ciudad Rodrigo, and with his
arrival there the curtain fell on the campaign of 1812.

That retreat has been considered by European critics
his finest feat of generalship. It fulfilled his own dictum
that the best test of a general is "to know when to retreat,
and to dare to do it." But while proud of his own performance—for which he was made a marquis—he was not
pleased with the behaviour of his troops, except in battle,
and signalized the end of the retreat by a scathing circular
on their indiscipline and misconduct. A little earlier he had
written home that they were "the finest and bravest soldiers
in the world". But now he sweepingly told them that they
were slack in all their duties—indicting the officers in
particular for neglecting to look after their men; and the
men, that they were "round-shouldered and slouching,"
while altogether too ready to go sick when they had to
march. But by this time he had so won their confidence
that they were ready to swallow anything from him, and
took his kicks as compliments. When in a tight corner they
acquired a habit of asking "Where's our Arthur?" For as
one of them said—"We would rather see his long nose in
the fight any day than a reinforcement of ten thousand men."

Although he was back once more on the Portuguese
frontier, and so superficially no further forward, actually
the Peninsular War was decided. For by abandoning the
greater part of Spain to concentrate against him, the French
had abandoned it to the guerrillas—and lost any chance
of shaking their grip. On top of this disaster came the news
of Napoleon's retreat from Moscow, which caused the
withdrawal of more French troops from Spain. Thus when
the next campaign opened, the situation had completely

changed. Wellington, now reinforced to 100,000 men—though less than half were British—was definitely on top of the French, who were very soon compelled to fall back behind the Ebro and reduced to the narrow hope of preserving the northern fringe of Spain.

Wellington launched his advance in May, and his confidence was expressed in his light-hearted cry, as he crossed the frontier: "Good-bye, Portugal." On reaching the Douro he was temporarily blocked by Joseph Bonaparte's army, but overcame this obstacle by dividing his force and sending the larger part on a wide turning movement through wild country that the French considered impassable. This manœuvre, he subsequently said, called for "more art" than any problem he had ever met. Joseph then retired behind the Ebro. Wellington levered him off this barrier by another extensive turning movement through wild country with his whole army—a move made practicable, thanks to seapower, by switching his base to Santander on the north coast. Joseph fell back to Vitoria, where he made a stand to cover the evacuation of the vast amount of baggage and loot he had collected during his reign in Spain.

Wellington saw the opportunity of cutting off the French army, and tried to seize it. For that big aim he took the risk of dividing his army when close to the enemy, relying on Joseph's passivity as well as on his own superiority of 70,000 to 50,000. With two-thirds of his army he crossed a fast-flowing river in face of the enemy, helped by their neglect to guard or destroy the bridges, but was stopped on the heights beyond. Meantime the other third, under Graham, made a circuit to the north and descended on the enemy's rear. But Joseph moved his reserve there just in time, and Graham allowed himself to be held in check until the rest of the French army, abandoning its position near Vitoria, had slipped away past his front. Wellington still hoped to catch him with a cavalry pursuit, but many of his men succumbed to the temptation of loot and the intoxication of wine. It was on this occasion that he described them as "the scum of the earth" and declared that it was "impossible to command a British army."

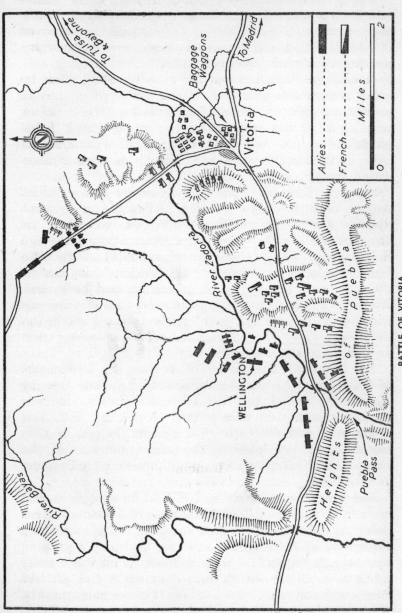

BATTLE OF VITORIA

The French army now retreated beyond the Pyrenees into France, where Joseph was superseded by Soult. While Wellington was still occupied in dealing with the fortresses of San Sebastian and Pamplona, Soult managed to raise the depleted French forces to a strength of over 70,000, and then unexpectedly re-crossed the Pyrenees in an effort to sever Wellington's communications. But Wellington was prompt to meet the threat, checked the French before reaching Pamplona—repulsing a two to one assault in his old defensive style—and then blocked several of the Pyrenees exits, so that Soult's army only filtered back into France with difficulty and heavy loss.

San Sebastian was captured by Graham at the end of August—another bungled siege, followed by another disgraceful sack, in which the town was destroyed. In October, Wellington tackled the frontier-line, along the Bidassoa river. Always at his best when he had a fairly wide front for manœuvre, he moved his divisions down during the night to a number of points on the near bank, and crossed it at first light, taking the enemy by surprise—all the more so because the main crossings were made in the tidal estuary, where the enemy had not imagined that anyone would risk a passage.

The French fell back to a position along the Nivelle, east of St. Jean de Luz. Wellington attacked this line in November, aiming first to fix the enemy's attention on their right, then pierce their centre and left, then swing west and pin their right against the sea. But his troops could not push through fast enough, and the French extricated themselves at dusk, retreating to Bayonne and the Nive.

Bad weather now intervened to hold up operations. But early in December—following the news of Napoleon's great defeat at Leipzig—Wellington struck again. He suddenly threw two of his divisions over the Nive, by a crossing upstream, in an outflanking manœuvre. Soult was equally quick to catch the British with their forces divided, and struck with concentrated strength first at one part and then the other. In each case he had a two to one superiority, but the British, changing over to defence, managed to repulse him. He then retired behind the Adour, and the weather closed down the 1813 campaign.

Prior to the last phase he had discarded the bulk of his Spanish troops—who, hungry for loot and eager to take revenge for what their country had suffered, had been behaving atrociously. Wellington, remembering how heavily the French army had paid for arousing the people against them, had felt that the importance of ensuring a smooth passage through France was worth the sacrifice of over a third of his numbers. But his action was more than a matter of policy—as he showed by resigning his titular position as Commander-in-Chief of the Spanish Army.

The destructive and sadistic tendencies of war were even more repugnant to him than the Napoleonic idea of the glory of war. He loathed barbarism, and detested anything like a mob—that was the root of his objection to democracy. He himself maintained the old courtesies of war, and sought to mitigate its inhumanity. He lent money to prisoners out of his own pocket to ease their lot. A little later in the advance, on reaching Orthez, he sent Soult a note suggesting, in the interests of the inhabitants, that if Soult would abstain from destroying the bridge over the Gave de Pau, he would promise that no British soldier should cross it. Soult trusted his word, and the bridge was preserved.

During the autumn, Wellington had been turning his mind increasingly to the problems of peace. He complained that little consideration had been given to them, apart from "loose conversation among Princes." It had been his view that once Napoleon was confined within the borders of France, his system would fall, since it was based on military power and the exploitation of foreign resources. But as he advanced into France, his desire for Napoleon's fall began to diminish. He found little eagerness among the people for a return of the Bourbon dynasty, and feared that its undesired restoration might merely pave the way for fresh revolutions, disturbing to the peace of Europe. He was thus moved to write to the Government that peace should be made with Napoleon, now that his power had been broken. "If Buonaparte becomes moderate, he is probably as good a sovereign as we can desire in France." *Moderation* on all

sides was the essential condition in bringing about peace—
he took the classical view of its virtue. But Napoleon's
continued intransigence brought Wellington, by the end
of the year, to realize the inevitability of adopting the next
best policy. "If *you* cannot make peace with Buonaparte
during the winter, *we* must run at him in the spring; and
it would be advisable to put one of the Bourbons forward in
that case."

In January, 1814, the Prussian-Austrian-Russian invasion
of France opened. Wellington considered the strategic plan
a bad one—his view was soon confirmed by the initial
reverses it suffered from Napoleon's ripostes—and feared
that Napoleon might soon be able to turn upon him with
overwhelming strength. So he decided not to push too deep
into France. In mid-February he manœuvred Soult out of
his position on the Adour, by a sea-flank crossing of the
river west of Bayonne, thus forcing him into the open.
Soult then withdrew eastward. Wellington followed, levering
him out of successive positions at Orthez and Tarber,
whence Soult made a hurried retreat to shelter within the
fortifications of Toulouse. Here Wellington took extraordinary risks, making a close-in flank march across the
front of the enemy's position on April 10, without any
serious attempt to distract their attention elsewhere. Such
a rash plan could only be justified by this confidence that
Soult would remain passive, but its execution also was
faulty, and except at one outlying point the assault failed—
with a loss double that of the defenders. The threat sufficed,
however, for on the night of the 11th, Soult retreated from
Toulouse. Unhappily, the loss was pure waste, for an hour
after entering the town, Wellington received news that
Napoleon had abdicated a week ago, and the war was over—
though there was to be an epilogue.

In a deeper sense, the campaign itself might be termed
uneconomic since 1812. For the subsequent period of
continuous offensive success was no more than a strategic
epilogue to the real issue of the Peninsular war. From the
time when Napoleon pushed into Russia while still entangled
in Spain, he had been doomed by the law of overstretch
unless he could achieve his complete aim at one end or the

other. For that, he had to secure not merely victory but peace, otherwise his eventual collapse was bound to come—unless he abandoned his aim and his hold at one end before his strength oozed away. His opponents, by contrast, had merely to prevent him from securing peace.

At the Spanish end, a statistical reckoning shows that the collapse was not produced by Wellington's battles. These inflicted on the French a total loss of some 45,000 only, including wounded and prisoners, and that loss was spread over five years—whereas the number of French deaths during this period averaged nearly 40,000 a year, according to Marbot. At the same time, the constant strain of the cruel guerrilla campaign was more wearing on their nerves than their intermittent defeats in battle. But Spanish resistance could hardly have been maintained without the moral and physical support of Wellington's presence in the Peninsula, while his operations, by distracting the French, repeatedly facilitated the spread of the guerrilla campaign.

When the curtain came down on the twenty-one years' war, and Napoleon had been deposited in gilded but not gilt-edged security on the Isle of Elba, Wellington was appointed Ambassador in Paris. Before settling down there, he went home on a visit—making a triumphal return to the city which had expressed such violent condemnation of his appointment to command. He was now made a duke.

In August he went back to his new duties in Paris. There he found himself less popular, even with those who owed the restoration of their power to him. Conscious of his own superiority, it was not in his nature to change his air to suit the atmosphere of courts or the sensitivity of foreigners. His reserve and his curt manner grated on their nerves, so that they could not forget his part in bringing about the defeat of France, while they failed to appreciate his efforts to prevent the victimization of France—or how much his capacity to rise above the common spirit of revengefulness owed to that irritating attitude of detachment. But it was better appreciated elsewhere. For when Castlereagh, who was representing Britain at the peace discussions of the Allies in Vienna, had to return home, Wellington was sent in his place. Britain's representatives played a vital part in

securing that the peace terms framed by the Congress of
Vienna were framed on the principle of moderation.
While France had to restore the foreign conquests made by
Napoleon, her own pre-war territory was left undiminished,
and no indemnity was demanded of her.

Before the Congress had completed its work, news came
in March that Napoleon had escaped from Elba and landed
in the south of France. Wellington at once urged the
British Government to despatch an army to the Low
Countries, but stayed in Vienna long enough to see the
Congress declare Napoleon an outlaw and organize a
fresh military alliance against him. So large were the
forces put in the field that his overthrow would have been
almost certain even if he had won the battle of Waterloo.

Wellington then hurried to Brussels, where he had two
months' grace before Napoleon advanced. The disbanded
soldiers of France, forgetting all the sacrifices his ambition
had caused, had rallied to him once again, and the recently
restored Bourbon King, Louis XVIII, had fled to Belgium.
By following him there, ejecting him from there, together
with the British, and regaining the Low Countries, Napoleon
hoped to gain a spectacular opening success that would
paralyse the opposing coalition and lead to the acceptance
of his initially rejected overtures for peace. Within two
months he had reconstituted an army of a quarter of a
million men, a total which was increasing weekly, and was
able to assemble a picked striking force of 120,000 for the
invasion of Belgium.

The British Army had been reduced or dispersed so
quickly in 1814 that only 30,000 men could be found for
Wellington's use, and four-fifths of them were raw troops.
The allied troops placed under his command amounted to
a further 60,000 men—Belgians, Dutch and various German
contingents—but the Belgian and Dutch forces included
many who had been in Napoleon's service, while only a
fraction of the Germans were fully trained. Surveying this
motley collection with disgust, Wellington described it as
the worst army, with the worst equipment and the worst
staff, that he had ever commanded. In later years he used
to say that if he had had his old Peninsular army he would

have swept Napoleon "off the face of the earth in two hours."

The Prussian army under Blücher amounted to nearly 120,000 men, but more than half of it consisted of recruits or militia, while its equipment was also poor. Still larger Austrian and Russian armies were on their way to join in the general invasion of France, which was intended to open early in July. Meantime the armies of Wellington and Blücher were widely distributed to protect the frontier of Belgium, the former covering the western half and its own line of supply from Ostend and Antwerp, while the latter covered the eastern half and its line of supply from the Rhine. The whole front stretched nearly ninety miles, and the depth of the Allies' dispositions was thirty–forty miles. They reckoned on having sufficient warning of any move by Napoleon to concentrate forward and meet him with their combined forces—a concentration which would take about three days.

Napoleon saw clearly that he must strike before the Austrian and Russian armies appeared, and aimed to strike at the joint between Wellington's and Blücher's armies, so as to drive a wedge between them and then crush them separately. He saw, too, that the chance depended on surprise—on whether he could bring up his own army from different parts of France and concentrate it within striking distance of the Allies' joint without their detecting his movements and aim. He hoped to profit by the way that their lines of supply ran divergently westward and eastward, so that if they were surprised and split by his stroke their natural tendency would be to fall back in different directions.

They had foreseen this possibility, and to meet it, Wellington had gone so far as to agree that, in the event of a retreat being necessary, he would abandon his own communications and withdraw along with Blücher towards the Rhine. But, with an Englishman's sense of the sea, he instinctively felt that Napoleon would try to cut him off from his own seaports. He had never yet fought Napoleon, and perhaps had not realized that Napoleon had an instinctive preference for operating on "interior lines," and piercing joints—especially when faced with numerically superior forces. Under the influence of that instinctively preconceived idea, Wellington kept his British divisions far out on his right flank, while his Netherland divisions were posted near the joint with Blücher's army—and he continued to keep a large detachment out on his right during the battle of Waterloo.

Wellington was handicapped to some extent by his scruples against sending covering patrols across the frontier before hostilities began. But his most expert intelligence officer, Colonel Colquhoun Grant, had gone into France, and it had been arranged that his reports were to be sent back through General von Dörnberg, the commander of the cavalry screen. Unfortunately, Grant was rather late in getting news of Napoleon's concentration, and when his warning message arrived on June 15, Dörnberg did not pass it on to Wellington, deciding that Grant's deductions were premature. Even so, it would seem that both Wellington and Blücher were the more easily taken by surprise because of over-confidence.

Napoleon had assembled his whole striking force in the angle between the Sambre and the Meuse, and had achieved its concentration close to the frontier with remarkable secrecy and speed. In the early hours of June 15 he advanced over the frontier, forced the crossings of the Sambre near Charleroi a few miles further on, and that evening the bulk of his force was massed beyond the river on a narrow front. Next morning it advanced in a Y formation, of two wings and a central reserve—which was ready to be swung in support of either wing as circumstances indicated. The right wing pushed up the Liége road towards Ligny, and the left wing up the Brussels road towards Quatre Bras. That expanding advance promised to widen the breach which had already been made in the Allies' front.

Blücher had been quick to recognize the danger—and to concentrate his own army—but slow to make it clear to his ally. It was mid-afternoon before Wellington received the bare and belated news that French troops were attacking the line of the Sambre. Still believing that Napoleon would come round his outer flank, he issued orders whereby the bulk of his forces assembled *west* of the road from Mons to

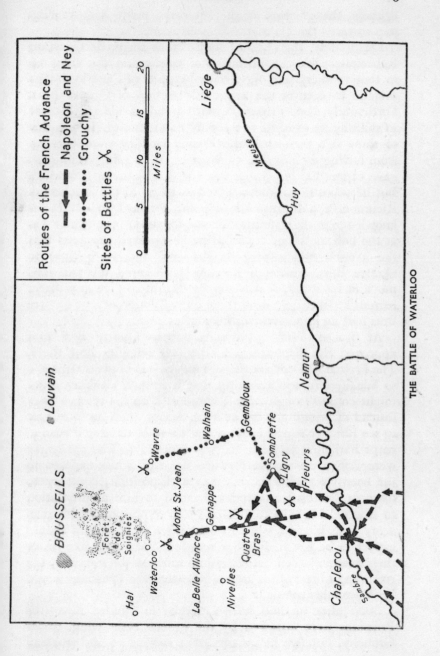

Routes of the French Advance

▬▬► Napoleon and Ney

••••► Grouchy

Sites of Battles ✗

Miles
0   5   10   15   20

Liége

Meuse

Huy

Namur

Louvain

BRUSSELLS

Forêt de Soignies

Hal

Waterloo

Wavre

Walhain

Gembloux

Mont St. Jean

Genappe

La Belle Alliance

Quatre Bras

Nivelles

Sombreffe

Ligny

Fleurys

Charleroi

Sambre

THE BATTLE OF WATERLOO

Brussels, though part of the left corps made a short side-step towards the Charleroi-Brussels road.

Fortunately, the chief of staff of that corps, de Constant Rebecque, took the initiative of continuing the side-step to that road by sending Prince Bernard of Saxe-Weimar's brigade to occupy the key road-junction of Quatre Bras. Fortunately also, Prince Bernard handled his small force so skilfully as to bluff the enemy as to its size. It was due to these two men that the French cavalry were checked from having a clear ride to Brussels. At 10 p.m. Wellington gave orders for his whole force to start moving eastward. But he was still so unconcerned as to go to the Duchess of Richmond's ball, instead of going forward to get closer knowledge of the situation, as was his usual practice. It was at the ball, at about 1 a.m., that he received the news that the French had captured Charleroi and were close to Quatre Bras. Although he now accelerated the eastward move of his army, it was too far distant to give any direct help to Blücher next day, though the fraction of it at Quatre Bras had an important indirect effect.

At 6 a.m. Wellington rode out to Quatre Bras and approved the dispositions of the two brigades now there. The French had not yet showed themselves in great strength, so Wellington, still thinking that a French flanking move might come through Mons, chose to keep his reserve back instead of bringing it up at once. About noon he rode over to see Blücher near Ligny, where three of the four Prussian corps had now arrived. He was shocked to find that they were drawn up on the forward slope of a hill, exposed to the enemy's artillery fire. Such a disposition, contrary to his own Peninsular practice, seemed to him an invitation to trouble. He said to Blücher: "Everyone knows his own army best, but if I were to fight with mine here, I should expect to be beat." Blücher retorted: "My men like to see their enemy." Wellington said no more at the moment, but remarked to one of his own officers that the Prussians would be "damnably mauled."

Soon after he had left—to return to Quatre Bras—the Prussians were attacked by the French right wing, under Grouchy. For five hours the battle swayed to and fro, and the issue looked uncertain, though the Prussian infantry were suffering excessive loss, as Wellington had predicted. Then late in the evening, Napoleon intervened with his reserve, and the battered Prussian centre broke—a collapse which led to a general retreat under cover of darkness. Blücher's defeat might have become an irretrievable disaster if Napoleon had been able to fulfil his afternoon intention of swinging his left wing, under Ney, round against Blücher's flank and rear. But that part of the plan had miscarried, owing to confusion of orders following initial hesitation.

Ney had been slow to advance in the morning when he could have overwhelmed the slender force at Quatre Bras and captured the cross-roads with ease, prior to an eastward turn. Perhaps he remembered too well the traps which Wellington had set in the Peninsular War. When Ney ordered his leading corps (Reille) to the attack about 2 p.m.—after lengthy reconnaissance and preparation—it quickly routed the Netherland Division there. But at this crisis Wellington's reserve was beginning to arrive, and by throwing the first two battalions into a counter-attack through the woods, Wellington bluffed the French to a standstill long enough for the rest of the reserve to occupy the position. Ney's renewed assault was repelled by a much stiffened defence.

Meantime, Ney's other corps (d'Erlon) had been diverted towards Ligny without Ney's knowledge. Furious at this step, and failing to grasp Napoleon's intention, Ney sent d'Erlon orders to return at once. So d'Erlon turned round, when he had almost reached the Ligny battlefield, and then arrived back at Quatre Bras too late to redeem the check which Ney had suffered there.

Next morning Wellington, receiving belated news of Blücher's defeat, withdrew from Quatre Bras to a position at Mont St. Jean, south of Waterloo, and about midway to Brussels. So skilfully did he screen his movements that his retreat was completed without serious interference from Ney. Napoleon was so angry when he arrived on the scene as to exclaim that Ney had "sacrificed France" by letting Wellington slip away. So it proved.

Wellington notified Blücher that he proposed to make a stand in the new position if Blücher could send him the support of one Prussian corps. Blücher, with characteristic comradeship and resolution, overrode the doubts of his staff and promised to send two corps next day—although they were later in arriving than had been hoped. In the end he brought three out of the four, and went himself at the head, spurring on the march with the appeal: "Lads, you will not let me break my word."

Wellington's defensive position was admirably chosen, so that the French had to attack uphill while his own troops, and their movements were sheltered by the crest of a low ridge. The open glacis of the forward slope was dotted with three separate clusters of buildings—the Chateau of Hougoumont on the west, the farm of La Haye Sainte in the centre, and the twin farms of Papelotte and La Haye on the east. Wellington threw out small detachments to occupy these points—like prongs projecting from his three-mile front—and used them to break up the attackers' formation. In all, he now had with him 64,000 troops to meet 70,000 of Napoleon's veterans. Wellington left a further 17,000 at Hal, ten miles away on his right, as he felt that Napoleon might try a flanking manœuvre that way rather than deliver a frontal attack. That detachment proved to be a useless, and dangerous, subtraction from his strength. Yet it should be added that on the morning of the 18th, several of the French generals—those who had met Wellington in the Peninsular War—warned Napoleon against attempting a frontal attack against Wellington's army in a defensive position. But Napoleon would not listen. A move round Wellington's flank might only drive him back towards Blücher, and Napoleon wanted to smash the British.

He was confident in the power of attack, when directed by himself, and retorted—"Because you have been beaten by Wellington you consider him a good general. But I tell you that Wellington is a bad general and the English are bad troops. This whole affair will not be more serious than swallowing one's breakfast." He was equally contemptuous of the possibility that the Prussians might intervene. For when it was reported that a waiter, who had served

Wellington at breakfast the previous day, had overheard an aide-de-camp refer to Blücher's coming, Napoleon scornfully said: "After such a battle as Fleurus (Ligny), the Allies couldn't join forces for at least two days—besides the Prussians are pressed by Grouchy's forces who are at their heels."

The battle opened about 11.30 a.m. on the morning of the 18th, Napoleon having postponed the start several hours in order to allow the ground to dry. To clear his path he began with attacks to break the right and left "prongs," but both attacks were repulsed—indeed, Hougoumont with its small garrison of 500 guardsmen, eventually reinforced to 2,000, absorbed the whole effort of Reille's corps of 13,000 throughout the battle. About 1 p.m., Napoleon, growing impatient, launched d'Erlon's corps of 16,000 men in an assault on the centre of the main position, following a massed artillery bombardment. But the crest of the ridge helped to shield Wellington's infantry line from the blast, whereas d'Erlon's dense columns offered an easy target. Although shrivelling under the fire, these columns succeeded in reaching the crest, and looked close to breaking through Wellington's front, but at that moment, Lord Uxbridge launched two British cavalry brigades (2,000 men) against them. The sudden impact on their disordered ranks burst them into fragments, and swept them back down the slope. At 3.30 p.m. Napoleon tried another battering-ram assault with diminished strength and no better result.

Seeing Wellington's line withdraw a little—actually to gain more cover from the bombardment—Ney jumped to the conclusion that Wellington was retreating, and led a whole cavalry corps forward. By the time it reached the crest, Wellington's infantry had formed into squares, against which the cavalry waves beat in vain, and they eventually flowed back down the slope.

Now, at last, the leading Prussian corps arrived on the battlefield and began to press on Napoleon's right flank, which drew off part of his reserves to check it. Realizing that the sand was running out, Napoleon threw in another massed cavalry corps to support the first, and carry it along

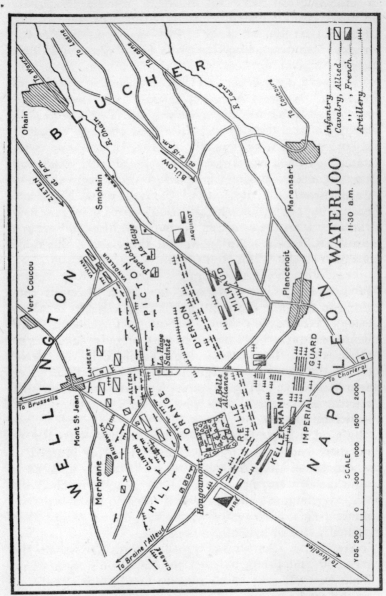

WATERLOO—THE ORDER OF BATTLE

in a renewed effort on a greater scale. This also failed. But a subsequent infantry assault managed to capture the farm of La Haye Sainte, and Wellington's line began to show the strain, needing all his resourcefulness to cement incipient cracks. Meantime, Blucher's flank pressure was increasing with the arrival of two more Prussian corps.

Becoming desperate, Napoleon risked most of his last reserves, 6,000 bayonets of the Imperial Guard, on a final gamble to break Wellington. After another intense bombardment, the assault came in three waves, about 8 p.m., across ground that was now a quagmire after so much trampling. Each wave was repulsed. Then Wellington rode forward to the crest, and raised his cocked hat as a signal for the whole line to advance in a general counterstroke. His army poured down the slope, sweeping Napoleon's shattered army before it, while the Prussians surged in from the flank. As the sun went down, the darkness swallowed not only an army, but an empire.

Waterloo, too, was both the zenith and the sunset of Wellington's military career. In his case the sunset was glorious. Yet his actual performance, as distinct from the fact of breaking Napoleon, was not so shining as some of his Peninsular achievements, especially Salamanca. He had made serious misjudgments beforehand, and it was partly due to these that the battle had been, as he remarked: "the nearest run thing you ever saw in your life." He had redeemed these mistakes by his cool judgment and heartening leadership on the battlefield, which justified his comment: "By God, I don't think it would have been done if I had not been there." Even Creevey, one of his arch-critics, to whom he said this on returning to Brussels, recognized it on that occasion as a great man's realism rather than an expression of conceit. But there was no brilliance of manœuvre at Waterloo. Victory had come through patience and puttying up holes.

Wellington's crowning triumph was not his supreme piece of generalship, but the final vindication of a method. That method was based on the calculation that, if the enemy could be induced to attack, defence was reasonably sure to prevail when the attacker's energy was worn down.

Fresh from the strain of the battle, it was natural that Wellington should be more conscious of his interim anxieties than of the final dividend his method had produced. But in reflection he summed up the lesson in the remark that Napoleon "just moved forward in the 'old style' in columns, and was driven off in the 'old style'." Wellington's tactics were typically English—in the true line of his nation's long-standing experience. They anticipated the proposed truth which that great pugilist, Jem Mace, expressed in his guiding principle: "Let 'em come to ye, and they'll beat theirselves."

An essay that is primarily concerned with Wellington as a soldier reaches its natural end at Waterloo. But it is worth emphasis that his subsequent political career showed the same characteristics as his military career, though affected by a less suitable environment and by increasing age. His mistakes can be traced to an insufficiency of foresight, and the way that his detachment separated his mind from the sparks of sympathetic imagination—for he was not so devoid of this faculty as his manner suggested. His successes, and the extent to which he retrieved his mistakes, can be traced both to the fundamental honesty and the inherent elasticity of his mind. Combined, these qualities modified the stubborn defence of his conservative position, producing the clear-sighted realism which enabled him to "know when to retreat and to dare to do it"—when it was the only way to maintain his essential aim, the preservation of good order and national peace.

His elasticity was too well subordinated to his principles, however, for him to be a great success as a politician. He was greater as a statesman, especially in the realm of international affairs, where the long-term prospects depended on whether arrangements were based on good principles. For that reason his greatest contribution was in the making of the peace settlement with France.

In the occupation of the conquered country he was as intent to protect the people from ill-usage as he had been when that policy had been a means to smooth the path of his invasion. He did all he could to curb the revengeful excesses of his allies—even to the point of posting a British sentry on the Pont de Jéna in Paris to hinder Blücher from blowing it up—while insisting that his own army must set an example of gentleness, courtesy and restraint. "We are Englishmen, and pride ourselves on our deportment, and that pride shall not be injured in my keeping."

When it came to drawing up the peace terms, he threw all his influence against the demand of Prussia and the other German states that France should be dismembered and compelled to pay a huge indemnity, to compensate their sufferings and safeguard their security. He realized with uncommon clarity the unwisdom of immoderation, and the fundamental insecurity of a peace based upon oppression. In the end only minor changes were made in the frontiers of France, and the indemnity was reduced to a mere £28,000,000. The outcome justified his policy of moderation.

It was because he really understood war that he became so good at securing peace. He was the least militaristic of soldiers, and free from the lust of glory. It was because he saw the value of peace that he became so unbeatable in war. For he kept the end in view, instead of falling in love with the means. Unlike Napoleon, he was not infected by the romance of war, which germinates illusions and self-deceptions. That was how Napoleon had failed, and Wellington had prevailed.

KITCHENER

By

SIR GEORGE ARTHUR

"WHO can now doubt that but for this man and his work Germany would have been victorious?" Such was the testimony borne by the soldier who led the great armies in the field to the soldier who raised and trained them, the tribute of the soldier who achieved victory to the soldier who organized it.

The story of Herbert Kitchener—and the creation of the armies which bore his name—is a simple story of a faithful servant of the Crown who looked a little further ahead than other men, chose what he believed the right path, and suffered no one to hinder him, and nothing to daunt him, from following it.

Until the close of the nineteenth century the name of Herbert Kitchener meant something to a few people, very little to society at large. There had been discoveries by a young R.E. officer in Palestine, but then Palestine was not often on the tapis; Gordon had written from Khartoum: "Whoever comes up here had better appoint Major Kitchener Governor-General," and again, "It is delicious to find not one civil word from any official person except Kitchener"; there were stories of how an officer of the Egyptian Army had gone ahead with the Nile Relief Expedition and, wearing Arab costume, had camped with Arabs to try and secure the information which Lord Wolseley required; when Khartoum fell Major Kitchener had been detailed to draft a report on the whole question of

EARL KITCHENER

From the portrait by
Sir A. S. Cope
By courtesy of the
Royal Engineers
Head Quarters Mess

the future of the Sudan; he had made a most favourable impression—an impression which proved to be lasting—on Queen Victoria at Osborne; he had represented England on the Joint Commission to delimit the Sultan of Zanzibar's frontiers and had told someone, who told other people, that Germany would not only be a serious competitor for territory in the great unknown continent but would some day come to blows with England and would probably not fight fair; he had been badly wounded in a fray with Osman Digna near Suakim, and Queen Victoria had asked for daily bulletins and had made him an A.D.C.; he had succeeded Sir Francis Grenfell as Sirdar, and, at the head of a band of picked and celibate British officers, was busily training the Egyptian Army for no less a duty than to avenge Gordon and free the Sudan from darkness and slavery; he had brought an erring Khedive to see the error of his ways; he had been ordered to retake Dongola and had done so; Lord Salisbury had said that if any General were to supersede Major-General Kitchener in the final stages of the campaign then in progress the Cabinet would have to change their Prime Minister; there had been a great fight at a place called Atbara, which required folk at home to refer to their maps—all these items were food for conversation in military and diplomatic circles and for those who had special relations with Egypt, but had not attracted any large public attention.

Then, on a September evening in 1898, there resounded up and down the country the news of a great victory won in a fight of a few hours, and as the story unfolded itself it was realized that, with the loss of about sixty British and 160 Egyptian lives, and for a sum which represented less than half a day's cost for Great Britain in the Great War, the Dervish power had been shattered, the Sudan re-occupied, nearly a million square miles brought under Anglo-Egyptian rule, and that a stain left on the British shield by the death of Charles Gordon had been wiped off.

And then the man who had planned and organized the river campaign and had struck the great blow was found to be something of a diplomat; he was to smooth over a rather awkward difficulty and play a leading part in inducing the

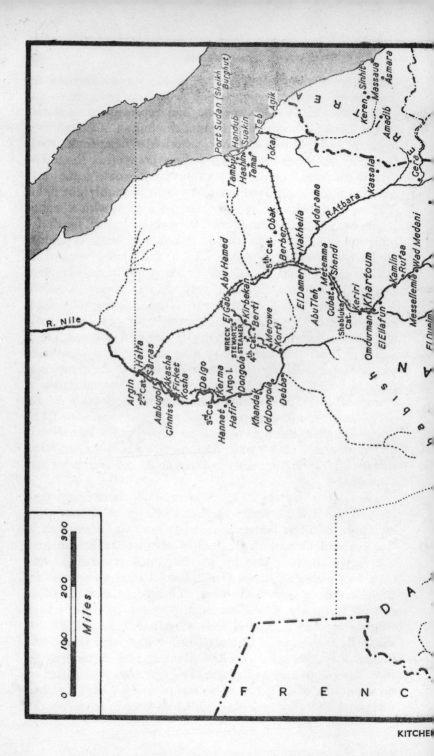

R. Nile

Argin
Halfa
2nd Cat.
Sarras
Ambugol
Akasha
Firket
Ginniss
Kosha
Delgo
Hannek
Kerma
Hafir
3rd Cat.
Argo I.
Dongola Steamer
Khandak
Old Dongola
Debba
4th Cat.
Berti
Kinbekan
Merowe
Korti
WRECK El Gab
STEWART'S
STEAMER
Abu Hamed
5th Cat.
Obak
Berber
Nakheila
El Damer
Adarama
R. Atbara
Abu Tleh
Metemma
Shendi
Gubat
Shablukat
Cat.
Kerini
Omdurman
Khartoum
Messellemia
Wad Medani
El Ellafun
Kamlin
Rufaa
El Dueim

Port Sudan (Sheikh Burghut)
Tambuk
Handub
Hashin
Suakin
Tamai
Teb
Agik
Tokar

Keren
Sinhit
Massaua
Asmara
Amadib
Kassala
Gera

S U D A N

D A R

F R E N C

SUDANESE

Miles

0   100   200   300

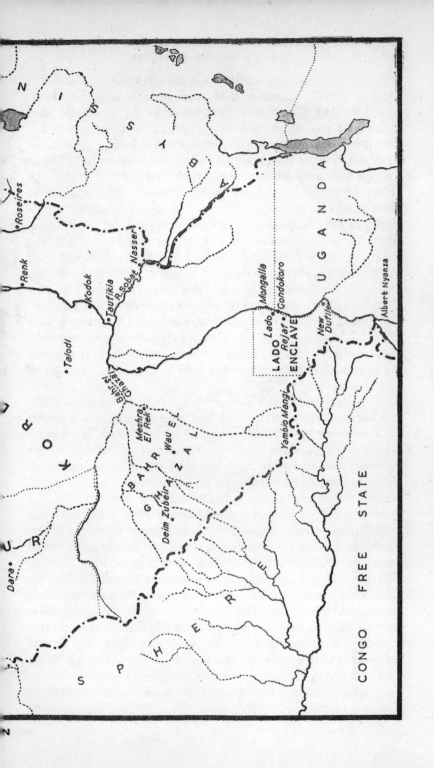

French to yield their claim to a desolate swamp in South Africa. Small wonder that the homecoming of Lord Kitchener of Khartoum (Kitchener of Khartum he said would be too ugly) was made the occasion of rapturous receptions, enthusiastic greetings, and the lavish bestowal of honours. To say that a soldier who knows everything about camps and very little about courts and clubs enjoyed the blaze of publicity and the plaudits which were rained on him would be beside the truth, but he exploited his popularity in the direction of hard cash to make good the purpose then nearest his heart—the permanent benefit of the brave blacks whose guardianship he had taken over from Gordon. The Sovereign endorsed the "Sirdar's Fund," the Prime Minister launched an appeal, the Stock Exchange invited him—a rare distinction—to address its members, and before the end of the year the Sirdar was back at Omdurman with £100,000 in his pocket, his plan for the new city in his head, and at the back of his mind the determination that Gordon College should benefit not the lads of Cairo but the lads of Kordofan.

The Anglo-Sudanese Agreement, signed in January, 1899, set out that supreme military and civil command was vested in Kitchener as Governor-General of the Sudan; his proclamations were to have the force of law, and the matters which claimed his attention, and none of which came amiss to him, ranged from telegraphs and land ordinances, general cultivation, the grain supply for starving districts, royalties and the liquor laws, to the building of a hotel and the restoration of the Palace at Khartoum; from pensions, indemnities and the bearing of arms to the appointment of an Anglican Bishop; from questions of frontier with Eritrea, the French and the Congo, to questions regarding the flag and rights of Egypt as compared with those of England; from superintending a flotilla of steamers on the headwaters of the Nile to devising a system of radiating the new city which was to spring up. The work was hard, but it was sweet, for it was work for the country he loved as his home and for the country he had been strong to redeem.

A busy year, and at the end of it came the hurried translation from one corner of Africa to the other, the appointment

—under new conditions—of Chief of Staff to Lord Roberts, and the campaign for which, truth to tell, a soldier who was last of all a fire-eater had throughout but little appetite. He warned eager officers, afraid that their arrival in South Africa would be belated, that the war would be long and laborious and fraught with more grief than glory; it was "a big business badly begun, and owing to our artillery officers' dislike of anything new, we are hopelessly behind the age." He endorsed Macaulay's dictum that there is nothing more cruel than languid warfare when from Bloemfontein he wrote to Lady Cranborne,* "People here do not seem to look upon the war sufficiently seriously; it is considered too much like a game of polo with intervals for afternoon tea."

And the longer the dreary warfare lasted—and it lasted for a year longer, as Kitchener scornfully said, in order to put 500 Dutchmen into prison at the end of it—the more convinced he was that if his sturdy opponents were to lose their independence they must be offered terms which they could honourably accept; neither legalism nor war-passion must stand in the way of a peace to be observed in the spirit as well as in the letter. So it came about that in the *pourparlers* at Vereeniging the Statesman was disposed towards the sternest measures, the Soldier stood firm for reconciliation. Lord Milner had wished a definite military conquest to precede any negotiations for peace; the Boers must be under no illusions as to who had won the war. Lord Kitchener, looking ahead, argued that a peace based on sheer exhaustion would preclude any real reconciliation and exclude any amicable incorporation in the British Empire. Even while his blockhouse system was being relentlessly pursued he had written home, "I hope I may be allowed to do away with any humiliating in the surrender when, and if, it comes."

Now he was sure that, if terms based on anything like goodwill could be arranged, the loyalty of new-found friends could be relied on, and we should have "an asset of first-rate importance to the Empire for whose honour and glory they may before long be fighting side by side with us." Least of all Kitchener entertained the theory, laid down just

* Later Marchioness of Salisbury.

then by the German Staff, that the intellectual and material resources of a sometime enemy State should be laid waste; rather had he steadily in mind that the change of status from a Republic to a British Dominion would leave democratic freedom unimpaired with British insurance thrown in.

Kitchener's share in securing a peace which was to forge an indissoluble bond suggests the part he might have played had he been one of his country's agents at Versailles. "I am not in the least afraid about our winning the War, I am very much afraid about our making a proper peace, and here I think I might be useful," he said more than once to the present writer. Speculation has often been busy as to the terms he himself would have proposed and the conditions he would have prescribed; he was, anyhow, clear that our bill of costs should be cut down to the lowest possible figure which would bear relations with our net expenditure, that it should not even then be stretched to the extreme limit of what Germany could pay; and that it should be inspired by no spirit of vindictiveness. But he would have insisted that the bill, having been "taxed" and sent in, must be met, and he would have been at pains to ensure that Germany, however sunk in moral corruption, should not seek by fraudulent finance to recover what she had been forced to lose in the field.

As in South Africa, so as Commander-in-Chief in India; one vision inspired the man, one simple purpose drew him on, and in following it every faculty had to be made the instrument of a resolute will. Kitchener was sure—he had been sure for many years past—that in time, if not in his time, there would be a great appeal to the arbitrament of the sword; although he kept silence, except to a few, a German menace to European peace—and something more— was constantly present in his mind, and he knew that our military arrangements were dangerously inadequate to our responsibilities. "Did they remember, when they went headlong into a war like this, that they were without an army and without any preparations to equip one?" was his cry in the fever of 1914, when he discovered how slender was our military force, how bare our military cupboard.

So much dust was raised by the controversy over the Dual

Control that it rather obscured the actual fruit of seven years' labour, of labour without the short leave of absence which was asked for and refused. "But for Lord Kitchener's work, India could never have possibly given the great work she has to the Empire during the War." So wrote a famous General of the Indian Army who fought in France, Flanders and the Dardanelles; and one remembers that, amid vast and various reforms, from an inchoate mass of battalions, squadrons and batteries distributed "higgledy-piggledy" among the armies of the three presidencies the Commander-in-Chief evolved a homogeneous army organized into nine Field Divisions and six Cavalry Brigades, that his constitution in India was to form the model for the salutary and skilful "Haldane" reforms prescribed at home, and that the Kitchener "Big Division" was to be adopted as the formula for regular and territorial divisions alike. So when, through four long years of bitter strife, the War Office made call after call on India for troops, response was always forthcoming, and even when she might have been thought to have been drained dry there could be despatched to Baghdad a complete and highly organized division of all arms, the Indian authorities providing the transport; and, be it remembered, India was the while sending home the whole residue of the British Infantry, excepting nine battalions, in exchange for a much smaller number of territorial troops.

In his administration of the Army in India Kitchener kept steadily in view the external demand which hereafter might conceivably be made on India's military resources. The defeat of Russia by Japan did something to induce the Czar to come to terms with England, terms which issued in the agreement over Persia in 1907, but Japan's triumph had been hailed throughout the East as a victory of an Asiatic over a European foe which broke the long spell of European dominance, and this, in Kitchener's belief, might well—as it did—lead to Eastern restlessness and revolt. And he saw with anxiety, if not with alarm, the dawn of another danger. Germany had quietly set afoot a process of peaceful penetration in Asia Minor, and her more outspoken politicians and professors were assigning to her the guardianship of the Ottoman Empire. The Berlin-Baghdad Railway was already denominated the Berlin-Byzantium-Baghdad-Bahn, but Bengal, not Baghdad, was marked as the terminus, and Germany was indulging herself in something more than a dream of enjoying both the hegemony of Europe and the control of India. And, as Kitchener reminded the authorities at home, in the event of any large conflict, Turkey's dusky hand would more than possibly be clasped in Germany's mailed fist.

If Wellington's military mind was always concerned with "what was happening on the other side of the field," Kitchener's eyes, strained to pierce the future, told him that the Kaiserliche policy rendered war between England and Germany a contingency to be reckoned with, in the East no less than the West, and that his handiwork in India must be such as to enable her to make a great Imperial contribution in the day when a mighty effort would have to be made.

The same train of thought pursued him as he passed on to set in order, and furnish, the military houses of Australia and New Zealand, and then, in three comparatively easy, and altogether enjoyable, years, to make Egypt proof against assault.

And then—a frenzied patriot fired a pistol in a back street in Bosnia and within five weeks five white nations were standing to arms.

Kitchener had often described himself as a lonely man, but probably he was never so alone as in his outlook on the character, the duration and dimensions of the struggle which had already started before he received the seals of the War Office. The accepted military plan had been that in certain eventualities, and on urgent demand, we should send overseas six Divisions of Infantry with a Cavalry Division and proportionate guns; that the Territorials should be responsible for the safety of these islands and that the Special Reserve should feed the Expeditionary Force.

In other words, our commitments were supposed to be limited to keeping a handful of troops in the field up to strength and looking after ourselves at home. Kitchener saw with one glance that the views of the politicians were wholly untenable and the provisions of the military authorities utterly insufficient, now that England, with something like fine recklessness, had thrown down a challenge to a fierce invader. It was not a question of reinforcing a perfectly trained and faultlessly equipped miniature army in the field, and of defending our own coasts from insult; there must be created, with the utmost rapidity compatible with efficiency, an Army which should speak fearlessly and effectively with the great forces of the German Empire. Without—literally without—an hour's delay Kitchener laid his plans for an army of seventy Divisions, coolly calculating—as he then told the present writer—that its maximum strength would be reached at the beginning of the third year of the war, just when the enemy would be feeling the pinch of a diminution of resources of man-power. The scheme, of course, ran quite contrary to the dogma that armies might be expanded, but could not be created when once a war had begun.

The Germans scornfully derided the Kitchener plan; G.H.Q. scoffed for a while at "Kitchener's shadow army", which could never become flesh and blood in time to take part in the fray; economists denied the possibility of any protracted European conflict; politicians prattled of a decision in the field before the end of the year; the Cabinet were aghast at the War Minister's predictions and proposals, while the French General Staff gracefully remarked that some leaders had called new armies into being, and other leaders had maintained existing armies, but that it was reserved for Lord Kitchener to perform the two feats simultaneously.

For this titanic task Kitchener had one priceless and indispensable asset: he enjoyed the confidence of everyone who mattered, from his Sovereign down to the humblest barbarian native among the King-Emperor's subjects; the trust in Kitchener, which almost savoured of a religious allegiance—and was of a piece with the long-drawn-out refusal to believe in his death—proved itself a chief factor in the resolve of the British people to spare nothing and shrink from nothing if the eventual victory which he had held up to their view could be secured. The closeness of the bond between the big soldier and his countrymen—which was all the tighter because not one in a hundred thousand had ever set eyes on him—became of peculiar importance because the only existing machinery for raising a large military force was by voluntary enlistment; the mutual trust between the man and the masses figured largely in the enrolling of an army, in fashion as no army was ever enrolled before.

Posterity, remembering a great figure who grows in stature as he recedes into history, will remember that in a supreme national emergency Kitchener called his fellow countrymen to the colours, and that three millions of them answered the call. They may have been moved by the instinct of self-preservation, they were certainly stirred to help a victim of aggression, but when all was said and done the signal to which they responded was a personal summons.

Posters and advertisements up and down the land carried the words that Lord Kitchener was confident his appeal to their loyalty to the King and love for their country would meet with immediate reply. And the country leapt to arms; rich and poor, squire and yokel, from moor and mine, from field and factory they flocked to the Standard to form what was to be popularly known, and even officially recognized, as the Kitchener Army. It is certain that neither his reputation as an organizer nor a soldier would have sufficed to command the faith of the people had they not been assured of the singleness of his aim and the strength of his motive. A leader is often, and often quite unjustly, suspected of working to gratify his own ambitions; Kitchener appealed to the public as entirely trustworthy because entirely selfless. This was in the minds of the Labour leaders when, after his death, they declared in the House of Commons that the workers "trusted Kitchener because they knew him to be straight." His motto was that the work and not the workman was the matter of real importance.

And if Kitchener was valuable in sustaining the spirit at home he was scarcely less so in vitalizing the alliance abroad. France felt that here was no insular Englishman but one who understood the real nature of a world struggle, who knew that the fight must be fought out in the great theatre of war and who was sure that if he wished to be safe in that East which he loved he should be strong in the West where Allies must stand fast on common ground. His hurried visit to

Paris to arrest the retreat of the Commander-in-Chief was not only the notion of a Minister determined that the policy of his Government should be carried out, but that of a soldier who understood war on the great scale.

The question was asked then, and has often been asked since, what difference it would have made to the conduct and duration of the War if Lord Kitchener had reached Russia; the Mission headed by Lord Milner and Sir Henry Wilson nine months later not only accomplished nothing but so entirely failed to appreciate the situation that they returned with a report of "All's well" when the Revolution was bursting out behind their backs. But the circumstances in midsummer, 1916, were different. Between July and December the Revolution became a fully organized movement, although at the last the hands of the organizers were forced, their plans were appropriated and altered and the result was Bolshevism, not constitutionalism. Kitchener knew precisely how things stood in Russia, that revolution was in the air and that concessions from above and reorganization from below were essential if a catastrophe were to be averted.

Such was the prestige of his name that Russia in some indefinable but undeniable way was relying on him to put things straight; such was the weight of that name that he had already not only been allowed, but invited, to criticize Russian methods with a freedom and to press his advice with an insistency which would have been tolerated from no other foreigner. If he had been unable to secure the concessions from above, all contemporary evidence went to show that he would have compelled the reorganization from below, and would have enabled a powerful ally to stand steady while hostilities lasted. At any rate, had he been obliged to count his journey as barren of success, he would have returned to complete his plans without further thought of Russian co-operation, and he could have reminded himself that in November, 1915, he had warned Joffre, at Chantilly, "You are relying on Russia standing by us to the end; I am calculating on her being 'out of it' within a year."

If an outpour of money be any indication of popular feeling it may be remembered that within a year of the tragedy of the *Hampshire* a sum of over £800,000 was subscribed by the subjects of the Sovereign to the memory of a faithful servant of the Crown. But, as *The Times* newspaper finely said, "The great armies which Kitchener called into being are his living monument, and no nobler monument has been raised to man." One, and only one, attempt was made to mar that monument. Early in 1916 Kitchener had suddenly to meet a representation, put forward by a section of the Cabinet, that he must choose between a diminution of the force of seventy Divisions and the reduction of our monetary advances to our Allies. He declined the dilemma; he did not think that England could present either of these conclusions to her Allies without proof positive that expenditure could not be reduced nor national income increased, and the soldier who had always caused economy to be the handmaid of efficiency gave proof that our pecuniary position could be improved to the extent of ninety millions— the sum required; and this without reduction either of our fighting forces or of the advances necessary to keep our Allies in the field. The discussion was sharp and short, and as a result the seventy Divisions were assured of their existence and of their drafts, and the Kitchener Armies could take their part in the Battle of the Somme which their creator knew was planned for the coming summer.

Kitchener did not live to see the end, but he willed and fashioned the means. There are many to aver that his part in winning the War was not yet played out, and that he would have had a large and valuable part in establishing the Peace; but at least as regards the creation and placing in the field of the armies who were to hold high England's honour and spell victory for the cause, he could review a work continuous through nearly half a century and only finished in the final hour allotted to him; for the last Division of the Kitchener Armies to go overseas took ship the very day on which he himself set out on the journey from which there was to be no coming back.

EARL HAIG

HAIG

By

THE RT. HON. WINSTON S. CHURCHILL

EARLY in 1919 Lord Haig walked ashore at Dover after the total defeat of Germany and disappeared into private life. There was an interlude of pageantry, of martial celebrations, of the Freedom of Cities, of banquets and the like; but in fact the Commander-in-Chief of the British Armies in France passed, as he left the gangway and set foot on the pier, from a position of almost supreme responsibility and glorious power to the ordinary life of a country gentleman. Titles, grants, honours of every kind, all the symbols of public gratitude were showered upon him; but he was given no work. He did not join in the counsels of the nation; he was not invited to reorganize its army; he was not consulted upon the Treaties; no sphere of public activity was opened to him.

It would be affectation to pretend that he did not feel this. He was fifty-eight—an age at which Marlborough still had four great campaigns to fight; he was in the fullest enjoyment of his gifts and faculties; he had been accustomed all his life to work from morning till night; he was full of energy and experience, and apparently at the moment when he was most successful, there was nothing for him to do; he was not wanted any more. He must just go home and sit by the fire and fight his battles over again. He became one of the permanent unemployed.

So he looked around from his small house at Bemersyde

beyond the Border and saw that a great many of his soldiers and brother officers were in the same plight so far as work was concerned, and that in addition many were stricken with wounds, and many more were hard put to it to keep their homes together. To their cause and fortunes then he devoted himself. They accepted him as their Leader in the disappointments of Peace as in the bitter trials of War. He acquired great influence over this immense and powerful body of men. Alike by example and guidance he led them away from all courses prejudicial or dangerous to the State, and did his best to improve their material conditions. He collected money on their behalf, he gave personal attention to grievous cases, he trapesed about the Empire weaving the soldiers of so many distant lands into the comradeship of a victorious army. Thus he occupied himself, and the world went on its way; and politicians dealt with all the interesting topics as they arose, and settled matters generally—or thought they did; and everybody seemed quite satisfied.

But we must understand that the great masses of ordinary work-a-day people, when in their busy lives they had time to think about things, wondered why it was that the Commander whose name was linked with hard-won but unlimited victory had no place in the hierarchy of the State. However, they did not know what to do about it, and he said nothing: he just went on with his work for the ex-service men. This, though it cheered his heart, by no means—once the organization was set up—occupied his time or gave scope to his abilities. So the years passed.

People began to criticize his campaigns. As soon as the war-censorship, actual and moral, was lifted, pens ran freely. There was no lack of material. There was deep resentment against slaughters on a gigantic scale alleged upon notable occasions to have been needless and fruitless. All this will long continue to be debated. However, Haig said nothing. He neither wrote nor spoke in his own defence. Some of his Staff Officers without his knowledge published a controversial rejoinder. The volume was extremely ill received by the press and the public. But neither the serious criticism nor the unsatisfying defence extorted any public utterance from Haig.

The next thing heard about the Field Marshal was that he had fallen down dead like a soldier shot on the battle-field, and probably from causes that had originated there. Then occurred manifestations of sorrow and regard which rose from the very heart of the people and throughout the Empire. Then everybody saw how admirable had been his demeanour since the peace. There was a majesty about it which proved an exceptional greatness of character. It showed a man capable of resisting unusual strains, internal and external, even when prolonged over years; it showed a man cast in a classic mould.

The qualities revealed by his life and conduct after the War cast a new light upon his contribution to the victory. One can see from a different angle and in a different medium the strength of will and character which enabled him to withstand the various intense stresses to which he was sub-jected. With his front crumbling under the greatest of Ger-man assaults, or with his own army collapsing in the mud and blood of Paschendaele, with an Ally always exacting and frequently irregular, with the Government at home searching high and low for someone to replace him, he pre-served at all times a majestic calm. He lived each day without departing from his convictions, or seeking sensa-tional effects, or courting popularity, or losing heart. He was equally sure of his professional qualifications and of his constitutional duty; and he acted at all times in strict accordance with these definite conceptions. When the news of frightful slaughters, often barren, and the ruin of opera-tions in which he had trusted, and for which he bore the awful responsibility, were reported to him, he was fortified by feeling that he had employed to the best of his ability the military training of a lifetime, that he was doing the duty assigned to him by the lawfully-constituted authorities, and that he was at all times equally ready to persevere or to be replaced.

A selfless, dispassionate, detached equanimity ruled his spirit, not only at moments of acute crisis but month after month and year after year. Inflexible, rigorously pedantic in his assertion of the professional point of view, he never-theless at all times treated the Civil Power with respect and loyalty. Even when he knew that his recall was debated among the War Cabinet, he neither sought to marshal the powerful political forces which would have come to his aid, nor failed at any time in faithfulness to the Ministers under whom he was serving. Even in the sharpest disagreement he never threatened resignation when he was strong and they were weak. Amid patent ill-success he never in his own technical sphere deferred to their wishes, however strongly those wishes were supported by argument, by public opinion—such as it was—or by the terribly unfolding facts. Right or wrong, victorious or stultified, he remained, within the limits he had marked out for himself, cool and undaunted ready to meet all emergencies and to accept death or obscurity should either come his way.

I had known him slightly, both in private life and in the Army since I was the youngest of subalterns and he a rising Major. At Omdurman and in South Africa we had served on horseback in the field together. We met on a different plane when I was Home Secretary and later First Lord of the Admiralty and he commanded our first and only formed Army Corps at Aldershot. Both on the Committee of Imperial Defence and at the army manœuvres I met him repeatedly, and we always discussed war problems. One remark he made to me at some Cavalry exercises which I was watching in 1912 has always seemed to me most revealing: "This officer," he said, speaking of a Brigadier, "did not show a sincere desire to engage the enemy." The occasion was a sham fight, but the saying was a key to his whole military outlook. Years afterwards in the height of the war, speaking to him of a naval episode, I repeated the expression with intent. His usually placid eye lighted in a compulsive flash, and he repeated the phrase with emphatic assent. "A sincere desire to engage the enemy." That was Haig. That was his message. That was the impulse which he imparted to his troops throughout his command till the last minute before 11 o'clock on the 11th of November, 1918.

He presents to me in those red years the same mental picture as a great surgeon before the days of anæsthetics, versed in every detail of such science as was known to him: sure of himself, steady of poise, knife in hand, intent upon the operation; entirely removed in his professional capacity from the agony of the patient, the anguish of relations, or the doctrines of rival schools, the devices of quacks, or the first-fruits of new learning. He would operate without excitement, or he would depart without being affronted; and if the patient died, he would not reproach himself. It must be understood that I speak only of his professional actions. Once out of the theatre, his heart was as warm as any man's.

"A sincere desire to engage the enemy." Woe betide the officer—Colonel, Brigadier or high General—who failed in that. Experienced, resolute men, with courage proved in the crash of battle, were sent home at an hour's notice for refusing to order—not to lead, for that would have been easier—their troops to certain destruction. Fight and kill and be killed, but obey orders, even when it was clear that the Higher Command had not foreseen the conditions; or go, and go at once, to the rear, to England or to the devil. That was the high-tension current which flowed ceaselessly from the Commander-in-Chief, himself assailed on every side, through more than forty months of carnage. All along the chain of responsibility from Army to Corps, from Corps to Division, from Division to Brigade and from Brigade to Battalion, this ruthless and often inevitably blind force was continually applied. And behind it all a man, a knightly figure, modest in demeanour, humble in spirit, self-forgetting and far above vulgar ambition, just, merciful, humane— such are the mysteries of human nature!

Moreover, the fierce internal pressures, resulting from such discordance, could find no outlet in personal action. Napoleon and the great Captains before him rode on the field amid their troops in the ardour of battle, and amid the perils of the storm. How gladly would Haig have welcomed the chance to mount his horse as he had done when a mere Corps Commander in the First Ypres, and ride slowly forward among the exploding shells! But all this is supposed to be forbidden to the modern Commander-in-Chief. He is lucky if even an aeroplane bomb, or some long-range projectile near Headquarters, relieves at rare intervals by its physical reminder the inward stress of mind. No anodyne of danger, no relief in violent action; nothing but anxiety,

suspense, perplexing and contradictory information; weigh-
ing the imponderable, assigning proportions to what cannot
be measured, intricate staff duties, difficult personal negotiations, and the mutterings of far-distant guns.

But he endured it all; and with such impassivity and
matter-of-fact day-to-day routine that I who saw him on
twenty occasions—some of them potentially fatal—doubted
whether he was not insensitive and indurated to the torment
and drama in the shadow of which he dwelt. But when I
saw after the war was over, for the first time, the historic
"Backs to the Wall" document written before sunrise on
that fateful April morning in 1918, and that it was no product of some able staff officer in the bureau, but written
with his own precise hand, pouring out without a check or
correction the pent-up passion of his heart, my vision of the
man assumed a new scale and colour. The Furies indeed
contended in his soul; and that arena was large enough to
contain their strife.

*   *   *

Douglas Haig embodied and lived up to the finest public
school tradition. He was, in fact, at the time he became
Commander-in-Chief of the greatest army Britain had ever
achieved, the head boy and prize pupil of the military
school. He had done all things requisite and proper. He had
fought as a squadron leader, served in the field as a staff
officer, played in the winning cavalry polo team, graduated
with distinction at the staff college, held an important
military appointment in India, commanded the Aldershot
division before the outbreak of war, and valiantly led the
First Army Corps and later the First Army for nearly
eighteen months of Armageddon. He had no professional
rivals at that time and none appeared thereafter during the
struggle. His realization of this was a strong prop to him in
the many ordeals, disappointments, and terrible disasters
which he had to face and endure. He might be, he surely
was, unequal to the prodigious scale of events; but no one
else was discerned as his equal or his better. So it all worked
down to blunt, grim, and simple duty, in the discharge of
which one may indeed make many errors or suffer grievous
misfortune, but which has to be done and which a man, if

called on, has a solid right to do. Lastly there was a strong
religious side to his character, and he had always cherished
the belief that he was destined to lead the British army to
victory.

Haig's mind, as one would expect from the credentials we
have cited, was thoroughly orthodox and conventional. He
does not appear to have had any original ideas; no one can
discern a spark of that mysterious, visionary, often sinister
genius which has enabled the great captains of history to
dominate the material factors, save slaughter, and confront
their foes with the triumph of novel apparitions. He was, we
are told, quite friendly to the tanks, but the manœuvre of
making them would never have occurred to him. He
appeared at all times quite unconscious of any theatre but
the Western Front. There were the Germans in their trenches.
Here he stood at the head of an army corps, then of an army,
and finally of a group of mighty armies. Hurl them on and
keep slogging at it in the best possible way—that was war.
It was undoubtedly one way of making war, and in the end
there was certainly overwhelming victory. But these truisms
will not be accepted by history as exhaustive.

If Haig's mind was conventional, his character also displayed the qualities of the average, decent man concentrated and magnified. This is only a part of a general's
equipment, but it is not necessarily an unimportant part.
His behaviour did not crumple under violent external
occurrences. He was rarely capable of rising to great heights;
he was always incapable of falling below his standards. Thus
the army, which was in fact our island race, gathered from
all parts of the world, looked to him with confidence through
many costly failures; and the military hierarchy, very complicated—almost a church—and in times of war of para-
mount importance, felt that in the Commander-in-Chief
they had someone on whom to rely. These are great matters.

Until the summer of 1916 the British Expeditionary Force
played inevitably only a fractional role in the stupendous
Franco-German struggle. We dwell with pride on Mons and
Le Cateau, on the turn at the Marne, the glorious defence
of the Yser and the Lys, on Neuve Chapelle, and upon our
important contributory efforts at Loos to the great battle in

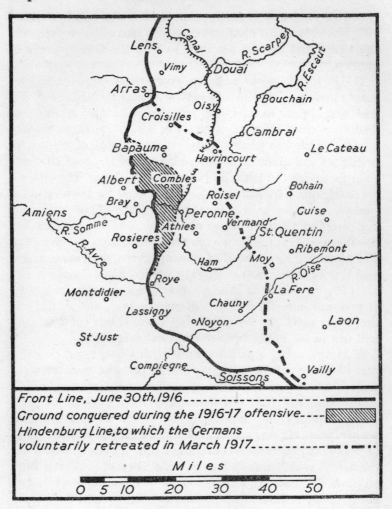

Front Line, June 30th, 1916 _____

Ground conquered during the 1916-17 offensive _____

Hindenburg Line, to which the Germans
voluntarily retreated in March 1917 _____

Miles

0   5 10   20   30   40   50

Champagne. These were times when our fighting personnel
was expanded far beyond our munitions. We paid in blood
and sorrow for the lack of cannon and explosive. Sir John
French, who is sometimes unduly slighted by the admirers of
Haig, bore the brunt of this. We can certainly say that if the
British Army had not been upon the front, France would
have been conquered. But even at the end of 1915 we were
but a sixth numerically, and perhaps but a quarter morally,

of the Allied front. It was not until the Somme in July, 1916, that we became a major factor in the vast land conflict. The next two years shows the British war effort, casualties and

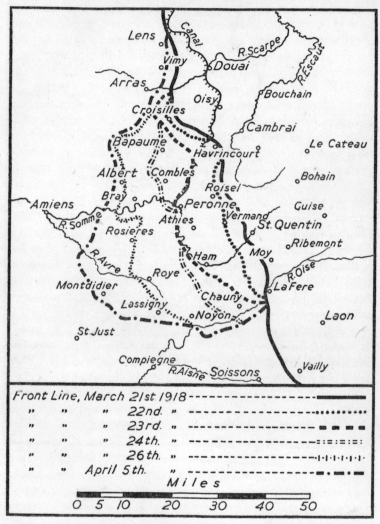

will-to-conquer as always equal to the French, and ultimately dominant. It was over this period that Haig presided. No one can say that it did not end in victory.

* * *

.B.G.—9

I saw and corresponded with him more frequently in the last year of his life than at any other period; and in a way— though I cannot pretend to intimacy with a personality so reserved—I got to know him better than ever before. Curiously, but characteristically on his part, this arose out of my writing a book on the war which, while it recounted the great achievements of the armies he led, nevertheless constituted a sustained indictment of the "Western School" of strategy which he embodied. I asked him whether he would like to read and comment upon the chapters dealing with his operations, adding that if so I must show him what was critical as well as what was appreciative. He accepted the suggestion readily, saying: "Never mind the criticisms. Let us get the facts right, and then people will be able to judge for themselves." There followed a very active inter-change of notes and comments, by which I was able to correct numerous commonly-accepted errors of fact. Throughout he manifested an entire goodwill, and treated the whole story from an impersonal and detached standpoint as if it dealt with events of a hundred years ago. I under-stood that this was because he was content with what he considered justice being done to the exploits of the British armies, especially in 1918, and that nothing affecting his own actions counted at all in the opposite scale. "No one," he wrote in a final letter, "knows as well as I do how far short of the ideal my own conduct both of the 1st Corps and First Army was, as well as of the B.E.F. when C.-in-C."

The nobility of this utterance in all the circumstances enables one to measure from yet another angle the real value of his services to the cause of the Allies.

But the greatest proof lies in the final phase of the war. The qualities of mind and spirit which Douglas Haig personified came to be known by occult channels throughout the vast armies of which he was the Chief. Disasters, disap-pointments, miscalculations and their grievous price were powerless to affect the confidence of the soldiers in their Commander. When in the autumn of 1918 the Government, often only too right before, doubted the possibility of early success, and endeavoured to dissuade him from what was feared would be a renewal of melancholy and prodigal

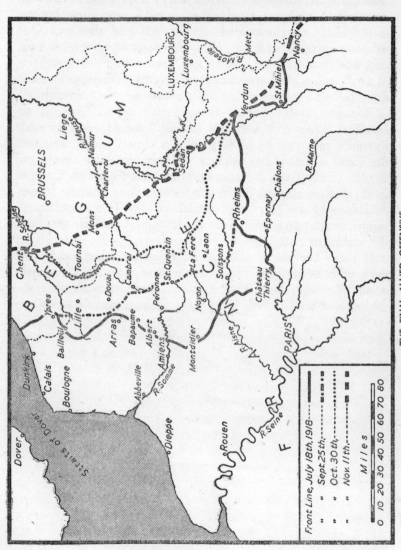

THE FINAL ALLIED OFFENSIVE

Front Line, July 18th, 1918——
" " Sept. 25th, —●—●—
" " Oct. 30th, ·····
" " Nov. 11th, ——————

Miles
0 10 20 30 40 50 60 70 80

slaughter; when in the most invidious manner they cast the
direct responsibility upon him, he did not hesitate, and the
war-worn, five-times-decimated troops responded to the will
and impulse of their leader and marched forward unswerving
to the awful convulsions of victory final and absolute. The
soldierly qualities of Foch, his wide range of vision, his vast
and fine combinations, could not have ended the slaughter
in 1918 unless they had been on several decisive occasions
deflected or reinforced by the entirely separate impulsion
of Douglas Haig. Foch's famous war cries, *"Allez à la
bataille," "Tout le monde à la bataille,"* would have carried
no more meaning to history than a timely cheer, but for
the series of tremendous drives and punches with which the
British armies from Amiens to Mons and from the Somme
to the Selle trampled down the fortifications and the brave
resistance of the best that was left of the German military
might, and spared mankind the slaughters which awaited
the unfought campaign of 1919.

If there are some who would question Haig's right to
rank with Wellington in British military annals, there are
none who will deny that his character and conduct as
soldier and subject will long serve as an example to all.

ALLENBY

By

Captain B. H. Liddell Hart

Few famous men have been the object of such extremes of
condemnation and admiration within the space of a few
years as Allenby. It may be replied that these extremes are
not so uncommon, that the crowd is always fickle in its
favours. But the verdict came not from popular opinion,
which knew him not until he was famous; it came from his
peers and his subordinates who were in close touch with him
during the four years of the World War. Most curious of
all was the sharp dividing line drawn by a journey through
the Mediterranean in June, 1917. For almost three years in
France he had been the target of strong criticism, lessening
only in degree in the later part of this time—criticism not
lightly to be discounted, because it came from many quarters
and from men whose honesty and judgment was, and still is,
held in the highest respect. Then he left to take over the
command of the Egyptian Expeditionary Force, and from
that moment on, his reputation became as radiantly white
as formerly it had been black. Nor was the change due to
military success. Men may win victories which crown them
with popular glory, but victory does not blind their co-
workers to the existence of their defects. It is proverbial
that no man is a hero to his valet, and few generals are
immaculate in the eyes of their staff and subordinate commanders, however loyal these may be in comment at the
time, or however much they may admire their chief on

balance. Yet Allenby in Palestine became, as a chief, not only preponderant in his good qualities, but *sans reproche* for any bad qualities. By no means a human enigma, his career is an historical enigma. By no means a romantic type, he conducted one of history's most romantic campaigns, in its site, sequence, method and result—the last Crusade.

An East Midlander by birth and having an ancestral link with Oliver Cromwell, Edmund Henry Hynman Allenby was born at Southwell in Nottinghamshire on April 23, 1861. Educated at an East Anglian school, Haileybury, he was intended for the Indian Civil Service, but failed in this stiff examination and, following his own inclinations, entered the Army instead. From the Royal Military College, Sandhurst, he passed to a commission in the Inniskilling Dragoons, whom he joined in South Africa during 1882. It has fallen to few young officers to go on active service so early in their career and to share in so many, if minor expeditions. A year after joining he was in the Zululand campaign which ended in King Cetewayo's surrender; in 1885 he served with the Bechuanaland expedition; and in 1888, promoted captain after less than six years' service, he was back again in Zululand to take part in the crushing of Dinizulu's rebellion. Thereafter, he passed into the Staff College where he was more celebrated for his appetite and hard riding than for professional distinction. But his popularity with his fellows led him to be elected master of the drag—over Haig's head incidentally. After leaving Camberley, his career took a slower course until the Boer War came to his relief. He then gave up a Staff appointment to go out again, in command of a squadron, to the land where he had first seen service.

Early in 1900, in charge of a small mixed column, he made a wide outflanking move against the enemy's communications which brought him to notice, and was a foretaste of that bold sense and conception of manœuvre which later distinguished him. He was in command of his own regiment during the advance to Pretoria, and of a column in the "sweeping" operations against the Boer guerrilla bands later, and at the end of the war was promoted lieutenant-colonel and given command of the 5th (Royal

Irish) Lancers. Yet in comparison with another great leader
of the World War, born in the same year—Haig, he had
lost ground despite having been a more successful column
leader. For although Haig had been commissioned three
years later than Allenby, he was a full colonel at the end
of the South African war, and a major-general less than
two years after. The difference created by that campaign
was to have a vital influence on the fortunes of the two
cavalrymen and on the destiny of the command in France
thirteen years later. Yet if Allenby was to forfeit the greater
prize, it may well have been to the advantage of his place
in history. And even that lost prize was nearly restored to
him by a turn of fortune's wheel, for it is within the knowledge of those who followed the devious undercurrents of
war politics in 1914–1918 that several times an eddy nearly
swept him into the place of the man who had overtaken and
passed him in South Africa.

Not until 1909, five years after Haig, did Allenby reach
major-general's rank—although, at forty-eight, he was by
ordinary standards, youthful for this rank. Next year he
became Inspector of Cavalry and the commander-designate
of the cavalry of the Expeditionary Force.

In training the cavalry of the Home Army, "the Bull,"
as Allenby was universally called, proved himself as determined and uncompromising in pursuit of his ideal of efficiency as he had been when in command of a regiment.
To the slack or incompetent he gave short shrift, but his
discrimination was not always as good as his intention.
And his impatience with diverging views and in sweeping
aside reasonable explanations not infrequently created,
among the best subordinates, a sense of injustice or aggrava-
tion, which was enhanced and gained point from the fact
that his handling of the cavalry on manœuvres was by no
means faultless.

On the outbreak of war in August, 1914, Allenby went
out to France as commander of the Cavalry Division, which
originally consisted of four instead of three brigades. Prior
to the opening battle at Mons on August 23, the Cavalry
Division—as distinct from certain intelligence officers of
Allenby's, whose reports G.H.Q. did not credit—had only

succeeded in giving the vaguest warning of the hostile
masses which were closing upon the little British Expeditionary Force. This failure to penetrate the enemy's screen

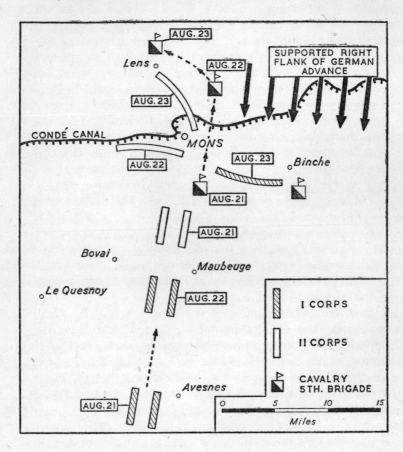

was due, however, mainly to the Commander-in-Chief,
who placed the cavalry at the outset on his right—the
flank of least danger—and intended it as his reserve. These
dispositions were not only a direct but an indirect source of
harm. For when Sir John French, on his way to the front,
called on Lanrezac, commanding the French Fifth Army on
his eastern flank, and explained his dispositions, Lanzerac
formed such a low opinion of a man who could thus place
his cavalry behind his infantry, when information and

security were all important, that he lost all faith in his British neighbour. Hence arose the friction and disunity of action between the neighbouring armies which persisted throughout the retreat.

After the British moved forward on August 21—pushing their heads, in ignorance, into the German noose—the Cavalry Division was moved over to the left flank. And when that tentative advance changed into defence at Mons, on the 22nd, Allenby's troops prolonged the British left, covering the exposed western flank.

In the early hours of the 24th, Sir John French issued orders for a retreat—to draw back if possible out of the noose—with the Cavalry Division covering the retirement of Smith-Dorrien's II Army Corps. When the II Corps halted at Le Cateau next evening, Allenby visited Smith-Dorrien and told him that the Cavalry Division was too scattered and the horses too tired for him to continue covering the retirement next day, and that the infantry must get away during the night if they were to avoid capture by the Germans, close on their heels. Allenby only gave this warning at 2 a.m., and it was impossible at such short notice for the infantry, footsore, and partly distributed in defensive positions, to get on the move again before daylight. Thus Smith-Dorrien's men were forced to stand and fight unsupported, escaping disaster only by their splendid resistance and at a heavy price. In the morning the cavalry continued their retirement, except the 1st (Briggs) and 3rd (Gough) Cavalry Brigades, which stayed behind independently to cover the right rear of the II Corps. When Smith-Dorrien's men fell back that evening, exhausted and disordered, it was fortunate that the German pursuit was tardy and then took the wrong direction; but it was also fortunate that Smith-Dorrien's left, the more exposed flank, was protected by Sordet's French Cavalry Corps—for there were no British cavalry on this vital flank.

It is necessary for the historian, however unwillingly, to correct a popular delusion which gained colour both from the Commander-in-Chief's dispatches and his later comment that "The cavalry, under Allenby's skilful direction, was effectively holding off the enemy's pursuit."

In blunt fact, Allenby, during the most critical phase, did not direct the cavalry operations in covering the retreat —because a large part of his division had escaped from his

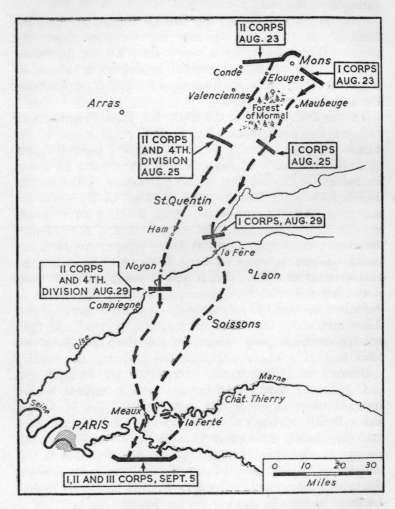

control. And as there was known friction between him and some of his subordinates, this escape was perhaps not involuntary—such, at least, is the belief of other eminent soldiers. Whether this be so or not, it is at least certain that at one time Allenby's Division, for practical purposes,

consisted of little more than himself and his staff. Not until
August 30 were three of the four brigades re-united under
his control, and the other—the 3rd—never rejoined,
remaining away on the right. On the eve of the Battle of
the Marne its commander, Gough, took the 5th Cavalry
Brigade under his wing, and on September 16 these two
brigades were officially designated the 2nd Cavalry Division.

When the British faced about on September 6, after
retreating a day's march farther south than their neighbours,
the Cavalry Division under Allenby was kept on the right
rear of the infantry during the first two days of the advance—
covering the flank, although the vital need was for the
British to retrace their steps at full speed and pierce the
weak joint of the enemy line opposite them. Only on
September 11, when the Germans had been in retreat for
two days, was the Cavalry Division tentatively unleashed
in pursuit by Sir John French, giving the Germans time to
recover and, on the 14th, block the British advance across
the Aisne—a resistance which ushered in four years of
trench-warfare. When the British Expeditionary Force was
transferred from the Aisne to Flanders—in the vain attempt
of the Allies to find and turn the Germans' open flank—
the infantry went by rail, but the cavalry by march route
through Picardy. During that move, on October 9, the two
cavalry divisions were fused into a cavalry corps, under
Allenby.

Directly on arrival the British advance began with the
II Corps, while the Cavalry Corps moved forward along an
arc to the north, covering the detrainment of the III Corps
and then advancing on its left—French having the idea
that the "plains of Flanders" were excellent ground for
cavalry shock-action! If the advance was short-lived, the
Cavalry Corps secured the valuable Messines-Wytschaete
ridges before the advance changed to a desperate dismounted
defence. Moreover, if they were stretched out perilously
thin, they had linked up on the left with the hard-pressed
defenders of Ypres, and thus a complete, if slender, barrier
was opposed to the German masses who were incessantly
hurled against it during the following weeks in the effort
to break through to the Channel ports. Although forced to

yield the Messines ridge, the dismounted cavalry, stiffened by infantry reinforcements, maintained their front unbroken until at last French relief came. In this "soldiers' battle" Allenby, like other generals, could do no more than strive to "putty up" the crumbling parts of his front; but in this process, cemented by ultimate success, he bore a responsibility only less than that of Haig.

In the trench-warfare which followed there was no scope for cavalry, and many cavalry soldiers began to change to the command of infantry formations, among them Allenby. Appropriately, it was during the crisis of the Second Battle of Ypres—the first gas attack—that Allenby was summoned to take charge of the threatened V Corps in the Ypres salient. If the immediate danger was averted, the drain of lives was heavy throughout the summer, perhaps heavier than necessary, and it is at least certain that the V Corps command acquired a reputation of ill-omen among the troops. So much so, that when a certain division, perhaps the best in France in 1915, received word that it was to be transferred to Allenby's Corps, the depression and moral decline were so marked that the consequences were pointed out to G.H.Q. and it was sent instead to another corps in the same area.

One source of complaint at Ypres was that the offensive spirit of the commander was not balanced by adequate investigation and knowledge of the situation. For example, a counter-attack was ordered to recapture a supposed strong point which was found to have no existence except on a paper plan, and only the moral courage of the local commander in disobeying orders averted a heavy and pointless waste of life—but nearly brought his own dismissal. The swelling strength of the British forces had already led to them being divided into two armies, and in the late summer of 1915 a Third Army was formed, when the British took over the French sector between the Ancre and the Somme. Monro, who at "First" Ypres had been a divisional commander in Haig's Corps when Allenby was the Cavalry Corps commander, was given command, but in October he was sent to take charge of the Dardanelles force, and Allenby stepped into his place—the last big appointment that Sir John French made before he was replaced as Commander-in-Chief by Haig.

Allenby was thus in charge of the sector where the main British offensive of 1916 was planned to take place, but some months before it was launched, Allenby's army was side-stepped to the north, between the Ancre and Arras, and a new Fourth Army, under Rawlinson, was inserted to conduct the main offensive on the Somme. Thus the Third Army's share on July 1 was limited to a subsidiary attack with two divisions against the Gommecourt salient, which met with an almost more bloody repulse than the main attack to the south. During the rest of the year Allenby had to remain inactive while the battles of the Somme were raging on his flank, a share of the offensive being now taken over by a new Fifth Army, under Gough, which had been pushed in between Rawlinson and Allenby.

But in the spring of 1917 an attacking rôle was at last assigned to Allenby, and when the time came almost the whole burden of the offensive fell to him. For the Germans' strategic retreat to the Hindenburg Line dislocated the intended renewal of the offensive on the Somme by the artificial desert which it had created for the armies of Gough and Rawlinson to cross. The German retreat had flattened out their former pinch-inviting salient, and from Arras south-eastwards ran the tremendous defences of the new Hindenburg Line. If Allenby could break through the old defences just to the north of where this line ended, he would automatically take it in flank and rear; but in anticipation of such a move the Germans had dug a switch-line from Quéant, near the northern end of the Hindenburg Line, through Drocourt, covering the rear of their old defences north of Arras. Thus Allenby's whole chance of strategic success depended on whether he could reach and break through this partially completed switch-line—some five miles behind the front system—before the German reserves could arrive in strength. Surprise was the only key which could open this gate. Because of this, the real drama of the Arras offensive lies in the preliminary discussions more than in the battle itself. Surprise had been almost discarded in the Somme offensive—indeed, this master-key

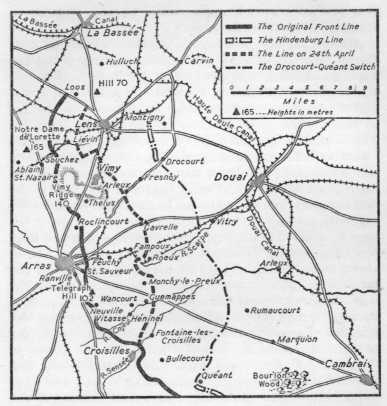

of all the Great Captains of history had been left to rust since the spring of 1915. Would it be brought out afresh in order to open the way to the Drocourt–Quéant switch within the brief time before the door was bolted and barred by the German reserves?

The two means by which surprise and time could be gained were by launching a mass of tanks, as at Cambrai in the autumn, or by a hurricane bombardment with gas, brief but intense. The first means was impossible owing to the slowness in delivering new tanks after the discouraging reports made upon them in 1916, so that sixty old machines were all that could be scraped together. Allenby and his artillery adviser were anxious to have the shortest possible artillery bombardment, and proposed that it should last only twenty-four hours. If this, according to later standards, was twenty hours too long, it was a tentative step in the direction of surprise. But General Headquarters were too material-minded to appreciate it, and had a deep-rooted distrust of such an innovation. Against their remonstrances, however, Allenby stood firm, until they hit on the device of promoting his artillery adviser to another sphere and replacing him by one imbued with their own views.

Allenby then gave way, and the plan of a five days' bombardment, preceded by three weeks of systematic "wire-cutting," was adopted—to the doom of surprise and the abnegation of a break-through. Allenby's yielding on this point against his own convictions seems hardly in keeping with his reputation for strength of character, although it may be urged that, as a cavalryman, it was not easy for him to overrule the advice of an artillery expert. But where experts differ a general is justified in basing his choice on his own common sense and in the light of the fundamental principles of war.

In smaller points he still sought for surprise, notably in opening up the underground quarries of Arras, St. Sauveur and Ronville in order to shelter two divisions which were to pass underground and leap-frog through the leading divisions. Another feature of the plan was that after the three assaulting Corps of the Third Army had broken the enemy's first system of defence, the Cavalry Corps and the XVIII Corps were to pass through in the centre between the human buttresses and drive forward towards the switch-line. Partly for concealment, the daring risk was taken of moving this pursuit force through the city of Arras, whose houses extended almost up to the front line. This plan, refreshingly ingenious, was vitiated, however, by two factors. First, the absence of initial surprise; second, the comparatively narrow front of the opening attack—little more than ten miles—so that the central bottle-neck was, in turn, so narrow that its end could be easily stopped. Ludendorff, in his Vilna offensive in the autumn of 1915, had revealed a better method—a dual penetration by two horns goring their way into the enemy front while through the wide gap between the horns the pursuit force unexpectedly issued.

A fundamental defect of the Arras plan, moreover, was

that its base was far wider than its fighting front—the routes
of supply and reinforcement all converging on Arras,
with the result that the narrow mouth of this bottle-neck
became utterly congested. When the initial attack failed to
make the progress anticipated, this congestion was increased
by the arrival of the cavalry in the forward area, although
it should have been clear from the experience of the Somme
that this advance was futile unless and until a wide path
had been swept clear of the enemy. The results of the
opening attack were greater and quicker, both in prisoners
and progress, than any previous offensive; yet they extin-
guished the possibility of a strategic break-through, for only
a miracle could have recovered the chance that had been
dissipated almost completely before the attack was launched.

In the attempt to redeem the fading strategic hopes,
Allenby's resolution was more marked than his understanding of modern fire-power. To assist his frontal advance
eastwards, he insisted that the divisions facing the Hindenburg Line should make a convergent attack from the
south-west, disregarding the fact—and the protests—that
they had insufficient artillery to subdue these formidable
defences. From this project, which must have cost a fruitless
sacrifice of lives, he was luckily dissuaded—circumstantial
evidence suggests that it was by the personal intervention
of Haig, who was visiting this sector. And when the distant
French offensive on the Aisne, to which the Arras battle
was the preliminary, proved abortive, Allenby's renewed
series of blunt attacks—some in conjunction with the
Fifth Army—were merely an object-lesson in the most
expensive way of trying to occupy the enemy's attention.
They were closed down on May 5, and next month
Allenby was sent from France to replace Sir Archibald
Murray—French's old Chief of Staff during the retreat from
Mons—in command of the Egyptian Expeditionary Force,
which had twice failed disastrously to break the Turkish
defences at Gaza.

That sea-voyage is a turning-point in Allenby's career
as well as in his reputation, both as commander and man.
The clouding obsessions of the later phase at Arras were
blown away, leaving the impressions of hard experience to

broaden and refine the original instinct for surprise. It is a
moot point whether, if he had stayed in France, he would
ever have adapted himself to the conditions of siege-warfare
as well as Haig ultimately did. And a recall to France, to
take the supreme command, was later a possibility. But
it is doubtful whether any other leader, if sent to Palestine,
would have been Allenby's equal in boldness of conception
and extent of success. For in this theatre of war, where the
historic methods of attack were still feasible when directed
with vigour, inspired by surprise and attuned to modern
weapons, Allenby found the right field for his gifts and
instincts.

In France siege-warfare was too firmly consolidated to
be dissolved by merely ringing the changes upon traditional
methods; in Palestine an alternative to siege-warfare was
possible, and it could be exploited if surprise was brought to
bear.

Gaza, on the coast, and Beersheba, thirty-five miles
inland, form the two natural gateways into Palestine, and
between them lie a series of ridges which form a natural
wall easily capable of defence. The British force, after
dragging its weary length across the Sinai Desert from
Egypt, had tried in vain to force the strongly fortified Gaza
gate. Beersheba, less artificially strong, was protected by
the difficulty of transport and water-supply for an attacking
force.

Experience had shown Allenby that even the most
difficult manœuvre was preferable to butting directly
against a blank wall. Grown receptive, he had no hesitation,
after study of the position, in adopting the plan outlined
in an appreciation made by Chetwode, the commander on
the spot, while improving its details by the light of his own
experience. With a heightened understanding of the axiom
that the success of an attack is in proportion to the firm
security of the "base" from which it is launched, he devoted
himself to intensive preparation—of communications, water-
supply, training—during his first three months on the
borders of Palestine, while the season was still unsuitable for
operations. Not less significant was that he moved General
Headquarters up from Cairo to the front, at Rafa, where

he could have his finger on the pulse of battle—and of his troops. It was not only a sound military move, but a wise human move, acting both as an ointment to sore feelings— for men could not help contrasting their hardships in the desert with the supposed enjoyment of Cairo amenities by the arbiters of their fate—and as a tonic, because the presence of their Chief was to the men a visible guarantee that they would not be thrown into the attack without due study and knowledge of the situation. Even to the natives of the country Allenby's coming carried a mystic significance, for the Arabic form of his name, "Allah en Nebi," meant "The Prophet of God," and thus appeared the complement, in the eyes of a superstitious people, to the old prophecy that when the waters of the Nile flowed into Palestine the land would be freed from the domination of the Turk— a condition that had been fulfilled by the construction of a pipe-line across the desert. Furthermore, Allenby's determination enabled him to insist on and obtain the force necessary for his plan, a reinforcement which his predecessor had not obtained. Thus Allenby obtained a full two-to-one superiority over his enemy—not excessive if he was to gain decisive results, and in view of the increased resisting power of a defender under modern conditions. The enemy, on their side, were also planning an offensive to drive the British back into the desert; but Allenby struck first. By thorough precautions for secrecy and many ruses, he misled the Turks as to the real point of attack. The defences of Gaza were bombarded from October 26 onwards, and as a deception to Turkish eyes the camps behind the British lines were left standing with rows of empty tents, whose occupants were on the move towards Beersheba. At dawn on October 31, two British infantry divisions attacked its defences from the south-west while two mounted divisions, Anzac and Australians, were closing on the town from the east, and in the afternoon a daring cavalry charge over the narrow trenches captured this gateway to Palestine, and its essential water supply. Next, to maintain the delusion that this attack was only a diversion, a strong holding attack was made on the Gaza defences during the night of November 1. The new enemy commander, Falkenhayn,

also aided Allenby's plan by throwing in his reserves in a
vain counter-attack to regain Beersheba, and thus had no
reserves left when, at dawn on November 6, Allenby's main
and decisive blow fell on the Turkish left centre and broke
through into the Plain of Philistia. The mounted pursuit,
hampered by lack of water, was also less able in execution
than the battle had been in conception, and by a prompt
retreat from Gaza the Turks avoided being cut off. Nevertheless, by November 14 the port of Jaffa had been seized—
giving Allenby sea-communication with Egypt—the Turkish
force driven apart into two divergent masses, and, leaving a
detachment to watch the mass which had retreated up the
coast, Allenby wheeled east for an advance inland against
Jerusalem. It was difficult to supply his whole force, and
so Allenby took the sound risk of pushing on at full speed
with a part to secure the mountain passes before the Turks
could block them. He succeeded, and although a stout
Turkish resistance, almost at the gates of Jerusalem, brought
his rush to a halt, he had passed the worst obstacles, so that the
arrival of reinforcements enabled him to capture the Turkish
trenches and open the way to the Holy City, which was
surrendered on December 9. Two days later Allenby entered
the city on foot by the historic Jaffa gate, specially reopened
for the purpose, thus offering a contrast with the theatrical
mounted entry of the Kaiser in 1898, for whose convenience
and glorification a breach in the city wall had been made.
Allenby's next step was to secure his hold on Jerusalem and
Jaffa by securing sufficient room for manœuvre in front of
these cities, and the repulse of Falkenhayn's misguided
attempt to retake Jerusalem enabled the British, on the
rebound, to gain ample space to safeguard their possession
of Jerusalem.

Allenby's advance was resumed in February, 1918, and
his first step was to make his eastern flank secure as a
preliminary to a northward move. Jericho and the river-line
of the Jordan had been gained when the crisis in France
caused by the German offensive—Ludendorff's last throw
for victory—forced Allenby to despatch thither most of his
British troops. The depletion was made up by troops from
India, and Allenby, undaunted, devoted the summer to

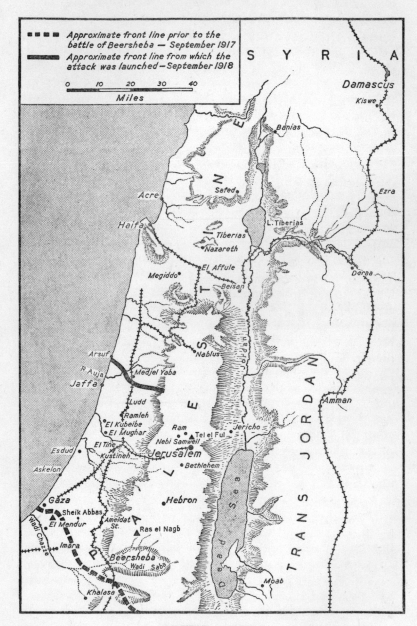

PALESTINE CAMPAIGN

the reorganization and training of these Indian units, building up a fresh striking force for the decisive stroke he had in mind. To pave the way, Allenby launched two raids east of the Jordan, in March and May, in order to create the impression that he intended to advance up the Hejaz railway, which ran parallel with and about 30 miles east of the Jordan, linking Arabia with Damascus. Allenby had already decided to make his real blow in the western flank in the coastal plain, where he could exploit his superiority in mounted troops, and his aim was therefore to draw the Turkish reserves over to the opposite flank. If neither of the raids was a full success tactically, they fulfilled their strategic object, for the threat led the new enemy commander, Liman von Sanders, to place one-third of his total force henceforth on the east of the Jordan. In this far-sighted strategy of "mystify, mislead, and surprise," Allenby had a new and important ally. Far away to the south, in Arabia, the Hejaz had risen in revolt against the Turk in 1916, under Hussein, the Sherif of Mecca. This pin-prick was converted into a dagger-thrust through the appearance of a young Englishman, Lawrence, with an acute understanding of Arab psychology and a genius for guerrilla warfare—based on an inversion of the orthodox rules of strategy. He persuaded Feisal son of Hussein and commander of the Arab forces, to neglect the Turkish armed forces in Arabia and to spread the revolt, like lighting a prairie fire, in their rear northward to Damascus, combining propaganda with continual raids on the long-drawn-out line of the Hejaz railway. To Lawrence's strategic ideas and his appeals for equipment and camels, Allenby was sympathetic—one more proof of his new receptiveness—and his support was an aid to Lawrence in dealing with more conventional and shorted-sighted members of his Staff.

The outcome was that in September, 1918, Lawrence and the Arab Army were both a psychological and a material aid to Allenby's plan. By circling round the rear of the Turkish Army east of the Jordan they cut the Damascus railway round the vital junction of Deraa, where the lines to the Hejaz and to Palestine diverged. Thus they not only attracted Turkish attention away from Allenby's real point of attack, but closed the only railway line of retreat and supply to all the Turkish Armies.

Allenby also turned to profit another new weapon— aircraft. On September 17 and 18, bombing raids cut the telegraph and telephone wires leading from the Turkish General Headquarters at Nazareth back along their line of communications, and on the night before the attack, September 18–19, a further raid on Afule destroyed the wires leading from General Headquarters to the front. Thus the directing power of the enemy's brain was paralysed.

Meanwhile the carefully shrouded preparations for the attack had been completed. Feinting towards the east bank of the Jordan to distract the enemy's attention afresh, the effect helped by a "dummy" concentration of troops in that area, Allenby secretly concentrated on the Mediterranean flank the mass of his infantry, and behind them the cavalry, concealed in the orange and olive groves. Dust columns had gone eastward by day, while troop columns marched westward by night. Thus he changed a two to one superiority on the front as a whole into a four to one superiority on the fifteen miles sector chosen for the decisive attack, leaving forces actually inferior to the Turks on the remaining forty-five miles of front. On the night of September 18–19, these forces attacked in the hilly centre to fix the enemy's attention. At dawn, after only fifteen minutes' bombardment, the western mass was launched, and after breaking through the Turkish defences, wheeled to the right. Thus they rolled the Turks back north-east into the hills, like a door on its hinges.

Through the open doorway the cavalry passed, riding straight up the coastal corridor for thirty miles before swinging east to cut the Turkish communications and close all exits of retreat. One division captured Nazareth, fifty-two miles distant, twenty-four hours later; another covered the seventy miles to Beisan in thirty-four hours, and thus blocked the best line of retreat across the Jordan to Damascus. Completely trapped, the main Turkish armies were rounded up, while Allenby's cavalry exploited the victory of Megiddo by a swift and sustained pursuit which, in conjunction with the Arabs, pulverized the Turkish Fourth Army, east of the Jordan, and gained first Damascus, and later Aleppo. On October 31, the capitulation of Turkey rang down the curtain on this brief and dazzling campaign, in which the British had advanced 360 miles in less than six weeks. Making all allowances for the British superiority in strength —against which must be set off the difficult country and the defensive power of modern weapons—this campaign must still rank as one of the masterpieces of military history, as classic in execution as in design. The clean-cut decisiveness of the result was the product of the clear-sighted selection of objectives and the nicely calculated distribution of force. The plan, like the execution, was distinguished by its fulfilment of and extreme emphasis upon the principles of mobility and surprise—both strategic and tactical—which have ever been the hallmark of the Great Captains. And it was Napoleonic, not merely in its shrewdly directed thrusts at the enemy's communications, but in its development of the British communications to coincide with the strategic plan, thus securing the offensive base from which the operations sprang and were maintained. In this campaign Allenby had a lesser superiority of strength than in his first and the difference of result is partly to be explained by the difference in the security of his communications.

Some who knew only the Allenby of Mons and its sequel, Ypres and Arras, have found difficulty in understanding the apparent transformation of 1918. Thus, on the one hand, there has been a tendency to discount this masterpiece unduly because of Allenby's superiority of strength; and, on the other, there has been a tendency, natural in view of the many other instances, to look for the brain of a Staff Officer behind the form of the Commander—to ask who was Allenby's Weygand, if not his Ludendorff. The fact that in this last year the Operations Branch was in charge of Bartholomew, whose ability was universally recognized, lent colour to such speculations, which, as often happens, were rather fostered than dissipated by the extremely discreet manner of Bartholomew, a second Weygand in his self-effacement. But, in fact, there are the strongest grounds for the verdict that, whilst the detailed working out of the plan owed much to this Staff Officer's gifts, the conception in its outline and pivotal points sprang direct from Allenby's own brain. Indeed, he had originally intended a less far-reaching manœuvre and a more limited envelopment. But returning one day from a ride spent in reflection, he made the announcement, the more dramatic because of its crisp directness, that he had decided to sweep straight up the coastal plain to near Megiddo, cross by the passes into the Plain of Esdraelon (ancient Jezreel) and, by securing the road and rail centres of Afule and Beisan, block the Turkish lines of retreat—drawing tight the neck of a bag which contained this whole force.

I would suggest that the evolution of Allenby from the bad General of 1914–1915 into the great General of 1918 is less surprising than appears on the surface: that the current can be traced throughout its course.

For, as early as the Boer War, Allenby had shown an almost unique instinct for surprise and mobility, which the strange conditions of siege-warfare only damped but could not extinguish—they flickered into flame before Arras.

Perhaps even his impatience and irritability in France sprang from this forcible suppression of his natural instincts. The historian may also note two other influences of possible significance: the disappearance in Palestine of the neuritis in the arm from which Allenby had suffered throughout the winter of 1916–1917, and the death from wounds of his only son shortly after he left France. Hard experience awakened him to the reality of the changed conditions of warfare, widened his understanding of material factors, taught him that obstacles could not be changed until they had first been undermined; and in the hour of final illumination he was sent to a theatre of war which might have been designed by Providence for the display of his natural gifts, now refined by experience. If he had advanced to meet the new conditions of warfare, Palestine brought back these conditions as near as possible to meet him, and the convergence produced a military classic—perhaps the last masterpiece of the old warfare in its medium, the foreshadowing of the new in its technique, and a reassertion of the unchanging principles in its governing ideas.

Moreover, Allenby had passed not only to a military region of greater freedom—from barbed-wire entanglements—but into an atmosphere of greater freedom. In Palestine he was a supreme war-lord, not merely one of the "Barons"—as the Army Commanders in France were somewhat aptly styled. And there is little doubt that he was cast by nature for an independent rôle, better and bigger in carrying out his own plans than in executing the orders of others; for, although not insubordinate, subordination cramped and irked the free play of his genius and the full development of his powers. Experience and the change of conditions, both material and moral, combined to improve and expand him, not only as a General, but as a leader of men, to make him less of a martinet and more of a magnet, less intolerant and more understanding, less obstinate, but no less resolute—in fact, to humanize "the Bull," whose coming many had feared, without diminishing, but rather refining, his inborn strength of character and purpose. Thus he not only achieved far greater results, but won far greater devotion.

In the Valley of Jezreel and the region of Megiddo, Allenby wrote a glorious last chapter to the old testament of warfare; at Nazareth he wrote the preface to the new. And the scope of his achievement, like the faith he inspired, was due to the light that had come to him on his journey to Damascus.

WAVELL

By

Major H. A. De Weerd

As the clouds of war hung over Europe in the summer of 1939, two generals were inspecting troops in Syria. News cameramen caught them riding in a gleaming black Renault past regiments of colourful French colonials and picturesque camel troops. One of the soldiers was world famous. He was small, sharp-eyed, trim-moustached, sixty-nine-year-old Maxime Weygand, former collaborator with Foch, co-victor with Pilsudski at the Battle of Warsaw, in 1920, and former vice-president of the Supreme War Council in France. The other man in the car was a comparatively unknown, one-eyed, compact British General of medium stature with a bull-dog chin. He was General Sir Archibald Percival Wavell, the British chief of the Middle East command. All eyes and cameras followed Weygand, who was expected to play the leading role if the war should spread to the Mediterranean. Wavell was the forgotten man in the hurly-burly of military publicity that attended the outbreak of war. Veteran newsmen in Cairo could not dig up enough about him in the files to make a respectable column. All they could say was that he was a student of the great Allenby, and that he was taciturn to the point of using words as if they cost a guinea each.

If relatively unknown, Wavell began the war with certain real advantages over better-known British soldiers, such as

EARL WAVELL

Gort (Commander of the B.E.F. in France) and Ironside (Chief of the Imperial General Staff). He did not have a reputation to lose! This was true, of course, only as far as the British public was concerned. Wavell was well known in the army for his service in World War I, for his knowledge of Russian and Middle Eastern problems, for his scholarly volume on the campaign in Palestine in 1917–18,* and for his Lees Knowles lectures on generalship at Cambridge University. He had put in years of work on a biography of Lord Allenby.† These evidences of scholarship and erudition, however, were forgiven by his brother officers because Wavell was not equally articulate in speech.

Wavell came from a military family. His father and grandfather were both professional soldiers. He was born in Essex, where his father's regiment was quartered, in May, 1883. As proper to a prospective officer, he was schooled at Winchester and Sandhurst, and took a commission in the Black Watch Regiment in time to see service in the Boer War. At the close of this war he was transferred to India. He served on the Western front (where he suffered the loss of his left eye) from 1914 to 1916, and spent one year as British military observer in the Caucasus. In 1917 he was sent as War Office liaison officer to the Egyptian Expeditionary Force, then under the command of General Allenby. This gave him an opportunity to observe this gifted and imaginative soldier at close range. In 1918, he took an active part in the Palestine campaign as Chief of Staff of the XX Corps under General Sir Philip Chetwode. During the two years in Palestine, Wavell learned many of Allenby's tricks of command, his skill in handling the polyglot British army that defeated the Turks in 1918, his brutal but effective way of maintaining discipline and morale. Above all, he saw a military mind of real magnitude—freed from the shackles of trench warfare—resort to ancient stratagems of war and deceive and destroy an enemy whose intrepid and tenacious fighting had hitherto held British armies in check. It was an experience no officer could forget.

In the period of retrenchment that followed the end of

* The Palestine Campaign. London, 1928.
† Allenby: A Study in Greatness. London and New York, 1940–41.

World War I, Wavell went back to England to command first a brigade and then a division at Aldershot. He was the principal author of *Field Service Regulations, 1935*, the last pre-war edition of that official manual. The War Office sent him off to Russia in 1936 and to Palestine and Transjordania in 1937.

In the year he served as commander in Palestine and Transjordania, Wavell had to deal with repeated anti-Jewish outbreaks of the Arab population. In this difficult and thankless post he demonstrated iron-handed firmness coupled with velvet-handed diplomacy, and gained fresh information about the theatre in which he was to serve in World War II. When the reform of the British Army was undertaken by Hore-Belisha in 1937–38, Wavell was called back to England to head the Southern Command. The fact that he was considered for the post of Chief of the Imperial General Staff (a position which went to Gort) indicated that he was being groomed for a vital command in case of war. As tension mounted in the summer of 1939, he was made Commander-in-Chief of the Middle East, a command that included Egypt, the Sudan, Kenya, British Somaliland, Palestine, Cyprus, and Transjordania.

Before departing for Cairo, in 1939, Wavell delivered three lectures on generalship at Cambridge University, which were distinguished for their urbanity, humour, and insight into human factors in war. Since these lectures serve to throw light on his subsequent career in North Africa, certain points in them are worth reviewing at some length. Wavell felt that the strategy and tactics imposed on the B.E.F. by conditions in France from 1914 to 1918, left no chance for the "imaginative planning, boldness in execution, and relentlessness in pursuit" that characterized great British military exploits of the past. "We must get the last of the Flanders mud out of our minds," he said. He did not think that the stationary war of trenches would be permanent, but felt that new developments would bring mobility back to the battlefield. Equipment and tactics were certain to change, but some essentials for a commanding officer were timeless.

Wavell stressed physical fitness and hardihood as primary

essentials of a successful commander. Officers as well as weapons should be able to survive unnatural tests and carry on. The General should have a touch of the gambler and be willing to run risks in order to win great gains. According to Wavell, sound topographic knowledge and the ability to prepare for moving and supplying troops over the terrain involved are the real marks of military understanding. He extended the indispensable requirement of personal courage to cover fear of new ideas as well as enemy bullets. As far as the technical side of soldiering is concerned, a modern commander should know a great deal more than the ancients. He should be familiar with aircraft and their performance, tanks and their capacities, armoured cars, wireless, smoke, chemical-warfare equipment, camouflage, propaganda, and military engineering. Above all, he must understand men.

Wavell's relationship with Allenby taught him that a commander could get the most out of his subordinates if he gave them freedom of action to the limit of their abilities. He stressed the necessity of taking every precaution for the comfort and safety of troops. The common soldier would tolerate, even admire, a tough and iron-handed leader, if he knew that the rigorous action was taken in his own interest. The kind of discipline Wavell wanted was the kind that insured that "where two or three men gathered together in battle there should be courage and enterprise in them." The ideal foot soldier should combine the qualities of a game stalker, a petty sneak, and a ruthless gunman. Individual resourcefulness and battle cunning in the common soldier should be sought by every means within the General's power. Moving men into battle in long waves, as Haig did at the Somme, was merely to sanction mass butchery. With an army toughened and trained for war the General could afford to drive the heart out of it, if necessary in order to save lives and insure victory. He likened the relationship between the General and the army to that between a horse and a rider. "The horse (the army) should be cared for (training and maintenance) in the stable as if he were worth £500. But he should be ridden in the field as if he were not worth half-a-crown."

It was a mistake, Wavell felt, for the British army to spend all its time studying the characteristics of foreign soldiers. In his opinion it would do well to analyze the national characteristics and aptitudes of Britishers and adapt them to the most formidable war methods which it could devise. He did not care to see a British army formed in German or French moulds. Wavell's lectures demonstrated that he was competent to analyse the craft of a military commander; it remained to be seen whether or not he could practice it successfully, for he had never exercised an independent command in the field.

Since Italy did not enter the war in 1939 there was no immediate fighting in the eastern Mediterranean. General Wavell's command in September, 1939, consisted of some 30,000 British and Colonial troops stationed in Egypt, Palestine, and Transjordania. They were equipped with a fair number of armoured cars and Bren gun carriers, but were allotted only the planes deemed obsolete for action in France. As the war went on, Wavell received reinforcements from India, Australia, South Africa, and Canada, which increased the size of his army by the time Italy entered the war. Wavell used the period of relative inactivity that preceded this event to train his troops in desert operations and to harden them by long marches. From his headquarters in Cairo he supervised the billeting and rationing of an army that embraced at least a dozen races and nationalities. He built up the strong morale and discipline required for sustained offensive operations.

Wavell's position in Egypt was delicate and complicated. The Egyptian government, never too reliable, hesitated to be drawn into the war. Cairo was a nest of Axis intrigue with spies as thick at the bar of the fashionable Mena House as flies around a mess-hall door. He had to keep happy troops and officers of widely different interests and nationalities, maintain friendly if distant relations with the Egyptians, and administer the immense military district under his command. Wavell followed Allenby's habit of spending as much time as possible with his troops, covering his vast domain by plane. His frequent trips were sometimes intended to throw Axis informers off the track. He lunched, swam, and hunted with King Farouk, often making a point of doing so just before some military stroke. He seldom risked a speech to the troops, but has shown that he could turn off an appealing order of the day when he had to. Like Allenby, he maintained distant relations with the troops, but they respected him and had complete confidence in his leadership. Even the monocle he wore in his right eye seemed natural and lacking in affectation to the otherwise scurrilous Australians: they knew he had only one eye! In the heat and confusion of Cairo his coolness and collected manner inspired confidence.

When Italy entered the war on June 10, 1940, the Egyptian theatre entered the zone of active operations. The collapse of France destroyed all joint Allied plans for the protection of the eastern Mediterranean. Weygand had been called back to France, and the tortuous policy of his successor, General Henri Dentz, made it clear that the French army in Syria could not be counted upon to defend even that area against Axis penetration. An Italian army of nearly 290,000 men was based in Libya under Wavell's old professional friend, Marshal Rudolf Graziani. It possessed 1,900 cannon, 779 tanks, 15,000 machine guns, and 10,000 trucks. This army had formerly faced the possible menace of a French advance from Tunisia. Now it could concentrate its full force against the frontiers of Egypt. In Italian East Africa (Eritrea, Italian Somaliland, and Ethiopia) was another fascist force of 120,000 white and native troops under the Duke of Aosta, the ablest of the sons of the House of Savoy. This force threatened Kenya, the Sudan, and British Somaliland. Graziani's army, however, was considered the real menace to Egypt. His well-known aggressive tendencies (he had conducted the rapid advance from Italian Somaliland into Ethiopia in 1936) suggested that an invasion of Egypt would soon follow Italy's entrance into the war. Actually Graziani was forced against his better judgment to advance toward Sidi Barrani by Mussolini.

General Wavell's adversaries drew first blood in the battle of the Middle East. On August 5, 1940, three columns of white and native troops under the Duke of Aosta invaded British Somaliland. Since Wavell's plans for the defence of this area had been made on the assumption of support by forces in French Somaliland, the blow could not be parried. The small Somaliland camel corps under Lieutenant-Colonel Arthur Chater (500 British and 500 native troops) put up a delaying action but was withdrawn by sea to Aden. The fascist forces entered Berbera on August 19. When the news arrived in Cairo, General Wavell did not break off his daily swim at the Mena House pool. Patience and imperturbability were qualities he also had included in his sketch of the ideal commander.

Against his main adversary in the west, Wavell adopted a policy of bluff and bluster. A few sharp engagements on the frontier convinced Graziani that Wavell had large forces at his disposal and was trying to lure the Italian army into a trap. Finally, in the first week in September, Graziani's army was ready to move. It left its bases at Bardia and Fort Capuzzo on September 12, and swept into Egypt through Halfaya Pass. Covered by Italian aviation, light Fiat tanks and armoured cars raced forward to Sidi Barrani. They covered the distance of 100 miles in five days. Here the Italian forces stopped to entrench, dig the necessary wells, and perfect communications. Water supply was a decisive factor, for the desert between Sidi Barrani and Mersa Matruh was waterless. Pipe lines were extended from Libya, which supplied the Sidi Barrani garrison with 335,000 litres of water daily. Roads were constructed which occupied the Italians until December, 1940. The 1st and 2nd (Libyan) Divisions and the 3rd Black Shirt Division were stationed in Sidi Barrani and in its outlying defences at Maktila. In support positions were the Catanzaro and Cirene Divisions, while the armoured division of General Maletti was stationed in two camps to the south.

As members of Wavell's staff studied the Italian position at Sidi Barrani, they came to the conclusion that it was vulnerable to attack. General O'Connor, Galloway and others embodied their views in a memorandum entitled: "Method of Attack on a Desert Camp." Their paper suggesting an indirect approach and attack from the flank and rear served as the tactical basis for Wavell's attack.

The operations that followed were made possible by a

number of apparently unrelated occurrences. First, Admiral Cunningham's torpedo bombers crippled the Italian fleet at Taranto, on November 11, cutting Graziani's sea communications; and Winston Churchill, with rare courage and foresight, sent first-line fighter planes and medium tanks from Britain in the face of a threatened German invasion. These reinforcements arrived in time to provide General Wavell with the equipment necessary to command the air over the desert and to put into action the 7th Armoured Division which was superior in quality to the Italian armoured force.* Numbers were heavily on the Italian side; no less than 60,000 men were concentrated in the vicinity of Sidi Barrani. Many more troops were in support at Sollum and Fort Capuzzo. The striking force of British and Imperial troops numbered less than 40,000, and there was only one tank division. But the morale of the men of the British army was extremely high; they were confident of their weapons, training, and leadership.

In the view of many military critics it was impossible to surprise an adversary on the sun-baked desert coastal plain. Armoured cars and reconnaissance columns could be spotted from the air miles away. The waterless rocky plain leading to Alexandria and stretching into Libya was regarded by both sides as an enemy to be overcome, rather than an ally to be used. Wavell was the first to see that the desert could be used like the sea to convey men and supplies to the decisive point if only the mechanical equipment were available and absolute mastery of the air obtained. The problem of supply, particularly water, was rendered simpler by the presence of the British fleet. It was an additional advantage that Mersa Matruh enjoyed rail connections with Alexandria.

For the first time in the history of World War II the full force of British power was to be thrown at the enemy in one area simultaneously. The fleet was to bombard Italian

* The now famous 7th Armoured Division fought in nearly every important engagement of the British armies in North Africa from 1940 to 1943. In 1940 it was hardly more than an armoured brigade. General Michael O'Moore Creagh was in command of the British armour in the first Libyan campaign but tactical control of the whole force was in the hands of Lieutenant-General Richard Nugent O'Connor, field commander of the army of the Nile. General Creagh fell ill just before the battle and Brigadier Caunter led the 7th Armoured Division.

positions from the sea and co-operate with the land forces. The air force was to prepare the way for infantry and tanks by neutralizing the enemy air force, and by bombing and machine-gunning enemy troop concentrations. An elaborate feint on the model of Allenby's Gaza manœuvre of November, 1917, was prepared. Dummy emplacements, a fake aerodrome, and a big artificial tank park constructed east of Maktila caused the Italians to expect a conventional British frontal attack on Sidi Barrani by way of Maktila. The attention of the Italian staff was fastened on the eastern approaches to their position. Meanwhile a real tank depot was hidden in the desert south-west of Mersa Matruh. In it, through the night of December 8–9, the 7th Armoured Division was concentrated. Winston Churchill sent an encouraging wire to General Wavell, quoting the scriptural phrase: "Seek and ye shall find, knock and it shall be opened unto you." Wavell's own order to the troops was a masterly appeal to their spirit and morale. He said: "In everything but numbers we are superior to the enemy. We are more highly trained; we shoot straighter; we have better weapons and equipment. Above all, we have stouter hearts and greater traditions, and we are fighting in a worthier cause——."

Throughout the bitter cold night of December 8–9, British troops and tank crews in the desert slept beside their arms and machines. A half-moon hid the approach of the British columns and sandstorms bit into the faces of the men. As the first streaks of dawn lighted the east, British bombers roared over the Italian positions protected by fleets of fighter planes. On the flying fields at Sidi Barrani, Sollum, Fort Capuzzo, and Bardia, hundreds of Italian planes were destroyed on the ground. Sweeping back, the planes took new bomb loads and returned to attack the Italian positions at Sidi Barrani. Ships of the Royal Navy appeared offshore and blasted Italian artillery parks. With Italian attention drawn to their coastal and eastern flank, the 7th Armoured Division rolled north-westward out of the desert. The Italians had placed minefields on their eastern and southern flanks but had only a wire barrier on the west. Through it the 7th Armoured Division crashed, catching the Italians with their armour still in parks. Many of the

Italian tanks never fired a gun or moved a tread. General Maletti was killed by machine-gun fire as he valiantly attempted to put his division into action. British armoured cars raced toward the sea at Bugbug, and by nightfall the Italian garrison at Sidi Barrani was surrounded. Two days later it surrendered. Forty thousand prisoners and an immense store of military booty fell into British hands.

As soon as General O'Connor saw that the work of the 7th Armoured Division had been completed he turned it westward. The Italian Catanzaro Division marching hopefully toward the sound of battle ran into the British tanks—and being helpless in that situation surrendered.

The most amazing thing about the success was the surprise attained. British intelligence had spread the impression that an advance by Graziani was expected in the near future. Axis newspapers had stated pontifically that surprise was impossible in the desert theatre. Newsmen in Cairo were kept completely in the dark until Wavell called them into his office at 10 o'clock in the morning of December 9, and informed them that the attack had been launched. Not a single correspondent (and they have proved remarkably effective in smelling out zones of impending action) had the slightest idea that a British offensive was contemplated.

The extent of the success at Sidi Barrani was frankly a surprise to Wavell. He had purposely worded the first announcements of the battle in modest terms, thinking that it would enable him to break off the operation without loss of morale in case of failure. In the preparatory stages of the operation the troops engaged had been informed that they were to undertake a routine training march. Once he saw the low state of Italian morale and studied the remaining Italian positions in Cyrenaica and Libya, Wavell decided that the situation justified a tremendous gamble. Since British losses were extremely light, he decided to throw his small striking force against the retreating fascists with the aim of capturing or destroying the whole Italian army in Cyrenaica. He even decided to pull out the 4th Indian Division and send it to General Platt for operations in Eritrea. He knew that relentless pursuit of a beaten foe called

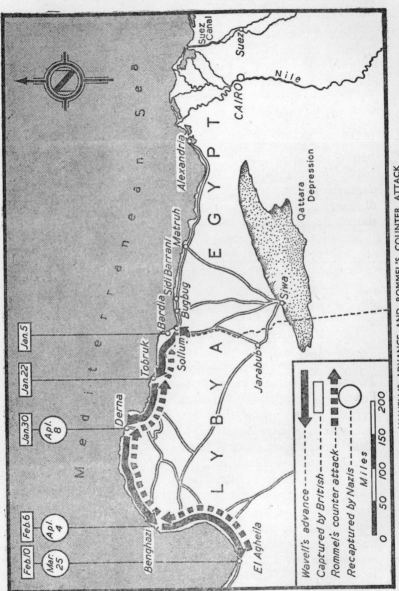

WAVELL'S ADVANCE AND ROMMEL'S COUNTER ATTACK

forth the greatest qualities in an army. Troops were naturally inclined to relax after the first victory. But Wavell decided "to ride the horse as if it were not worth a half-a-crown." He gave orders for an immediate continuation of operations. From this point on, Wavell's great victories of December, January, and February, took on the form of magnificent improvisations. There was no time to prepare each new movement with the care and detail of the Sidi Barrani operation. So, favoured with the terrain involved and command of the air, Wavell repeated an encircling manœuvre at Fort Capuzzo, Bardia, Tobruk, and Benghazi. Graziani proved helpful by acting on the World War I doctrine of fighting battles for territory. As a result, parts of his army were captured or destroyed in each defended area. This system of isolated fortress positions failed completely. The most daring stroke of the whole campaign was Wavell's decision to send the 7th Armoured Division cross-country to cut off the retreat of General Tellera's forces some fifty miles south of Benghazi. They caught this column of 112 tanks, 216 guns, 1,500 trucks and 20,000 men on the open road and bluffed and fought it into surrender. It was one of the most audacious and brilliant operations of the war.

The rate of Wavell's advance into Libya did not equal the speed of German blitz campaigns elsewhere, but for a British advance it was rapid. Bardia was taken on January 5, Tobruk on January 22, Derna on January 30, Benghazi on February 6, and El Agheila on February 10. By that time 134,000 Italian soldiers had been killed or captured and an immense quantity of arms had fallen into British hands. Most welcome of all was the fact that the victories were accomplished with British losses of less than 3,000 men. The only reinforcements received by the striking force after taking Sidi Barrani were in infantry and artillery. The main brunt of the advance fell on the 7th Armoured Division which, after fighting over 500 miles of rough terrain, was due for an overhaul. Wavell's victories were celebrated around the world, and he suddenly became "the most famous British General." Even the Germans spoke of his ability with respect.

According to Alexander Clifford, a British observer who

covered the entire war in North Africa, "Wavell's army won because it was superior in the only two spheres where it could be superior: in quality of leadership and quality of individual fighting troops. Victory came through non-material, impalpable things, largely qualities of the mind: through a disciplined audacity, an intuitive awareness of when and where risks could be taken——." It took Graziani, who had never before been on the receiving end of mechanized war, eight weeks to learn that it was futile to fight for "places." By the time he learned this lesson his army had dissolved and he was replaced by a German leader, General Erwin Rommel.

When Wavell's forces reached Benghazi, many expected that the advance would continue into Tripoli. These hopes were based on an ignorance of the real situation in Libya. The public had little knowledge of the relative weakness of Wavell's striking force. Almost unnoticed was an occurrence in the Straits of Pantelleria on January 10, which changed the whole character of the war in Libya. On that day a British convoy, passing through the Straits under protection of cruisers and the aircraft carrier *Illustrious*, was attacked by nazi dive bombers operating from Catania in Sicily. Despite heavy losses from anti-aircraft fire, the German pilots attacked with such desperate resolution that the British cruiser *Southampton* and the destroyer *Gallant* were sunk. The *Illustrious* was severely damaged. After that, the surface forces of the British navy ceased to operate freely in this theatre. With immunity from surface attack, German mechanized equipment was shipped to Tripoli. In February and March a mechanized force headed by General Rommel was concentrated west of Benghazi. Luftwaffe squadrons appeared on the Libyan front. General Rommel soon possessed superiority in both mechanized and air strength. The swiftness of this transport performance on the part of the enemy was ominous. General Wavell's advanced positions could no longer be held. The African force of General Rommel (who kept the Italian General Garibaldi at his headquarters as concession to Italian pride) struck at El Agheila on March 25, forcing the British to retreat. The British and the neutral press played it up as a mere fluctuation in the battle; but, when the same force took Benghazi on April 4, the strength of Axis forces in this area could no longer be concealed.

General Rommel was a commander of long experience, tough and resourceful. He served throughout World War I, and in the Polish, Flanders, and French campaigns. His sweeps into Cyrenaica were bold and extremely well organized. On the night of April 8, a small detachment of his motor-cycle troops armed with tommy-guns cut off a British convoy. In the confusion they captured three of General Wavell's most valuable assistants, General O'Connor, General Philip Neame, and General Michael Gambier-Parry. It was a heavy blow to the Middle East Command.* On April 14, General Rommel's forces, which had passed up Tobruk, moved across the Egyptian border at Sollum.

The British public watched with dismay the loss of the territory occupied in Libya, but it did not lose confidence in Wavell. Unlike Graziani, who lost the same territory, Wavell saved his army from destruction or capture. Leaving a strong garrison at Tobruk, he withdrew to his old positions at Sidi Barrani and Mersa Matruh and awaited the Axis thrust. It should be remembered that while Wavell was being driven out of Libya he was at the same time carrying out the conquest of Italian Somaliland, Eritrea, closing in on the Italian forces in Ethiopia, and preparing to aid Greece against an impending invasion of the Nazis.

Though fighting of an indecisive character broke out on the frontiers of Egypt and Kenya as soon as Italy entered the war, Wavell did not begin his programme for the conquest of Italian East Africa until his Libyan drive had reached its crest at Benghazi. There were far-reaching political as well as military reasons for the campaign. South African leaders (particularly General Smuts) were eager for a conquest of Italian possessions in Africa. The British occupation of the entire Red Sea littoral, the shores of the Gulf of Aden,

---

* Churchill's witty attempt to explain this surprise could not conceal its importance. In describing the event he used the hackneyed phrase of the Air Ministry, "From these operations three of our generals failed to return." Generals O'Connor and Neame escaped from captivity in the confusion following Italy's withdrawal from the war in September, 1943.

and the approaches to the Indian Ocean might encourage
the United States to remove this area from the combat zone
and thus facilitate shipment of arms and munitions to the
Middle East. The military motives for the conquest were
not so pressing. The Duke of Aosta was isolated from Italy
and, like a cut flower, was certain to fade with the gradual
exhaustion of his supplies. As long as his army was in being
it constituted a menace to the security of the Sudan, but he
lacked strength sufficient to operate alone against Egypt.
The task of destroying his forces and occupying his territory
involved moving troops across immense distances and
extremely difficult terrain.

The British forces available for these movements were very
small indeed: they numbered less than 50,000 men. Only a
limited number of tanks and Bren gun carriers could be
allotted to the forces, and air support in all the southern
operations depended on the small South African air force.
In general, the troops and weapons employed were merely
those that could be spared from other more vital theatres
in the Middle East. When the conquest was practically over,
one British wit (paraphrasing Churchill's splendid tribute
to the R.A.F.) quipped: "Never have so many been defeated
by so few."

The attack on the Duke of Aosta's forces began from four
directions in February, 1941. One British column advanced
from Moyale in Kenya toward Mega and Negelli in
Ethiopia. A second column from Kenya (commanded by
General Sir Alan Cunningham) crossed into Italian Somaliland, bridged the Juba River, and advanced on Mogadiscio.
The main Italian resistance in this colony was broken in the
battle over Mogadiscio in which 10,000 Italian prisoners
were taken. General Cunningham's column then moved
north-west along Graziani's old route into Ethiopia, capturing Gabredarre and Jig Jiga. After the latter strong point
was captured, part of Cunningham's column turned to the
north-east to assist a British force which had landed at
Berbera on March 17, to reconquer British Somaliland. The
remainder of Cunningham's column pushed on to Harar and
Diredawa, where it cut the Addis Ababa–Djibouti railway
on March 30. A third British column advanced from the

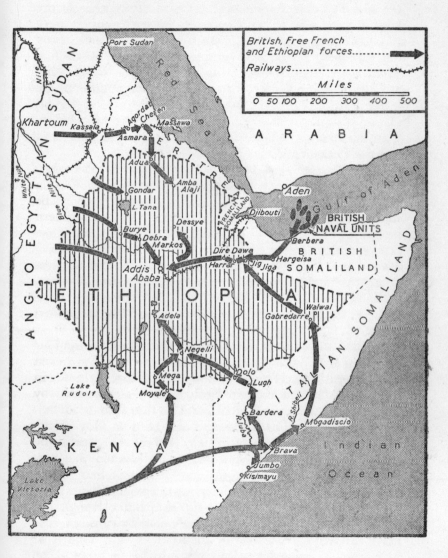

WAVELL'S EAST AFRICAN CAMPAIGN

Sudan in the direction of Burye, Debra Markos, and Addis Ababa, which was occupied on April 6. Here this column made a junction with General Cunningham's force and turned northward to attack the Italian garrison at Dessye. A fourth British column, operating out of Kassala in the north, invaded Eritrea and captured Agordat on February 2. The main Italian resistance in this colony was encountered at Cheren, where the fascists put up their most stubborn and intrepid fighting of the campaign. Here the added strength of the 4th Indian Division which Wavell sent to General Platt after his victory at Sidi Barrani may have turned the balance in favour of the British. This mountain stronghold was not taken by the British until March 28. Its fall enabled the British to divide their forces in Eritrea. One half of the column moved northward to occupy Massawa and Assab; the other half drove southward to hem in the Duke of Aosta at Amba Alaji. Here, on May 19, the Italian viceroy surrendered the fragments of his army. Scattered bands of Italian and native troops continued to resist, but the conquest of the Italian East African Empire had been completed in seven months.

These victories revealed the hollowness of Italian military pretences. Fascist troops in some cases were found to be equipped with artillery which had been used in the Tripolitan war in 1912. The Duke of Aosta repeated Graziani's error of fighting for places and his army was reduced piecemeal. In general, the morale and fighting spirit of the troops in Italian East Africa was higher than that shown by Graziani's army in Libya. The British campaign was carried out methodically and, considering the distances, terrain, and forces involved, it was a rapid conquest. General Wavell was successful in co-ordinating the movements of four widely separated columns and in keeping the wild tribesmen of Haile Selassie from butchering helpless Italian colonists. The seven-month conquest of three Italian colonies ranks with the greatest British colonial campaigns.

A great soldier is not to be judged by his victories alone. Defeat and frustrations are often required to bring out the truly superior qualities of a military leader. Wavell was to have his share of disaster. The vastness of his military domain

presented problems and vexations great enough to tax the
strongest mind. Axis plans for the Spring of 1941 brought
him into conflict with a formidable German army in the
Balkans.

The Italian army had blundered into defeat in Albania
and required early rescue. Throughout the winter of 1940–41
and in the early Spring, German penetration of the Danubian
and Balkan countries went on. Hungary, Rumania, and
finally Bulgaria submitted to nazi military occupation. These
steps were preliminary to a German stroke at Greece. To the
surprise of all, including the nazis, Jugoslavia refused to
join the Axis camp. This upset in German plans seemed to
offer the prospect of a joint Jugoslav-Greek-British front
against the Axis in the Balkans. If Jugoslavia fought, the
Allies could count on a paper force of 1,300,000 men.
Churchill took the great risks involved in a Balkan campaign
for political and prestige reasons. He ordered a British force
to Greece. An expeditionary army of 60,000 British troops
and approximately 100 fighter planes (commanded by
General Sir Henry Maitland Wilson) began to land in
Greece in March. There were hopes that this force would
stiffen Greek and Jugoslav resistance and have an encouraging effect on Turkey.

An Allied victory over a large nazi force of thirty-three
divisions (including six armoured divisions) and two fleets
of the Luftwaffe was hardly to be expected, but a prolonged
resistance was anticipated which would use up German men
and material. The terrain involved seemed favourable for
defence against a mechanized attack. The Greeks had
recently shown and the Serbs had frequently proved their
high military qualities. But there were many factors that
operated against a successful collaboration by the Allies. By
preserving a "correct" attitude toward the Axis up to the
last minute, Jugoslavia had refused to take part in British
and Greek staff conversations. As a consequence the Allies
were forced to fight without adequate liaison.

The bold and brilliantly executed German attack on
April 6, soon shattered all hopes of a prolonged Allied resistance. German air power again proved decisive. Blitzkrieg
tactics confused the Jugoslav army and cut it into helpless

parts in seven days. With their left flank exposed by the sudden collapse of Jugoslav resistance, the British and Greek forces were driven into retreat to escape encirclement. So rapid was the German advance in the north that Greek armies in Albania were cut off and forced to surrender on April 23. Australian forces under General Sir Thomas Blamey made a heroic stand at Thermopylae in order to safeguard the evacuation of the main British forces. Despite savage bombing from the air, 45,000 of the 60,000 British troops were successfully withdrawn from Greek ports by the end of April.

As at Dunkirk, the B.E.F. had to abandon most of its heavy equipment, and the haggard men who reached the security of Egypt and Crete spoke in bitter terms about the lack of air support. The Balkan disaster was rendered endurable only by the escape of the major part of the British army. The Australian troops bore the brunt of the fighting; and, to still the rising criticism in that country, General Blamey was appointed to the post of second in command to General Wavell. Unfortunately, numbers of the Australian troops evacuated from Greece were sent to Crete for "rest and refit," where they soon found themselves for the second time victims of German air superiority.

The Greek disaster, like most other disasters in war, did not come singly. General Wavell at the same time had to face a dangerous rebellion in Iraq which was inspired by nazi intrigue and which aimed at disrupting the Allied oil supply in the eastern Mediterranean. It also threatened to open the back door to Palestine and the Suez to Axis penetration. The problem of suppressing the revolt was particularly difficult because of the dangers inherent in the Arab situation in the Middle East and because of the distances involved. By a remarkably speedy transport performance, tanks and armoured cars landed at Basra were able to occupy Baghdad on May 31 and put an end to the revolt. By this time, however, a new disaster had befallen General Wavell's forces in Crete.

The British had been in occupation of Crete for eight months. Suda Bay provided the navy with an excellent deep-water harbour in which heavy and light craft could be based.

Its flying fields permitted British bombers to menace Axis lines of communication in Libya. It was a strategic prize of the first importance and should have been defended with all the resources available. A shortage of anti-aircraft artillery, however, prevented adequate protection of the three principal flying fields. The garrison of 50,000 British and Greek troops possessed some tanks and artillery but it was lacking in modern automatic weapons. The defences erected were designed primarily to repel a traditional landing from the sea. Beaches were wired and mined. Pillboxes and machine-gun nests guarded the strategic points. The defence of the island was entrusted to General Bernard Freyberg, V.C., a New Zealand veteran of World War I, known for his personal courage and enterprise.

On May 20, 1941, after a savage ten-day bombing attack, German parachute and glider troops were dropped from fleets of transport planes that followed close upon the heels of German bombers. So rapidly were these troops reinforced from the air, and so perfect were their equipment and organization that the Greek and British infantry were gradually pushed from their defensive positions around the airports and Suda Bay. It was the strangest battle of the war. German troops were supported by the air but had no tanks or artillery. British fighter planes withdrew after the first day of attack because their flying fields could not be defended. This left the Greek and British defenders without air support. In the end superior German direction, unremitting air support, and constant reinforcement by additional parachute troops and infantry carried in transport planes (many of which deliberately made crash landings) proved decisive. There was not time to reinforce the British garrison from Alexandria before the crisis was reached and, even had there been time, the forces that arrived would have been engulfed in the growing confusion in Crete. General Wavell was forced to make the distasteful decision to cut his losses and evacuate the island. Fifteen thousand dazed and beaten men reached Egypt on June 1. Like the men evacuated from Greece, they spoke about the savage power of the German air force. For the second time it became painfully clear that the British armies in the Middle East could not be expected to meet the German

Wehrmacht with any prospect of success until approximate equality in the air had been attained.

There was a strong outburst of criticism in Britain and Australia over the Greek and Crete disasters. The public took little comfort from the fact that the Iraq rebellion had been crushed at the same time. In both campaigns the Australian troops seemed to have been left "holding the bag." Though there was no official protest by the Australian government, it was widely felt that "a fresh mind might prove to be useful in the Middle East Command." British commentators were forced to praise the brilliance and execution of the German attacks on Greece and Crete. It was pointed out that one of the alleged reasons for inadequate British air support in the Greek campaign was shortage of suitable flying fields. Yet, after being in possession of the same Greek flying fields for less than three weeks, the Luftwaffe used them to mount a heavy and sustained air offensive. Air Marshal Longmore and General de Guingand agree that Wavell was much more optimistic about the British chances in the Greek campaign than members of his staff. On a staff paper which dealt with the difficulties of a campaign in Greece, Wavell had written a quotation from General Wolfe: "War is an option of difficulties."

The public accepted the validity of Churchill's explanation that the fighter plane squadrons had to be withdrawn from Crete because of the lack of adequate anti-aircraft guns to protect their flying fields. They could not understand, however, why these fields had not been rendered useless for the Luftwaffe. It was felt that eight months could have been used by the British forces in Crete to pour a lot of concrete and take other measures to increase the defences of the island.

The fact that German planes had used French airports in Syria to support the Iraq rebellion seemed to point in the direction of a nazi penetration of that country at the close of the Crete campaign. There were rumours that German armoured cars and mechanized equipment had been landed at the port of Latakia. The obvious dangers to the British position in the Middle East made it necessary to forestall this step by military action. Accordingly, on June 8, a small force of British and Free French troops under General Wilson moved into Syria. The announced aim was "occupation," not invasion. At first the advance was slow and every effort was made to win over the Vichy forces by propaganda. Peaceful penetration failed, however, and serious fighting delayed the advance of British and Free French columns. American newsmen who witnessed the Allied advance in Syria described the armies as "lacking in modern equipment." The pace of the Allied advance was therefore disappointingly slow. The capture of Damascus on June 21, was almost lost sight of in view of the startling German declaration of war on Russia on the following day. The Syrian campaign did little to enhance British military prestige in the Middle East.

General Wavell supervised one more important military movement before his career as commander in the Middle East was suddenly terminated. On June 15, he sent forward strong armoured forces supported by infantry to test the strength of the German-Italian position at Sollum. The aim was something more than a reconnaissance in force, for an attempt was made to encircle the Afrika Korps at Halfaya Pass. Indian troops skilled in hill fighting attacked the German and Italian outposts with great resolution, but the German organization for support of the advance posts was too effective. The attack bogged down. Meantime General Rommel met the British encirclement manœuvre by tanks with an encirclement of his own. A tank battle on a considerable scale followed, in which the British forces withdrew after very heavy losses. "There had been miscalculations and mistakes," said one British reporter. Writing long after the event, General de Guingand said that this operation never had the slightest chance of success. He took it as a mark of Wavell's greatness that he immediately stopped the operation when he saw the situation at first hand.

It was under these rather depressing circumstances, and after the German war on Russia was a week old, that General Wavell was suddenly transferred to the command of India. Judging his performance solely on the basis of his two-year tenure as Commander in the Middle East, one can safely draw the following conclusions. Wavell was the first British soldier in World War II to grasp the full lessons of the

German campaigns in Poland and France and apply them to the conditions of desert fighting. He was the first British soldier in this war to co-ordinate effectively the full power of British sea, land, and air forces in a single campaign. His success in handling the many races and nationalities making up the Allied armies in the Middle East was conspicuous. The Libyan victories were the cheapest triumphs ever won by a British force against a European adversary—if not the cheapest in all British military history. Even though the territorial gains in Libya were quickly lost to General Rommel, Wavell still had to his credit the destruction of Graziani's army and the conquest of Eritrea, Italian Somaliland, and Ethiopia. His victories cheered and inspired the whole British Empire and the neutral world at a time when the Axis powers seemed invincible. Italian military prestige suffered blows from his hand that were almost fatal. When he left Cairo there was no part of the British Mediterranean Empire in Axis hands.

To newsmen in India, Wavell admitted the mistakes of his period of command in the Middle East with admirable candour. He said that he had miscalculated the speed with which the Germans were able to pour troops into North Africa. In this circumstance he described his plan to hold Cyrenaica with partly trained and partly equipped troops as a " mistake."*

Wavell's position in India assumed new significance when Japan entered the war on December 7, 1941. The balance of power was so heavily weighted against the United Nations in the Pacific that Wavell was forced to stand helplessly by while Japan overran Malaya, the Dutch East Indies, the Philippines, and Burma. He was able to protect the Indian frontier.

On June 18, 1943, Field Marshal Wavell was raised to the peerage and appointed Viceroy and Governor-General of India to succeed the Marquis of Linlithgow. He chose Viscount† Wavell of Cyrenaica and Winchester as his new

---

* General de Guingand believes that Wavell's successors in the Western Desert up to Montgomery's time were not able to follow up their initial victories in Cyrenaica because they failed to appreciate the opportunities that the "Bengazi bulge" offered for successful enemy counter-attack.

† He was later, at the end of his term, to become Earl Wavell.

title. This sudden elevation to an important political post was accompanied by a change in the Indian command, General Sir Claude Auchinleck replacing Wavell as Commander-in-Chief in India. On August 25, 1943, a South-East Asian Command was established under Vice-Admiral Lord Louis Mountbatten to direct operations against Japan in this theatre.

Looking back on the extreme perils through which Britain has passed in the late war and seeing the dangers that menace her in the future, Wavell urged his countrymen to fall back upon their ancient sources of strength. In the introduction to his second volume of the life of Allenby he wrote:

> There were dangers ahead even before the disaster of the present war shook us from our complacency and ignoble ease. Country life had given place to town life; courage and toughness seemed rated lower than of old; cleverness was being reckoned of more account than character; leadership was gained by caution rather than by daring; pleasure and personal advantage were being set before duty. The dangers and hardships of to-day are helping to bring back the old standards of courage, self-sacrifice and hard work. These qualities will be very necessary in the great task before us of rebuilding a shaken world.

ALEXANDER

By

CAPTAIN CYRIL FALLS

THE province of Ulster has always been a notable source of officers for the British Army. In the late war, however, it produced a crop of seniors which is remarkable in view of the small proportion of its population to that of the British Isles as a whole. First and foremost, there is the greatest military figure which the nation threw up throughout the course of the war, Field Marshal Lord Alanbrooke, Chief of the Imperial General Staff from Christmas, 1941, until after the end of hostilities. His predecessor in that office, Field Marshal Sir John Dill, was also an Ulsterman. Field Marshal Sir Claude Auchinleck is of Ulster blood. And the two soldiers under whose command British armies fought their principal battles, Field Marshals Lord Alexander and Lord Montgomery, spring from Ulster families.

It is from the leading families of the Anglo-Scottish colony "planted" in Ulster in the early seventeenth century, in the reign of James I, that the commanders have mostly sprung. The Brookes have been big landowners and important figures ever since, and a nephew of Lord Alanbrooke, Sir Basil Brooke, is Prime Minister of Northern Ireland. The Montgomerys, a more wide-spread clan, have also been prominent ever since the Plantation, and only a few years back produced another Chief of the Imperial General Staff, the late Field Marshal Sir Archibald Montgomery-Massingberd, born a Montgomery.

VISCOUNT ALEXANDER

Detail from the portrait
by Maurice Codner
By courtesy of
the artist

Yet though the Plantation of Ulster set its stamp upon the province, and though many of the great families of that time have endured, there have naturally been social changes as in other communities. Some of the foremost Plantation families have died out, or fallen into obscurity, or emigrated, while others not then so prominent, originally perhaps tenants of the greater landlords, have worked themselves up by trade or other means to great positions. The Alexanders are among the Plantation families, but their most important branch to-day owes its place to a self-made man, who founded its fortunes in the latter part of the eighteenth century, over a century and a half after the Plantation. This was James Alexander, one of the earlier of the nabobs who acquired opulence in the East Indies and returned home to found a great family with it. James bought a large estate, mostly in Tyrone, and established himself at Caledon House, in the southern part of the county on the Armagh border. He became M.P. for Londonderry in the Irish Parliament. A supporter of the Government, he became first Baron, then Viscount Caledon. Then came the Union and the abolition of the Irish Parliament on January 1, 1801. Honours were distributed with a lavish hand to those who helped to bring it about. James Alexander was one of them, and he received a further step in the peerage, being created Earl of Caledon. Acid critics described him as a *parvenu*, but from what we know of him it is certain that that worried him little.

Field Marshal Lord Alexander is the great-great-grandson of this James Alexander. He is the third son of the fourth earl and brother of the fifth, their mother having been Lady Elizabeth Graham Toler, daughter of the third Earl of Norbury. He was born in 1891 and educated at Harrow School and the Royal Military College, Sandhurst. There is no evidence of his having been outstanding at work. He was, however, both at school and at the R.M.C., good at games, especially cricket, but his chief fame in the world of sport and athletics was as a long-distance runner. He established records in the Harrow steeplechase, and later on, the mile and two miles at Sandhurst. He kept up his running, and after the First World War, which bound up the muscles

of many athletes and players of games, won a military
cross-country race. Even in the early part of the late war,
when he was Commander-in-Chief, Southern Command,
and approaching the age of fifty, he used often enough to
turn out for a run.

From Sandhurst, Harold Alexander entered the Irish
Guards, a comparatively new regiment with its own private
traditions to found, though it inherited the traditions of the
Foot Guards. The Grenadier, Coldstream, and Scots
Guards were old-established regiments, but the Irish
Guards had been created only in 1901. The Welsh Guards
did not come into existence until 1915. The Brigade of
Guards is distinguished for its drill, discipline, and sense
of duty. Regimental service set its stamp upon Alexander
and, without confining his mind or character within narrow
limits, gave them a certain cast which there can be no mis-
taking when it is encountered. He became, and has remained,
very much a guardsman, very much a son of "the Brigade."

The ensign thus launched upon his military career was
good-looking, alert, cool-headed, strong and very fit,
though only of middle height or even a little below it. He
was also even-tempered and kindly; but though he had
many friends of diverse kinds, was not in those days, and
perhaps could not be called now, hail-fellow-well-met with
the world in general. He was indeed considered somewhat
shy and aloof. He was and has remained an extremely
smart-looking officer in the best sense of the words. Never
did belt, or field boots—when he attained to them—shine
more brightly than his. One would almost say that his cap-
band, gorget patches, and medal ribbons were brighter in
colour than those of anyone else. And yet all this is without
a trace of dandyism. That is no paradox because dandyism
is a matter of personality. With Lord Alexander it was
simply a question of uniform worn as well as it can be.

There is no certainty that he would have risen high had
his career been cast in the Victorian age of small wars
before the South African War at the turn of the century.
The Guards saw only a limited amount of service in those
wars, and it does not appear that he had any particular
bent for the staff work which would have brought him

special appointments. On the other hand, he was probably not one of the men whose temperament would have chafed at the ceremonial of the Guards in time of peace, so that he might have remained with his regiment and retired fairly early, or even stayed with it until his allotted time was up. He would, with opportunity, certainly have been a good sound staff officer, as he proved during a short period between the two great wars; but if he was to go to the top it would have to be as a commander in the field. It befell that he had only a few years of regimental duty before the First World War broke out. On August 12, 1914, he went to France as a platoon commander with the 1st Battalion, the Irish Guards.

It is impossible at this period to write of his personal experiences in the war; all that can be done is to give his record. He fought at Mons, in the great retreat, at the Marne and in the advance on the Aisne. When the British Expeditionary Force was transferred to the north, he took part in the desperate battle of Ypres, where he was wounded. He received from the French the order of a Chevalier of the Legion of Honour, an exceptional decoration for a subaltern. Having recovered from his wound, he saw a short period of service at home with the 2nd Battalion of his regiment, and returned to France with it almost exactly a year after his first arrival in the country, on August 15, 1915. He was now a captain and a company commander. That autumn he took part in the bloody and disappointing battle of Loos and was awarded the Military Cross.

The first half of 1916 was for him a period of trench warfare. New battalions of Guards were formed and the Guards Division was created, one of the finest fighting instruments in any army. With it he took part in incidents of the fierce and long-drawn-out battle of the Somme, receiving the D.S.O. for his services. He was an acting major in 1916, and was promoted to that rank in August, 1917, being then one of the youngest substantive field officers in the British Army. In March, 1917, with the temporary rank of lieutenant-colonel, he returned to his 1st Battalion to command. In October, he took over command of the 2nd Battalion and remained with it for the next twelve months. He was slightly wounded on October 9 in the third battle of Ypres, but was present at the battle of Cambrai in the following month, when the Guards Division saw some of the hardest and most prolonged fighting of its relatively brief existence.

Early in the following year, British divisions were reduced from twelve to nine battalions. In the case of nearly all of them this was effected by reducing brigades to three battalions apiece and breaking up the surplus three battalions to provide much-needed reinforcements. The Guards battalions were, however, too valuable to be disposed of in this manner, so a brigade was withdrawn from the division and attached to another, the 31st. With this division Alexander took part in the resistance to the German offensive on the Lys in that phase of the fighting known officially as the battle of Hazebrouck, where the whole of his brigade won for itself imperishable glory. He did not take part in the final strokes of the victorious campaign at the end of the year. He had been appointed Commandant of the X Corps School, holding this post for the last month of the war, his sole period of service outside the regiment during its whole course. He emerged from the war with a truly remarkable record. In addition to the D.S.O., the M.C., and the French Legion of Honour, he had received the Russian Order of St. Anne, and had been mentioned five times in despatches. He was a marked man, and henceforth, as he went up the military ladder, was to be always one of the youngest men of his rank in the Army.

Further interesting employment came to him immediately. He served on the British Food Misson to Poland and the Baltic Political Mission from March to June, 1919, and in the following month took over command of the Baltic Landeswehr. These men were practically all of German descent, with no love for the British. Yet Alexander won their confidence as completely as he had that of his own Irish Guardsmen. The curious phase of warfare in North Russia in which he took part, with its divided loyalties and cross currents, provided invaluable military education. Not long afterwards he had another interesting experience. Posted to command the 1st Battalion of his regiment once more in April, 1922, and promoted lieutenant-colonel in May, he was in the Army of Occupation at Constantinople for the better part of eighteen months. At the time of the Chanak crisis, when the Turks under Mustapha Kemal threatened to cross from Asia Minor and attack Constantinople, two other battalions of the Guards were sent out, and the Irish Guards then joined them to form a Guards' brigade. It was not on the whole a particularly creditable incident, since none of the face-saving negotiations and stipulations could hide the fact that in the end we yielded to force, but once again it provided experience of great value to a young officer destined for high command.

A quiet spell followed. From September, 1923, to April, 1924, the 1st Battalion was stationed at Gibraltar, and after that Alexander was at home for a long time to come. In January, 1926, he went to the Staff College, considerably senior in rank to the great majority of his fellow students. From 1928 to 1930 he was commanding the regiment and regimental district. Then began the period of service in India which was to prove his capacity for higher command, though there was already little doubt about that among those who had watched his career. That career had so far been regimental, and it was obviously with troops that he was to shine. But he commenced work in India in a staff appointment, G.S.O.1 to the Northern Command, in 1932. Before going out he married Lady Margaret Bingham, daughter of the fifth Earl of Lucan. Two sons and a daughter have since been born of this marriage. In 1934, as a colonel with the temporary rank of brigadier, he took over command of the Nowshera Brigade in the Peshawar District. And in the very next year there were two "small wars" to prove his mettle.

The first is officially known as the Loe Agra Operations. It was an affair of a type common enough. The area of Bara Totai-Agra, south and east of the Swat river, nominally part of a "protected area," had never in fact been fully absorbed, and in 1934 a dissident faquir crossed the Swat with a *lashkar* and drove out the local levies. The Nowshera Brigade, backed by some district troops, including artillery, and with air support, was ordered to reoccupy the territory and establish a post at Loe Agra. Alexander marched through the Malakand Pass, sniped and harrassed by the way. He was attacked on February 23, 1935, but entered Loe Agra on the 25th after a march through terrible country. Twenty or thirty of his loaded mules fell over precipices by the way. The brigade was withdrawn too soon, and the faquir, raising a new *lashkar*, again chased out the levies and re-entered Loe Agra. Back came Alexander to eject the invader. This time he left two battalions behind, but again the faquir returned, and a company, heavily attacked on a height above Loe Agra, had to be extricated. On April 11 he carried Loe Agra by storm after a twenty minutes' bombardment. This time the victory was consolidated, a motor road being driven through to Loe Agra from Kot before the regular troops were withdrawn. The region was re-absorbed into the Malakand Protected Area. Sir Philip Chetwode, the Commander-in-Chief, wrote that the operations "were in every way admirably directed by the commander." What chiefly struck observers was the manner in which Alexander, with no previous experience of fighting in this country, gripped its intricacies. Few realized how thorough had been the private apprenticeship to Indian mountain warfare to which he had subjected himself. He was appointed a Commander of the Star of India, and mentioned in despatches.

The Mohmand Operations west of the Swat later in the year have less personal interest for his biographer. They were on a much bigger scale, but were conducted almost to the finish, in the absence of a senior officer who was on leave, by a brigadier, who added substantially to his already high reputation. His name was Claude Auchinleck. The operations were carried out in terrific heat, and before they had been brought to an end Alexander was laid aside by one of the rare attacks of sickness which have attacked this very fit man all through his career. He was not present at the decisive action of September 29, when a battalion of the Guides in his brigade got into an awkward situation, over the brow of a ridge out of sight of the artillery and subjected to heavy counter-attacks by the Mohmands. But Alexander's previous work had reinforced the esteem in which he was already held. He was recommended by Chetwode for the C.S.I. for this expedition, but soon afterwards the award came through for the earlier campaign of Loe Agra.

Alexander had gone to the First World War in 1914 as a subaltern. Twenty-five years later he set out to take part in the second as a major-general. The division which he commanded was the 1st, which he had taken over at Aldershot in 1938. It formed part of the I Corps, commanded by his fellow-Ulsterman, Lieutenant-General Dill, who was later succeeded by Lieutenant-General M. G. H. Barker on becoming Vice-Chief of the Imperial General Staff. The I and II Corps went straight up to the frontier of neutral Belgium, the 1st Division taking up a position south of Roubaix on October 3. It was far from the enemy, but the possibility that the Germans would violate Belgian neutrality, as in 1914, had to be borne in mind, so the work of fortification at once began.

This was to be the strangest and least satisfactory of campaigns, some eight months of stagnation followed by an advance into Belgium, a hasty retreat to the sea, and re-embarkation almost in a matter of days. The weather that winter was exceptionally bad and the soil was heavy. At times it became so wet that work had practically to stop, but the troops were kept as busy as possible, and brigades in turn had spells in line with the French on the front facing the Germans. Meanwhile that plan, which has been so strongly criticized since, was worked out. If the Germans entered Belgium the Allies would advance to the line of the Dyle, covering Brussels and Antwerp.

The long-awaited German invasion took place on May 10, 1940. At once the B.E.F. moved forward, and, without serious interference from the air, established itself on the Dyle, the 1st Division on the left of the I Corps line. The front was scarcely established before it had to be abandoned as a result of the German break-through on the Meuse, on the French front. On May 16, the order was issued for a withdrawal by stages to the Escaut, and, after a halt on the Dender, Alexander withdrew to that line on the night of the 18th, the enemy having now reached Saint-Quentin.

By the 23rd he was back on the old frontier defences near
Roubaix, the Germans being at Saint-Omer and around
Calais. By the 28th he was on the Lys near Armentières.
The attacks on the B.E.F. were mainly directed against its
long right flank as the French caved in, and later, after the
Belgian collapse, against its left flank also; the 1st Division,
facing east, was not seriously attacked until the later stages
when it was defending the approaches to Dunkirk. Alexander
must, however, have created a strong impression by his
conduct of the retreat; for after the front had been withdrawn to the perimeter, the 1st Division being on the Furnes
Canal, it was he who was ordered by Lord Gort to take over
the final defence and conduct the last stage of the evacuation.
On May 31 he handed over his 1st Division and assumed
command of the I Corps, the only one remaining.

His coolness and imperturbability during that last critical
and tragic phase have become legendary. It was a moment
when something more than sound leadership was called for;
it was also necessary to inspire the tired troops with the
feeling that matters were less desperate than they appeared,
to call for a last effort from men who were only just physically
capable of producing it. He went about his task with an air
of quiet confidence, his manner giving no hint either of the
perils of the moment or of those of the immediate future. He
was, to use the trite but unavoidable phrase, an inspiration
to all who came in contact with him. The withdrawal went
on, and though losses were suffered, they remained unexpectedly small. Early on June 3 he made a tour of the
beaches in a motor boat and, finding that there were no
more British troops to be evacuated, then left himself.

The next task was that of reorganizing the troops and
preparing to meet the invasion which seemed almost
inevitable. On his return to England, General Brooke went
back for a very brief period to his old position as Commander-in-Chief, Southern Command, but was then
appointed Commander-in-Chief, Home Forces. Alexander,
still not fifty years of age, took his place with the Southern
Command at Salisbury. From the point of view of resistance
to invasion, this command was not quite equal in importance
to the South-eastern and Eastern—though the lie of the

French coast at Cherbourg was a feature not to be forgotten —but as regards training it was second to none. Before special areas elsewhere were cleared for battle training, Salisbury Plain was the principal area in the country for the exercises of armoured forces. A new aspect of training was, however, appearing. The need for an extreme realism, including the bold use of live ammunition of all natures, had been recognized. Alexander took a leading part in these new methods of instruction and of hardening troops, and made a great success of them. The methods which were followed long after he had left the country to command in distant theatres owed a great deal to him. Their success was amply proved by the improved showing of formations going into battle for the first time. In the circumstances of the late war, there was little prospect of being able to harden troops under conditions of active service as had been the case in the First World War. It was therefore more than ever important that troops proceeding to a theatre of war should realize the nature of their task and encounter without perturbation of mind the alarming and unsettling circumstances of a modern battle.

While Alexander was training his troops in the winter of 1941-42 in the pleasant country of south-western England, the Japanese attack in the Far East had brought about British and American disasters. That suffered by Great Britain in Malaya was the more serious and the more humiliating, perhaps the worst in the history of the nation. And it was clear to those with vision that the loss of Singapore was not going to mark the end. The Japanese were going to win more great victories, and there was as yet no sign that their progress in Asia and across the waters of the Pacific could be brought to a halt. There did, however, appear to be a hope, even if a slender one, that Burma might be saved. Early in March, 1942, when the attack was well under way, Alexander was sent out to take command of the forces operating in that country.

On February 2, the Japanese, advancing from Siam, had captured the port of Moulmein, crossed the estuary of the Salween on the 10th to take Martaban, and on March 7 captured Pegu, west of the Sittang. It was considered

necessary to evacuate Rangoon, but the order was delayed
until Alexander had actually taken over, and it was only by
a narrow margin that the British avoided envelopment and
broke through to the north. Our two divisions, with some
reinforcements just received, now had to swing round and
face south against the northward drive of the Japanese from
the direction of Moulmein and Rangoon. One column withdrew up the Sittang towards Toungoo, the other up the
Irrawaddy towards Prome. To cover the withdrawal, a
well-timed and hard-pressed counter-attack was first
launched through the town of Schwegyn and was successful
in checking the Japanese pursuit. Alexander now had at
his disposal two Indian divisions already depleted and two
small Chinese divisions which had moved into Burma by
way of the Burma Road. At the end of March, one of these
took over the British front at Toungoo to allow the British
to concentrate on the Irrawaddy. These Chinese troops
put up a stout defence for several days, and when the
Japanese, using their favourite tactics, by-passed their
position, they succeeded in breaking through to the north.

Next the Japanese succeeded in blocking the British line
of retreat on the Irrawaddy, but after a stiff fight south of
Prome, they were driven off the road. Both forces were now
more severely hampered than ever because the enemy
succeeded in catching a large proportion of the British aircraft which had been covering them on an airfield in
central Burma and inflicting very serious losses upon them.
It had become manifest that central Burma could not be
held and that there was but small prospect of clinging on
even to the northern part of the country. The next feature
of the campaign was marked by the attempt of the enemy
to seize the oilfields of Yenangyaung intact, while Alexander
fought for time to destroy them. He succeeded in this task,
and, with Chinese aid, also extricated some thousands
of his troops cut off by another Japanese turning movement.

So the retreat continued, steadily and successfully, until
the disaster of the end of April, when a Japanese column,
using true *Blitzkrieg* methods, broke through the Chinese
at Taunggyi, swept through to Mandalay and captured
Lashio, the terminus of the Burma Road, thus cutting the

Chinese off from their base. All Alexander could now do was to withdraw into Assam across the Chindwin, moving as slowly as possible to give India time for preparation. He fulfilled his task in both respects, and the Japanese in fact never seriously menaced India. He had kept his little army together on short rations in a retreat of 800 miles, the last section through dense, roadless forest and over steep mountains. The verdict of those who knew best as well as of the world in general was that his achievement had been extraordinarily fine, and he had the unusual experience of coming out of a disastrous campaign with a greatly enhanced reputation.

He went straight to the scene of another disaster. He was in Egypt, on his way home, at the time of the fighting at El Alamein, to which our forces had been driven back after suffering a heavy defeat. The Commander-in-Chief, General Auchinleck, suggested in a message home that it would be well to make a change in the command in the Middle East and mentioned Alexander's name. He was appointed to the command, with a newcomer, a man somewhat senior to himself, Lieutenant-General B. L. Montgomery, to take over the Eighth Army.

The prospects were by no means bad. Auchinleck had definitely stopped the enemy, who, as soon as he had used up the captured British stores, began to suffer from shortages. It was, indeed, a remarkable feat on the German side to have maintained during the late summer and autumn a force of some twelve divisions so close to the Delta in face of British air superiority. The German commander, Rommel, owed a great deal to the Italians, whom he despised, but whose seamen, especially those of the merchant fleet, showed skill and daring in keeping up the flow of supplies. On the British side, strong reinforcements in men and material, including the invaluable American Sherman tanks, had arrived. Rommel's last thrust towards Alexandria was completely defeated by Montgomery, though it somewhat delayed his preparations for his own great stroke.

The tactical detail of the battle of El Alamein and of the pursuit across North Africa which followed does not form part of the biography of Alexander. They were conducted

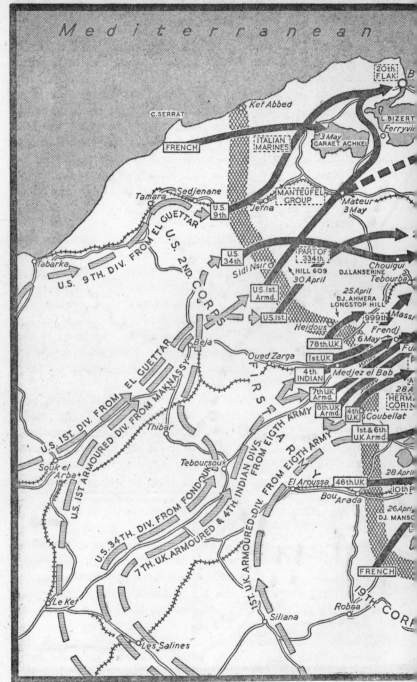

THE T...

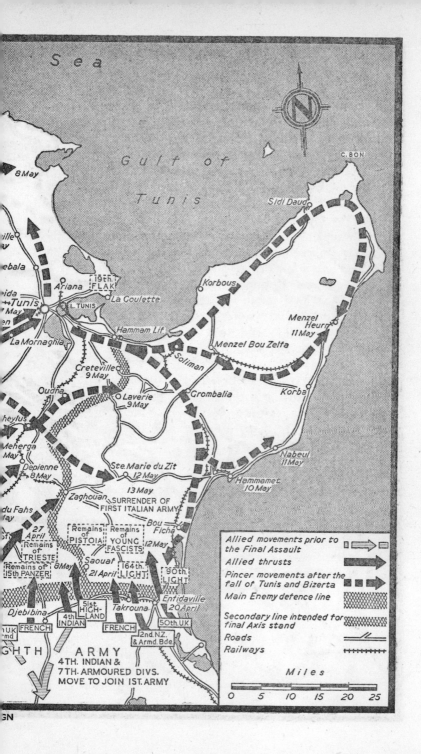

S e a

Gulf of

Tunis

8 May

C. BON

Sidi Daud

19th. FLAK

Ariana

Korbous

Menzel
Heurm
11 May

+Tunis
May

ida
+Tunis
May
en

L. TUNIS

La Goulette

Hammam Lif

Menzel Bou Zelfa

La Mornaghia

Creteville
9 May

Soliman

Korba

Oudna

Laverie
9 May

Grombalia

heylus

Nabeul
11 May

Meherga
May

Depienne
8 May

Ste. Marie du Zit
12 May

Hammamet
10 May

du Fahs
May

Zaghouan

13 May
SURRENDER OF
FIRST ITALIAN ARMY

27
April
Remains
of
TRIESTE

Remains
of
PISTOIA

Remains
of
YOUNG
FASCISTS

Bou
Ficha
12 May

Remains of
15th PANZER

8 May

Saouaf
21 April

164th.
LIGHT

90th.
LIGHT

Djebibina

51st
HIGH-
LAND

Takrouna

Enfidaville
20 April

UK
md

4TH.
INDIAN

FRENCH

FRENCH

2nd. N.Z.
& Armd. Bde.

50th. UK

GHTH   A R M Y
4TH. INDIAN &
7TH. ARMOURED DIVS.
MOVE TO JOIN 1ST. ARMY

GN

| Allied movements prior to the Final Assault |
| Allied thrusts |
| Pincer movements after the fall of Tunis and Bizerta |
| Main Enemy defence line |
| Secondary line intended for final Axis stand |
| Roads |
| Railways |

M i l e s

0   5   10   15   20   25

by his army commander, Montgomery, under his general supervision, and it can be taken that he interfered very little at this stage. On the administrative side, a heavy responsibility fell upon his command, especially in the pursuit, but he had in his senior administrative staff officer, Lindsell, a man of first-class ability in this all-important branch of warfare. The Eighth Army's assault was launched on October 23, but it took ten days of bitter fighting to breach the deep and heavily-mined position between the sea and the marshy Qattara Depression. Then the British armour broke through. The Germans retreated headlong from their seemingly impregnable defences, leaving tens of thousands of Italians and a fair proportion of their own people behind. By November 4 Rommel was in full retreat to Agheila, where he had held up the British advance in the previous January. He had lost 30,000 prisoners, at least as many in killed and wounded, and vast quantities of material. On December 13 he fell back towards Sirte, and after some rear-guard actions, halted at Buerat, half-way between Sirte and Misurata. Here he stood until January 15, 1943, Montgomery's advanced guard being occupied with organizing its supply lines and picking up mines. Rommel got away with little further damage, and the Eighth Army entered Tripoli on the 23rd.

The pursuit was conducted by Montgomery, and from Alexander's point of view, there is only one question to be considered. Would it have been possible to intercept the retreat of the enemy by means of a landing from the sea? It is on this point that foreign criticism has fastened. Rommel it is said, was allowed to join the German forces in Tunisia, as he desired, with comparatively little further loss after the battle of El Alamein. If he could have been caught on the road the struggle there would have been over in half the time and the invasion of the Continent would have become practicable proportionately earlier. It goes without saying that the matter was discussed. But it was considered impossible to mount such an operation in sufficient strength, and it is not at present possible to dispute that verdict. The official history will be studied with interest from this point of view.

February saw Rommel's army back in Tunisia and Montgomery's facing the Marcth Line, which constituted its southern defences. Then there opened a new phase for Alexander. The campaign in Tunisia had gone by no means as well as had been expected since the Allies had landed in Algeria. The last episodes had been disquieting. Making the most of his interior lines, Rommel withdrew his armour from Montgomery's front and threw it into an attack, together with troops already in Tunisia, on the Americans at Sidi Bou Zid. The Americans lost the Kasserine Pass, and at one moment it looked as if the rail junction of Tebessa would go the same way. But Rommel did not persist. It was the old problem of interior lines, how far to exploit success against one section of a divided enemy before turning on the other. Some say that Rommel should have gone further and that he had lost his nerve. At all events he was now preparing a stroke against Montgomery, a stroke which was to be defeated. Its failure led to the departure of the German commander, who was a sick man.

It was after the American set-back that Alexander took over the post of Deputy to General Eisenhower, the allied Commander-in-Chief in Tunisia, with the special task of co-ordinating the operations of the Allied forces within the country with those of the Eighth Army now standing at its gates. He assumed command on February 20. He required another seven weeks to bring the campaign to an end, but when that was accomplished, it was as thorough a job as any in the history of war.

He suffered some minor rebuffs before he had his way and worked himself into a favourable position to strike the final blow. He launched the decisive attack on May 6, two infantry and two armoured divisions under the orders of General Anderson, commanding the First Army, assaulting the German position astride the Mejerda on a front of only 3,000 yards. The German front buckled completely. The armour pressed almost straight on to Tunis, and at the same time the Americans on the left flank were equally successful and broke into Bizerta. This was not quite the end, because the enemy still hoped to withdraw a large proportion of his forces for a last stand in the Cap Bon

peninsula, east of the Gulf of Tunis. On the 10th this hope
was frustrated. The First Army broke through the powerful
defences east of Tunis and swept across the base of the
peninsula to the sea of Hammamet. The Navy and Air
Force prevented evacuation. The Axis forces were doomed.
The final count of prisoners taken after May 5 was 248,000,
of whom three-fifths were Germans. All the material,
including 250 tanks, 558 aircraft, and over 1,000 guns, fell
into the hands of the victor.

There was no decoration for Alexander for the Tunisian
campaign because he had only just received, in the previous
November, the highest existing, the Grand Cross of the Bath,
for his part in the Egyptian campaign. And the Grand Cross
had come in the same year as promotion to the lower order,
the K.C.B., awarded for his work in Burma. (The companion-
ship of the order he had received in 1918.) But he had won
something as valuable: the admiration and trust of the
officers and men of the armies, British, American and French,
whose operations he had directed.

The next task was to gain possession of Sicily at the earliest
possible moment as a stepping-stone to Italy. Alexander
had begun to prepare for the task before finishing the
campaign in Tunisia, but there was much to be done. And,
however soon the naval and military forces were ready, it
appeared rash to cut short the preliminary bombardment
from the air. Whether or not the invasion could have been
put forward slightly in order to gain a little more of the
priceless boon of summer weather is another of the matters
which can be fully discussed only when the archives are
opened; the present opinion of those best acquainted with
the administrative side is that it could not have been. The
landings of British and American troops under Montgomery
and Patton took place in the small hours of July 10 along
one hundred miles of the south coast between Syracuse
and Licata. The trifling resistance of most of the Italian
troops suggested that the invasion might have been carried out
with less preparation, but it would have been a heavy responsibility to gamble on the Italians fighting worse on their own
soil than they had in North Africa. In any case the task of
assembling the various forms of shipping was the bottle-neck.

The campaign requires little description here. Depending entirely on their own efforts, the Germans fought a long and dogged rear-guard action on the slopes of Mount Etna, commanding the wide Plain of Catania, while organizing evacuation of the island across the Straits of Messina. They packed the straits with anti-aircraft artillery, which made interference from the air with their movement very difficult, and without doubt they got away a disagreeably large proportion of their forces under this "umbrella." First the Americans from the west, then the British from the south, reached Messina on August 17. Practically all the Italian troops in the island had either surrendered or donned civilian clothes and disappeared. Over a thousand hostile aircraft had been taken and more than half that number destroyed, and the enemy had also lost 260 tanks and 502 guns.

The next task before Alexander was the conquest of Italy. The details of the invasion are so mingled with political considerations that it is an almost impossible task to disentangle the two sets of threads in a biography as brief as this. Even before the end had come in Sicily, the Italians had begun negotiations in Lisbon for an armistice, and a convention was signed at Syracuse by General Eisenhower's representative, General Bedell Smith, and the Italian General Castellano on September 3. If time had been wasted, this had nothing to do with Alexander, whose task was to launch the invasion as soon as possible. He landed troops of the Eighth Army in the "toe" of Italy that same day and put forward his second landing, south of Naples, which was to have taken place on the 15th, to the night of the 8th–9th, simultaneously with the announcement of the armistice. Many of the terms of the armistice became inoperative owing to German action, and the plan to drop an American airborne division on the Roman airfields fell through because the Italians allowed the Germans to occupy them without opposition. It was fated that the Italian campaign was to develop into a slogging match.

However, all went well at first. The Eighth Army, practically unopposed, swept up the "foot" of Italy and further forces landed at Taranto in the "heel" with Italian assistance. The Eighth Army under Montgomery pressed forward at the rate of thirteen road miles a day until it made touch with the Fifth American Army under Mark Clark, which had landed on the Salerno beaches south of Naples.

Before that happened, however, this latter army had fought one of the most vital battles of the war. On September 13 the enemy launched a fierce counter-offensive and at some points drove the Allies back to the beaches, which were under heavy fire. It was touch and go. The Germans, indeed, thought that the battle was won, but they began to crow too soon, prophesying immediate evacuation. Perhaps it was the fire of the British battleships under the command of Admiral Sir Andrew Cunningham which decided the issue, though the air forces also did splendid work and the land forces fought grimly. On the 16th the Allies could pass to the offensive again, and by night the enemy was in retreat.

Naples was occupied on October 1, by which time the Eighth Army on the Adriatic side had possession of the great Foggia airfield. The advance continued in bad weather across mountainous country and deep-cut rivers running to the Adriatic and Tyrrhenian Seas on either flank. Doggedly the two armies fought their way forward until late November brought a halt. The way was barred by the Garigliano on the west coast, further inland by the grim masses which have become known under the general title of "Cassino," and east of the Apennines by the Sangro. The Sangro was crossed by the Eighth Army, but it was then held up by bad weather. In the west the attack stuck fast.

On January 22, 1944, Alexander made an effort to break the deadlock by landing a strong force on the beaches of Anzio, about half-way between his front line and Rome, the objective which it had been hoped at one moment might be secured by Christmas. The operation had been carefully prepared and high hopes had been founded upon it, but it produced no success whatever that winter. The hostile commander, Kesselring, seems to have been prepared to make a deep withdrawal if necessary, but found he could hold both the original front and this new lodgement. It was

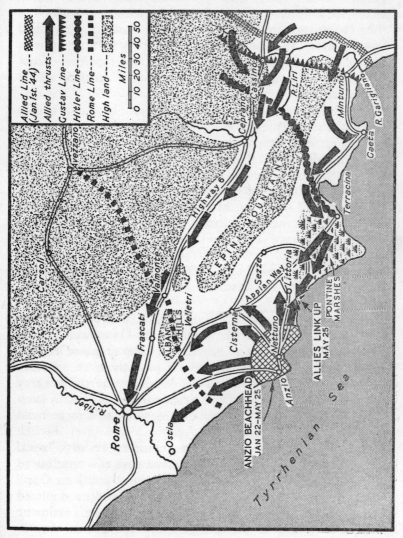

THE ITALIAN CAMPAIGN

a bitter disappointment, and naturally Alexander came in for his share of the criticism which was rife in the United Kingdom. He and his Army Commander on this flank, Mark Clark, were both early on the scene at Anzio, but they could not break the ring. On the contrary, the Allied forces had to withstand a series of heavy counter-attacks, certain of them extremely dangerous. But the Anzio front held and the Germans were heavily mauled in their efforts to disrupt it.

The Anzio holding was after all to prove its utility and to justify the strategy upon which the landing had been based, but not until the spring, and there was much bitter, costly, and generally ineffective fighting in the Cassino region in the interval. On May 11, during the hours of darkness, the allied armies launched one of the best conceived offensives of the war. All went "according to plan" in the truest sense of that often misused phrase. The enemy suffered his heaviest defeat of the war in Italy. A number of his divisions were cut to pieces and he was driven to a hasty retreat with big losses in prisoners and material. On June 4, two days before the invasion of France, the Fifth Army entered Rome.

The advance continued, though at a reduced pace. The Germans contrived to make a partial recovery and to restore some order in their retreating forces. Of even more importance was the fact that the armies in Italy were seriously weakened by an expeditionary force being removed to carry out a landing in the south of France in aid of the invasion through Normandy. The total strength of this force from the Mediterranean was three American and seven French divisions. It began its landing on August 15. Its withdrawal killed Alexander's brilliantly conceived plan of a continuous pursuit followed by a break through the "Ljubljana Gap" into the Danubian plain. Meanwhile Alexander's depleted forces, after a signal victory in the region of Lake Trasimene in the last week of June, had come up against the so-called "Gothic Line" in the northern Apennines, a very strong position. A general offensive was launched on September 10 with the object of breaking through into the plain of the Po. A disappointment followed. The German works were overrun, but the mountains themselves checked the advance until the winter broke. In December, General Sir Henry Maitland Wilson, Supreme Allied Commander in the Mediterranean, went to Washington as senior British military representative, and Alexander took his place. An American, General Mark Clark, succeeded him in command of the army group in Italy. Alexander was thus further removed from the operations and had other matters besides those of Italy on his hands, but he continued to lay down the strategy of the campaign. He was promoted to the rank of Field Marshal.

The winter operations made heavy demands upon the troops, but the measure of success was limited. On April 9, 1945, however, another general offensive was launched. This time the success was complete, though only after hard and prolonged fighting. The hostile front broke; both armies crossed the Po simultaneously; and shortly afterwards resistance completely collapsed. Meanwhile German emissaries had come to Alexander's headquarters with proposals for surrender on the part of the German commander-in-chief, whose area covered parts of Austria in addition to the Italian theatre. On May 2 the enemy laid down his arms. Thus the armies of Italy, which had been fighting in that country for nine months before the landing in western France, secured the first great wholesale surrender.

Alexander's reputation stood high at the end of the war. As it was probable that Montgomery would remain in Germany, it was generally expected that Alexander would succeed to the office of Chief of the Imperial General Staff. Instead, however, he was in 1946 appointed Governor-General of Canada, and his acceptance of that post made it probable that he had said farewell to military life, although field marshals remain theoretically on the active list. He was raised to the peerage with the title of Viscount Alexander of Tunis. In the same year he was created a Knight of the Garter and a Knight Grand Cross of the Order of St. Michael and St. George.

He had proved himself the ideal leader of an international group of armies. The easy affability which might be thought necessary for such a position was not his, but it is doubtful whether, where soldiers are concerned, this quality ranks as high as is generally supposed. The soldier, whatever his rank, looks first of all in such circumstances for reliability. The international commander who would win the trust of the various sections of his troops, supposing him to have proved himself efficient, must next inspire them with confidence that he has no favourites, that he spares none, including the troops of his own nation, and that he would not dream of attempting to advance the particular interests of his own nation at the expense of the nations providing his other contingents. When dealing with Alexander, all nationalities could rest assured that this was the case. And the longer they remained under his orders the greater became their respect and affection for him.

As a strategist he is entitled to a high rank. It may be that he did not possess the extraordinary power of appreciating a situation and deciding upon the best of several alternative courses which was displayed by Field Marshal Lord Montgomery. In the case of Alexander it would appear that plans were commonly worked out upon the system which is most usual in the British Army: the commander tells his staff his general intentions and bids it work out the possibilities, perhaps giving it two alternatives. He then considers the scheme or schemes presented to him, makes the adjustments which appear to him to be necessary, and finally decides upon his course of action. Montgomery, after long reflection, made up his mind first what must be done and then bade his staff work out the detailed plan to conform with his intentions. It was the staff which suggested the adjustments. If the staff were to declare that he had demanded the impossible, he might have to revise his ideas, but he would not easily resign himself to doing so, and it was never likely that this would be necessary, because he possessed so clear a sense of the possible in war. The difference must not be pressed too far. It was slight and might not apply to all operations, but as a generality it may be called valid.

The same plan might well be arrived at by the two methods. Certainly Alexander's two outstanding operations, the final offensive in Tunisia and the spring offensive of 1944 in Italy, could not have been bettered by any commander or on any other conceivable plan. As for the carrying through of the plan—which Marshal Foch used to insist was far more important than the plan itself—there was no commander in the late war who did that more thoroughly. War is not for the dreamer who can merely conceive, but cannot put his conceptions into effect. The successful commander is a man who never takes his hand from the work for a moment; who sees his conception through from the first step to the last; who has a temperament sturdy enough to stand up to constant disappointment, accident, and the weaknesses of subordinates; who works calmly and with steady nerves amid a friction which would finally drive the highly-strung demented. There Alexander was strong.

MONTGOMERY

By

Major H. A. De Weerd

One afternoon early in August, 1942, two German fighter planes were returning from a raid behind the British lines on the El Alamein front. By a malicious turn of fate one of the pilots happened to spot a lumbering R.A.F. Bombay transport plane scudding along under a low ceiling. Dipping his wings to attract the attention of his companion, the leading fighter swept down on the hapless transport with blazing machine-guns. The pilot of the Bombay manœuvred his slow plane in a desperate effort to escape. He finally dived toward the ground, and attempted to land in order to save his passengers. The second fighter swept down like a hawk. Just as the wheels of the Bombay touched the ground a long burst of incendiaries ripped through the plane. The transport burst into flames, careened wildly over the rough ground, tipped upside down, broke up, and burned furiously. Among the seven British officers who perished in the blaze was Lieutenant-General W. H. E. (Strafer) Gott, who had just been chosen to command the British Eighth Army. He had left the front that afternoon for a well-deserved rest in Cairo before taking up his new post.

The "best desert fighter" in the British army, Gott's tragic death was just another example of the fantastic string of misfortune that followed the Eighth Army after Wavell's transfer to India. Gott's death was a tremendous loss but, as is sometimes the case when the hand of fate topples the carefully laid plans of men, it made possible one of the most amazing careers in the annals of the British army. It led to

VISCOUNT MONTGOMERY

Detail from the portrait
by James Gunn
By courtesy of
Viscount Montgomery

the appointment of General Bernard Law Montgomery to the command of the Eighth Army.

The circumstances of Montgomery's appointment are worth setting down at some length, since they give us a standard by which to judge the results of his command. General Neil Ritchie had commanded the British Eighth Army from the time that Cunningham lost control of the battle of Sidi Rezegh in November, 1941, until late in June, 1942. During his command he drove Rommel to El Agheila, in December, 1941, but was forced back with heavy tank losses to the line Gazala–Bir Hacheim. When Rommel assumed the offensive in May, 1942, Ritchie had been unable to relieve the gallant Fighting French garrison at Bir Hacheim, had stumbled into Rommel's tank trap at Knights-bridge, on June 13, and was unable to provide an effective defence of Tobruk, which fell on June 20, with a loss of 30,000 men. When the battered remnants of the Eighth Army retreated from Mersa Matruh, General Auchinleck relieved Ritchie and took personal charge of the final British defence position at El Alamein. There, after heavy fighting in July and August, the two tired armies lapsed into positional warfare.

Auchinleck never quite "clicked" as a commander in the Middle East, despite his capacity as an organizer. He possessed real courage, ruthlessly sacked his friends when they failed, and did a brilliant job of deepening and holding the El Alamein line, but the army never quite appreciated him. Neither did the correspondents or the staff at Cairo, who wistfully recalled the splendid open-handed manner of Wavell. When Auchinleck attempted to "vitalize" the High Command by moving the staff out of Cairo into tents on the fringe of the desert, scurrilous troops sardonically referred to G.H.Q. as "the short-range desert force." Though large-scale reinforcements were on the way to Egypt in July, Rommel was still at the gates of Alexandria. The British fleet based at Alexandria had steamed into hiding, and Cairo was openly preparing to receive the Afrika Korps. New blood was needed to restore the situation in the Middle East. Churchill decided to place Alexander in command and give the Eighth Army to General Gott who had come through two years of fighting in the Western Desert with a brilliant reputation. No other commander seemed equally qualified to restore the morale and fighting power of the army.

Not that the Eighth Army had lacked promising officers—but many of them had been lost by enemy action or accident. O'Connor, the brilliant field commander, had been captured early in 1941; Russell and Pope were killed in a plane crash; Jock Campbell, the magnetic and audacious leader of the 7th Support Group, was killed when his car overturned on a narrow road; Gatehouse, Briggs, and Lumsden were wounded by the bombs of a Stuka; rising young officers like Garmoyle and Coombes were gone; and now Gott was dead. Surely the Eighth Army lived under an unlucky star. The troops felt this and often sang a plaintive song which some nameless musical wag originated on Wavell's first retreat:

> Oh, Sidi Barrani!
> Oh, Mersa Matruh!
> The Eyties will get there,
> Then what will we do?

Now not only the "Eyties" but the Germans were at El Alamein and the fate of the whole Middle East hung in the balance. The choice of the right command for the Eighth Army was a matter of inestimable importance. Churchill picked Montgomery.

Men remembered that Alexander had been the last man off the beach at Dunkirk, but that was an evil memory. He had commanded the last stages of the Burma campaign but that also was a campaign without glory. As for Montgomery —he was frankly an unknown. No one noticed him when he registered at Shepheard's Hotel, in Cairo. They noticed him the next morning, however, when he left for his first inspection at the front at 0500 hours. Something new had been added to nervous, defeatist Cairo! His first order to the troops read: "We will fight the enemy where we now stand; there will be no withdrawal and no surrender." From that moment on the Eighth Army never looked back.

After they had time to look up his record and size up the new commander in the flesh, the Eighth Army found that it had a somewhat astonishing person at its head. Slightly

above average height, Montgomery was a slender, hard,
hawk-like, energetic man, with piercing blue eyes, long nose,
and sparse, sandy hair. His habits were frankly disturbing.
He neither smoked nor drank, but quoted scripture; prayed
regularly; detested unnecessary noise; set aside two-minute
periods before conferences for coughing; demanded utmost
punctiliousness of his officers and men; conducted violent,
whirlwind inspection trips; showed a weakness for bizarre
headgear; wore fantastic combinations of clothes; painted
his nickname "Monty" on his personal reconnaissance tank;
and insisted on lecturing his officers at odd and inconvenient
hours. Montgomery had "character" and an innate sense of
the dramatic. Within a few weeks he was known to every
man in the Eighth Army.

Montgomery, the son of a Colonial bishop, was born
at Moville, County Donegal, Ireland, on November 17, 1887.
After graduating from Sandhurst he entered the Royal
Warwickshire Regiment, was twice wounded in France
during World War I, and served with occupation troops in
Germany and Ireland. In 1934, he was a colonel instructing
at the Staff College in Quetta, India. He commanded
the 9th Infantry Brigade at Portsmouth in 1937 and led a
Division in Palestine during the disorders of 1938-39.

When World War II broke out Montgomery commanded
the 3rd Division in France and brought it through the hell
of Dunkirk. After the evacuation he commanded the V Corps
for a time before taking over the south-eastern Command.
He apparently did not study war to the exclusion of all other
things until after the death of his wife (Betty Carver) in 1937.
"My wife and I used to do things together," he once told
newsmen, "now—I like birds!" He apparently not only
studied military history but also investigated the psychology
of command in large armies because he was able to do in a
few weeks what Auchinleck had notably failed to do in
many months—he made a lasting impression on every man
in the Eighth Army. This was no mean feat; that army was
one of the strangest racial mixtures ever placed on a single
battlefield. It was composed of Britons, South Africans,
Australians, New Zealanders, Indians, Greeks, and French-
men.

Up to the time he proved himself in victorious battle against the Afrika Korps at El Alamein, all Montgomery had to work on was his sense of the dramatic, his drive, and his unmistakable concern for the welfare and preparation of his troops. His trips of inspection were endless; his regime of violent exercise and realistic training was so severe that the men looked forward to the prospect of battle with a sense of relief. He is said to have invited a small group of officers to a Spartan meal, lectured them for two hours, and then remarked in bidding them farewell: "I trust that you are militarily revitalized!" Back in England, in 1941, he made all the officers in command up to the rank of Brigadier do a seven-mile run once a week. In Africa his regime was even more exacting. As one American officer said: "Montgomery put an army that was already supposed to be veteran through a physical-conditioning programme equal to that of the commandos. After that the Germans could not stop the Eighth Army."

Everywhere he spoke to the troops and officers. "We have got to get a spirit into every man in the Eighth Army that burns like a flame!" He described his plans to the officers with utmost frankness. "War is a simple thing. The ABC of modern combat is common sense!" He made every man in the army a partner in his project—the defeat of Rommel and the destruction of his army. He told the plan of El Alamein to the whole army so that every man understood the part he was to play. All Montgomery's major orders to his corps commanders from El Alamein to Tripoli were oral. He had no use for elaborate paper plans. A superior commander should not sit up nights wrestling with paper work and files. It would be better, he said, to go to bed or read a good book. He kept a picture of Rommel in his headquarters to remind him constantly of his mission. Morale in the army soared like an ascending rocket. The effect of Montgomery's assumption of command was described by Churchill as nothing short of "electrifying."

Though it does not detract in the least from Montgomery's magnificent achievement in raising the effectiveness of the Eighth Army to the pitch of fighting efficiency shown in October, it should be said that for the first time the Eighth

Army was really getting the equipment required for modern combat—and getting it on an ample scale. Ritchie had to fight German tanks with two-pound anti-tank guns. He had to meet German Mark III and Mark IV tanks with inferior British and early American models. He never had enough of the excellent 25-pound field guns to make up for his other deficiencies, and above all he had no self-propelled guns. Major-General Daniel Peinaar, commander of the South African Division, used to say: "Give me a good self-propelled assault gun—never mind the armour—and I'll drive Rommel out of Libya." While Rommel was beating Ritchie in May and June of 1942, large-scale reinforcements of men and equipment were being sent from Britain and the United States. Three well-trained British Divisions—the 44th, 50th, and 51st—left England for Egypt during these months. Large numbers of British six-pound anti-tank guns arrived to augment the less effective two-pounders. Enough 25-pound field guns were sent to provide one gun for every twenty-three yards of front. American planes swelled the superiority that the R.A.F. already held in the air. Finally, brand-new American Mark IV (General Sherman) tanks and 105 mm. self-propelled assault guns arrived in numbers to give the Eighth Army superiority in the quality as well as in the quantity of its armoured equipment. The Mark IV tanks and 105 mm. assault guns were to be General Montgomery's tactical surprises. After the battle of El Alamein, General Alexander told American officers that the American Mark III (General Grant) tanks saved the Eighth Army from disaster in June and July, 1942, and that the Mark IV tank made the victory at El Alamein possible.

Montgomery also had "brains" at the top of all parts of the Eighth Army. His Chief-of-Staff was Francis de Guingand; his intelligence officer was Lieutenant-Colonel E. T. Williams, a former Oxford don. With Lindsell in charge of supplies, Gatehouse and Lumsden in command of his tanks, and with Freyberg, Moreshead, and Wimperley in command of infantry divisions, Montgomery had the best subordinate commanders any leader could have wished for. He insisted on the best staff and rear establishment possible on the ground that "an army commander's administration in the

rear should be on a scale commensurate with what he hoped
to achieve at the front." Officers who did not meet his high
standards were dealt with frankly. "You are a good officer,"
he would say, "but you are not good enough for me."

The position that Montgomery took over extended from
the Qattara Depression northward to El Alamein from
which it took its name. It was a forty mile line which ran
through Himeimat, Deir El Munassib, Ruweisat Ridge, past
the Hill of Jesus toward Thompson's Post and the sea. There
were some concrete pill-boxes on the British side but mostly
well-concealed artillery and infantry positions in great depth
covered by extensive wire entanglements and minefields.
Land mines had become a major factor in fighting and they
were used on a prodigal scale by both sides. According to
General de Guingand, the principal change that Montgomery made in the organization of the Eighth Army was
to restore the division to its basic position as chief combat
unit. All special columns were abolished. An armoured corps
was formed to counter Axis armour, and air-ground co-
operation was made absolute, not provisional as before.

It is noteworthy that Montgomery saw the strategic
importance of Alam Halfa, an undefended ridge of high
ground in the rear of the El Alamein position, on his first
visit to the front. With rare instinct he concluded that Alam
Halfa would be a main objective of Rommel's coming attack.
He immediately set about to make this position into a death
trap for Rommel's armour, planting "false-going" maps
which showed firm ground in a sandy approach area in such
a way that they were sure to fall into enemy hands. Rommel
swallowed the bait and burned up precious tank fuel trying
to follow this false approach. Montgomery's defensive battle
of Alam Halfa, August 30 to September 7, 1942, was a minor
classic. Rommel did everything Montgomery wanted him
to do and was badly mauled. Montgomery could then plan
for his attempt to crush the Afrika Korps in October.

The forces available in the Eighth Army consisted of the
X Armoured Corps (two armoured divisions plus the 2nd
New Zealand Division), two armoured brigades, and six
infantry divisions: 9th Australian, 4th Indian, 1st South
African, 51st (Highland), 44th and 50th British; together

with Fighting French and Greek detachments. Montgomery
turned his newly-arrived British divisions into veterans by
training them alongside the battle-tried units that survived
the retreat to El Alamein. The exact strength of the R.A.F.
under Air Marshal Coningham is not known, but it was
sufficiently powerful to attack Axis supply lines with at least
700 bombers prior to the infantry assault and then pin the
enemy aviation to the ground.

The Axis forces on the Alamein front in October, 1942,
consisted of two German panzer divisions (the 15th and
21st), the German 90th Light (Motorized) Infantry Division,
the German 164th Light Infantry Division (flown from
Crete), two Italian armoured divisions (the Ariette and
Littorio), and the Trieste Motorized Infantry Division which
made up the XX Mobile Corps, plus the Trento, Brescia,
Pavia, Bologna, and Folgore Infantry divisions. The effective
strength of this force on October 23 may be estimated at
90,000 men, 600 tanks, 400 guns, 900 anti-tank guns
(including 88 mm. dual-purpose guns), and 600 planes.

The directive which Mr. Churchill gave to Generals
Alexander and Montgomery was simple and brief. It read:
"Your prime and main duty will be to take, or destroy, at
the earliest opportunity, the German-Italian army commanded by Field Marshal Rommel, together with all its
supplies and establishments in Egypt and Libya."

General Montgomery's plans for carrying it out were also
simple. He had observed that whenever Ritchie waged a
battle of confusion against Rommel, the Eighth Army took
a beating. This time he was to make sure that the British
plan was simple enough to carry out in spite of enemy interference. Once action was joined the initiative should never
be surrendered to the enemy. This would prevent the kind
of disorganization that had cancelled British advantages in
earlier battles. He replaced Rommel's radio technique of
directing battles by a policy of making every man in the
Eighth Army understand the whole plan of battle.

In order that he might have entire freedom to carry out
his preparatory steps, Montgomery built up a "reserve army"
in the back areas out of odds and ends. This secured his
bases against an unexpected enemy attack. Then he pulled

out two armoured divisions and the 2nd New Zealand (the Ball of Fire) Division and formed them into a special assault corps called the X Armoured Corps. This force was equipped with newly-arrived American tanks and self-propelled assault guns and put through a vigorous training programme for its break-through mission in the coming battle.

General Montgomery's plan of battle sought to achieve maximum surprise and deception. Feints were to be made by the 4th Indian Division at Ruweisat Ridge, by the 50th and 44th Divisions north and south of Deir El Munassib, and by the 7th Armoured Division south of Himeimat. The 9th Australian Division was to pin down the 164th, 90th, and Trieste Divisions along the coast. The real attack was to come in the north at Tel El Eisa where the X Armoured Corps was to use a break-through gap to be prepared by engineers and infantry. The sector chosen for the break-through was the strongest part of the German front. The point of attack apparently expected by the Germans was at Ruweisat Ridge farther south. Adopting a modification of Allenby's Gaza deception of 1917, Montgomery formed a truck park in the rear of the break-through point. Each day German reconnaissance planes watched the training area of the X Armoured Corps far behind the lines, but each night squadrons of Mark IV tanks disguised as trucks were moved into the truck park and an equal number of trucks were withdrawn. As the preparatory stages of the infantry assault and mine-lifting operations at Tel El Eisa proceeded, the whole force of the X Corps was in position to strike.

Far from suspecting a decisive British attack, so it appears, Marshal Rommel took time out in September for a trip to Berlin, leaving General von Stumme in command of the Afrika Korps. At Hitler's Sportspalast speech on September 30, he appeared as a guest of honour. There was no lack of confidence as he talked to German newsmen. "We hold the gateway of Egypt with full intentions to act. We did not fight our way forward in order to be thrown back. You can depend on it that we shall hold fast to what we have taken."

Montgomery's pre-battle dispositions not only deceived the Germans as to time of the British attack, but caused

General von Stumme to divide his armour. He sent the 21st and Ariette Divisions south to meet the threatening British concentration in that area and held the 15th and Littorio Divisions in the north. If the British attack came where General von Stumme expected it would, at Ruweisat Ridge, he hoped to crush the British penetration by bringing his armour together like the jaws of a pincer. After the battle joined, his successor found that it was too late to effect a junction in full strength. The Afrika Korps thus prepared for its own defeat.

General Montgomery's order of the day on the eve of battle read: "When I assumed command of the Eighth Army I said that the mandate was to destroy Rommel and his army, and that it would be done as soon as we were ready. We are ready now. The battle which is now about to begin will be one of the decisive battles of history. It will be the turning point of the war."

Promptly at 2130 hours on Friday, October 23, a tremendous British artillery barrage crashed down on Axis positions along the Alamein front. It fell upon the forward positions, battered the enemy command posts, and cut their communications. Under cover of this bombardment and of smoke screens, infantry and engineer patrols went forward to lift anti-tank mines and clear barriers. Then infantry advanced in strength. Ranging far and wide over Axis positions the bombers and fighters of the R.A.F. carried out over 1,000 sorties, against enemy airfields, communications centres, troop concentrations, and supply depots. It was the heaviest and most sustained air attack launched up to that time in the Middle East. Later, when the troops advanced across the area over which the R.A.F. operated, they found 550 Axis planes either destroyed or abandoned on enemy flying fields.

For seven days and nights the artillery-infantry action continued with engineers constantly extending the gap through the Axis minefields. General von Stumme was killed in action on October 26, and the command of the Afrika Korps passed to General Ritter von Thoma, who made a desperate effort to concentrate his armour in the face of an impending British break-through. Finally, on November 1, the 2nd New Zealand Division, with brigades from the 50th and 51st Divisions (brought up from the south after feinting in that area), broke through the last Axis line at Kidney Ridge. The 51st Division had belated revenge that day for its losses at St. Valery in 1940. The stage was set for the advance of the X Armoured Corps. It struck the Afrika Korps like a thunderbolt.

Never before had the British concentrated so much armour and fire power in a single mass. Hundreds of tanks rolled forward over Kidney Ridge on the morning of November 2. As one observer described the scene: "Each tank tore itself a bow wave and a wake of streaming dust that the sun caught and tipped with crimson. They spread out toward the sea and in toward the desert—a racing, roaring army of steel straining their petrol guts in rocking thunderous motion." As they reached the vicinity of El Aqqaqir, General Thoma met them with the bulk of his armoured strength. It wasn't enough. Unprepared for the fire power, mobility, and armour of the new Mark IV tanks, and above all, for the hitting power of the 105 mm. assault guns and concentration of supporting British anti-tank guns, General Thoma lost the main body of his armour in a single day's fighting at El Aqqaqir and fell captive to General Montgomery.

According to the British official account there were two decisive stages of the El Alamein battle. "The first was the infantry break-through. The second was the great tank battle at El Aqqaqir. The first made the second possible, and the second sealed the success of the first. The first was completed in just over nine days. The second in as many hours. When it was over, El Aqqaqir was a cemetery of Axis armour, and the Battle of Egypt was in fact won. The rest was pursuit."

General Montgomery's decision to make the break-through in the north paid big dividends in the tank battle. It prevented the enemy from employing his favourite methods of armoured counter-attack on the flanks. Montgomery's choice of battlefields forced the Axis to make frontal assaults on the X Corps, and in the daylight hours of November 2, General Thoma's tanks were outfought by

British tanks and assault guns. Losses were heavy in the X Corps but since the British remained in possession of the battlefield many disabled tanks were repairable. Every German tank that dropped out of the fight through damage or lack of fuel was a complete loss. After the battle 260 enemy tanks were counted on the field at El Aqqaqir.

That the tank battle of El Aqqaqir decided the issue was immediately indicated by German and Italian infantry action. To quote the British official account:

> On November 2, the day of the tank battle, there were already signs of infantry withdrawal all along the front. On November 3 these signs became very definite. In the south the Italian divisions could not retreat far, for they were abandoned by the Germans, who commandeered all transport for their own men. Hardly a man of the six Italian infantry divisions escaped. Droves of prisoners were taken. The German 164th Light Division also lost heavily. Even though the Germans were the first to retreat after the battle was lost, they left behind over 8,000 prisoners apart from their killed and wounded. The Battle of Egypt cost the Axis 75,000 men, over 500 tanks, and over 1,000 guns.

Total British casualties to November 11 were 13,600 killed, wounded, and missing.

In the words of Mr. Churchill, the "bright gleam of victory" at El Alamein "caught the helmets of our soldiers and warmed and cheered our hearts." Combined with the magnificent victories of the Red army and the Allied landing in French North Africa, it assisted in wresting the initiative from the Axis. At last, the Eighth Army had produced leadership capable of exploiting to the full the human and material resources available. General Montgomery outwitted and outfought the Afrika Korps. British tactical methods were at last equal if not superior to those of the enemy.

The disposition and leadership of the Afrika Korps at El Alamein were faulty, a fact which Montgomery good-naturedly pointed out to captured General Thoma. He expressed regret that Thoma was not Rommel because he had always "wanted to talk over things" with the latter. He regarded Rommel as a good fighter but no superman, pointing out that he had a tendency to repeat his tactics. Whether Rommel was personally responsible for the decision

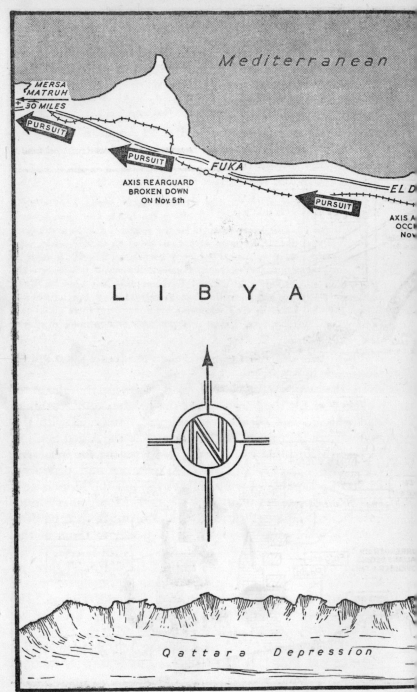

MERSA
MATRUH
30 MILES
PURSUIT

PURSUIT

AXIS REARGUARD
BROKEN DOWN
ON Nov. 5th

Mediterranean

FUKA

EL D

PURSUIT

AXIS A
OCC
Nov

L I B Y A

Qattara Depression

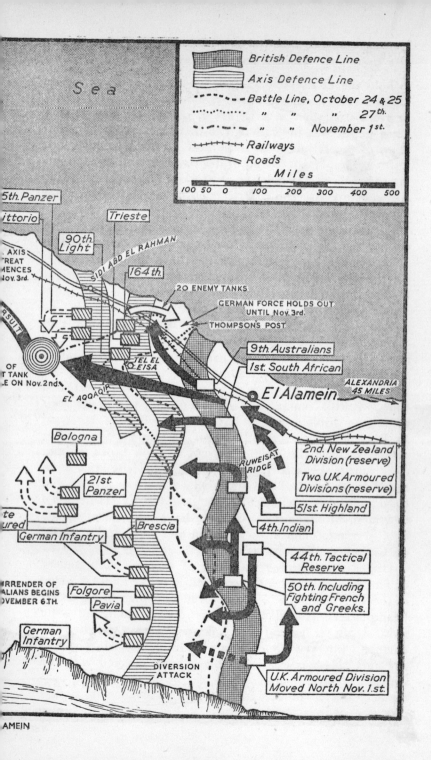

Sea

British Defence Line
Axis Defence Line
Battle Line, October 24 & 25
" " " 27th.
" " " November 1st.
Railways
Roads
Miles

100 50 0 100 200 300 400 500

5th. Panzer

ittorio

90th. Light

Trieste

SIDI ABD EL RAHMAN

AXIS REAT ENCES ov. 3rd.

164th.

20 ENEMY TANKS
GERMAN FORCE HOLDS OUT
UNTIL Nov. 3rd.
THOMPSON'S POST

RSUIT

9th. Australians
1st. South African

OF T TANK E ON Nov. 2nd.

TEL EL Q. EISA

EL AQQAQIR

El Alamein

ALEXANDRIA 45 MILES

Bologna

RUWEISAT RIDGE

2nd. New Zealand Division (reserve)

Two U.K. Armoured Divisions (reserve)

21st. Panzer

te ured

German Infantry

Brescia

51st. Highland

4th. Indian

RRENDER OF ALIANS BEGINS OVEMBER 6.TH.

Folgore

Pavia

44th. Tactical Reserve

50th. Including Fighting French and Greeks.

German Infantry

DIVERSION ATTACK

U.K. Armoured Division Moved North Nov. 1st.

AMEIN

to hold the El Alamein line, or whether he was acting on Hitler's orders, cannot be determined. If a British attack in great strength was anticipated, then a defence in very great depth was indicated. The mere possession of a few miles of desert might be important for Axis prestige, but it was not important from a strategic standpoint. By attempting to hold a thin strong line at El Alamein the leader of the Afrika Korps risked the destruction or capture of his main forces.

For two long years the Eighth Army had tried in vain to destroy the Afrika Korps. More than once it came close to achieving this end; but Rommel's skill in mechanized war, his capacity for keeping armour concentrated, his flair for tactical improvisation, his excellent transport and tank-repair service, and the superior quality of his armour and anti-tank guns turned prospective British victories into defeats. The Eighth Army learned mechanized desert warfare in the harsh school of lost battles. In previous campaigns the Eighth Army had possessed superiority in the air, but this in itself was insufficient to prevent German victories. Earlier British commanders had a tendency to commit their armour in driblets, only to have each small force destroyed by Rommel's concentrated armour. It took repeated bitter defeats to teach British tankers not to fight tanks without close anti-tank support. Never before Montgomery's command did the ground and air forces work in absolute unison. Co-operation was replaced by command at El Alamein. To newsmen, Montgomery said: "We have just one plan, one idea in mind. There is no army on one hand and air force on the other. We work as a unit."

Under the warming influence of success, Montgomery expanded visibly. After the completion of the infantry phase of the El Alamein battle he received newsmen in his desert headquarters. He talked to them easily, balancing a fly swish deftly on the end of one finger. "I have defeated the enemy. I am now about to smash him—how do you like my hat?" He was wearing a black beret covered with the insignia of several units. Suddenly he broke off the conference, heaved himself into his reconnaissance tank, and disappeared in a cloud of dust.

When pressed for his secret of success in battle, Montgomery laid down the following requirements for a good general:

1. Have a good chief of staff.
2. Go for simplicity in everything.
3. Cut out all paper and train subordinates to work on verbal instructions and orders.
4. Keep a firm grip on basic fundamentals; the things that really matter.
5. Avoid being involved in details; leave them to your staff.
6. Study morale; it is a big thing in war. Without high morale you can achieve nothing.
7. When the issue hangs in the balance express confidence in the plans and in the operations, even if inwardly you feel not too certain of the outcome.
8. Never worry.
9. Never bellyache.

Before each battle he issued an order to the troops telling what he intended to do and why. As the campaign progressed he showed them in subsequent orders how his plans had worked out through their efforts. This practice had a cumulative effect in building up their confidence in him until nothing he asked for seemed impossible. He assured the army he would never order them into battle unless he was satisfied that the operation had a reasonable chance of success. As a result no general ever had a more devoted army under his command.*

Despite all Montgomery could do, part of the Afrika Korps escaped destruction by a hasty retreat. Further heavy losses in men and equipment marked the Axis attempts to put up rearguard actions at Fuka (November 6), Matruh (November 8), and Bug Bug (November 10). Over the dusty roads to the west, in an endless stream, the trucks of General Sir Wilfrid Lindsell (the Eighth Army's supply officer) rolled forward. But in spite of herculean efforts, the Eighth Army was never able to bring the remnants of the Afrika Korps to decisive battle. Two heavy rains held up British tanks and fuel trucks. The retreat continued through Cyrenaica and Libya into Tripolitania.

* Typical examples of Montgomery's orders to the Eighth Army can be found in Major Peter W. Rainier's *Pipeline to Battle: An Engineer's Adventures with the Eighth Army* (New York, 1944), pp. 297–302.

Names associated with former triumphs and defeats came into the news in succession: Halfaya Pass, Sollum, Tobruk, Derna, Benghazi, and El Agheila. Montgomery made a bold effort to cut off Rommel at El Agheila by sending the 5th and 6th New Zealand brigades across the desert behind the retreating Germans, but the line to be held at Wadi Matratin was too long and Rommel filtered through.

Thirteen weeks after he began to advance General Montgomery entered Tripoli and put an end to the fascist dream of empire in North Africa. In thirteen weeks he had advanced 1,300 miles and reached objectives that had been beyond the strength of Wavell, Cunningham, and Ritchie. After months of desert campaigning, Montgomery insisted that the Eighth Army appear in spotless order in the victory parade in Tripoli. This gave rise to the story (doubtless apocryphal) that Churchill jokingly said to him in Tripoli: "If you keep this up, they'll say about you, 'Montgomery, indomitable in defeat, invincible in retreat, insufferable in victory'." The victory parade over, Montgomery moved his army forward toward the Mareth line guarding the Axis flank in Tunisia.

Montgomery's victory at El Alamein and the advance to Tripoli were parts of a larger Allied plan to drive the Axis out of Africa. American and British troops landed in French North Africa, on November 8, 1942, but failed to take the all-important ports of Tunis and Bizerte in their first improvised advance. German and Italian troops were transported to Tunisia in numbers sufficient to check this venture, and the campaign settled into bad-weather positional warfare in which each side built up its strength. Meantime, Rommel had withdrawn the remnants of the Afrika Korps behind the dismantled Mareth line and awaited the advance of the Eighth Army. Large-scale Italian infantry and tank reinforcements (later called the First Italian Panzer Army) gave Rommel a formidable force. To offset this somewhat, the possession of Tripoli gave Montgomery harbour facilities for receiving supplies by sea from Egypt.

Taking advantage of Montgomery's slow approach to the Mareth line, Rommel struck swiftly with part of his forces against the American position at Gafsa, on February 14,

1943. Breaking through the thin line at Faïd and Kasserine passes, he threatened the great Allied supply bases at Thala and Tebessa but was turned back on February 22.

Perhaps his easy progress in the first stages of the Gafsa–Faïd–Kasserine operation caused Rommel to become careless. Switching his forces back to the Mareth line he tried the same tactics on Montgomery near Medenine, on March 6. The almost insolent manner in which he handled his armour showed that he had learned little from previous contacts with the Eighth Army. Montgomery cleverly decoyed him on. Forward British gun crews abandoned their pieces in mock terror when the German tanks appeared. Without waiting for further reconnaissance, the German tankers swallowed the bait, closed their hatches, and roared in for the kill. Then, suddenly, Montgomery's real tank defences were unmasked. A wall of fire blasted the leading column and stopped the advance cold. When the enemy retreated they left fifty-two wrecked tanks on the field. It was now the Eighth Army's turn to resume the offensive.

Allied military operations in Tunisia were co-ordinated by the reorganization of February 20, 1943, which placed General Eisenhower in over-all command of Allied forces in North Africa. Direct command of the armies in Tunisia fell to General Alexander as head of the newly formed 18th Army Group composed of the British First Army, the British Eighth Army, the United States II Corps, and the French XIX Corps. The Allied air forces in this theatre were reorganized two days earlier under the supreme command of Air Marshal Tedder. This effected a division of forces into a strategic air force under Major-General Doolittle, a tactical air force under Air Marshal Coningham, a coastal command force under Air Vice-Marshal Lloyd, and a photographic wing under Colonel Roosevelt. In the light of future developments it seems safe to say that these reorganizations made the overwhelming victory of May 6–13 possible.

Though the reorganization of the air forces did not materially change General Montgomery's relations with Air Marshal Coningham, with whom he had worked in closest

harmony since El Alamein, it extended the benefits of the
system for air-ground operations which these two men had
worked out to the rest of the forces in Tunisia. General
Eisenhower sanctioned the general policy that the air programme in North Africa should be determined upon and
carried out by the air officers but insisted upon real integra-
tion of air and ground operations. The experience of El
Alamein showed that until the enemy air force had been
cut down, no effective air support to ground troops was
possible. Thus the main weight of Allied air power in North
Africa was directed first at the bases of Axis air power and
the lines supplying it. Then, after a working command of
the air had been attained, Allied air power was thrown into
direct support of ground operations. This arrangement
enabled Air Marshal Tedder to achieve a concentration and
flexibility in the use of the air weapon which the Axis could
not match.

An example of how this concept of air-ground co-operation
worked out in practice is to be found in the operations of
the Eighth Army which led to the forcing of the Mareth line.
Though the forts of this former French defence zone had
been disarmed, the position was still one of great natural
strength. Finally, on March 20, Montgomery was prepared
to attack the Mareth position. Allied air forces in northern
Tunisia kept German air power under heavy attack, allowing
Coningham, who virtually lived at Montgomery's headquarters, a chance to use his tactical air force in direct
support of the Eighth Army. When the frontal attack at
Wadi Zigzaou failed, Montgomery varied his usual frontal
push and right hook; he threw the New Zealand Division
under General Freyberg around the left flank of the Mareth
line in a brilliant march over rough terrain toward El
Hamma. When this movement met with initial success,
Montgomery boldly reinforced success and sent the 1st
British Armoured Division to support the flanking movement. General Messe, who succeeded Rommel on the
Southern front, hastily countered by sending crack German
and Italian armoured forces and infantry to defend El
Hamma and the approaches to Gabes. On March 26 the
battle for El Hamma reached a climax. Coningham threw

every plane that could carry a bomb or fire its machine guns into the battle. A sustained air attack on the Axis position, which featured the employment of Hurricane "tank busters," cracked the defence wide open. Here it was that the 164th German Light Division was caught moving on a road and cut up by fighter-bombers, paving the way for the advance of British armour and infantry.

The victory at El Hamma undermined the Axis position on the Mareth line and forced a withdrawal to Wadi Akarit. A surprise attack on the moonless night of April 5 by the 4th Indian Division cracked the Axis position at Wadi Akarit, driving the Afrika Korps northward to its final position at Enfidaville on April 24.* The Axis line then ran from that point to Pont-du-Fahs–Medjez-el-bab to the sea west of Bizerte. Arnim placed his strongest forces opposite the Eighth Army—a tribute to that army and its leaders.

Banking on the legendary reputation of Montgomery, General Alexander boldly detached the 1st Armoured Division from the Eighth Army and sent it northward to reinforce Anderson's First Army. He also sent the United States II Corps across the lines of the British First Army to a position from which it could menace Sedjenane and Mateur. Thus, using the threat of Montgomery's all victorious Eighth Army at Enfidaville, General Alexander concentrated a decisive superiority against Arnim in the north. He even transferred the 7th Armoured and 4th Indian Divisions from the Eighth Army to Anderson in the last stages of the battle.

After ten days of savage fighting in the north, the British First Army and the American II Corps broke through the Axis positions behind a moving carpet of bombs, crashed into Tunis and Bizerte, and overwhelmed the Afrika Korps. By May 6 all organization in the Axis forces in the north disappeared. Mass surrenders followed; on May 13 the campaign was over.

General Alexander is a hard man to please and General

* For an account of this brilliant attack led by the 2nd Gurkhas, see Lieutenant-Colonel G. R. Stevens, "The Gurkhas at Fatnassa," in the *Army Quarterly*, XLVII, pp. 191–197, January, 1944.

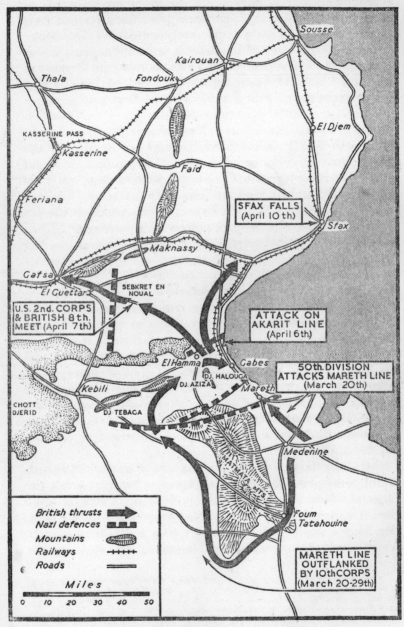

THE TUNISIAN CAMPAIGN (March-April, 1943)

Montgomery is not an easy man to get along with, yet at the end of the Tunisian campaign the former remarked: "When you have a good army commander leave him alone. All I have to do is tell Monty what I want and he goes ahead and does it. I never have to worry about him." Together, Alexander and Montgomery made a combination whose achievement gave a new sense of pride to British arms everywhere.

Asked by an American correspondent to sum up the lessons of the Tunisian campaign, Montgomery replied: "First concentrate your forces; second, knit your ground and air forces together. That's it. Knit ground and air together. Knit them together absolutely."

In his opinion it was necessary to win the "air battle" before you could win the ground battle. Accordingly, Montgomery urged that theatre air forces be commanded by air officers guided only by the broad general directives of the theatre commander.*

In July and August, 1943, Montgomery led the Eighth Army through some of the hardest fighting of the Sicilian campaign. At the close of that campaign his troops were the first to break into the fortress of Europe. On September 3, the day on which Italy signed the armistice, his troops landed at Reggio Calabria. When the United States Fifth Army and the British forces made a daring landing at Salerno, his troops finally forced the enemy to release his grip on the Allied beachhead. From that time on until December 24 he directed operations on the eastern side of the peninsula.

On Christmas, 1943, it was announced that General Montgomery would command the ground forces under General Eisenhower's new command. It was a task he welcomed with scriptural phrases. No appointment could have been more popular with the British people. They knew that it was largely Montgomery's personality and leadership that

---

* The memorandum he wrote on this subject was so impressive that much of his language was incorporated directly into Field Service Regulations F.M. 100-20, *Command and Employment of Air Power*, which the United States War Department issued after the Tunisian campaign. This is the first instance in modern times in which the words of a foreign officer were embodied directly in American doctrine.

gave the British army the skill and spirit required to defeat the Afrika Korps.

Montgomery introduced something new into British military history—army esprit de corps. There had been regimental esprit de corps before but not a spirit that distinguished a whole army. In his Christmas message to the Eighth Army on taking leave of them, he said: "Wherein lies the strength of this great army? It lies in its team spirit, in the firm determination of every man to do his duty, and in its high morale. This army is a great family with a spirit the like of which has seldom been seen before."

It was a relief to Montgomery to be assigned command of the ground forces for "Overlord." Fighting in Italy was not to his liking. It afforded little scope for his particular genius, pinning an enemy down to a given front and then making the necessary preparations for his destruction. There was always another river line or mountain defence position for the Germans to fall back upon in Italy. He left before the heart-breaking assault on Cassino and the long-drawn out agony of Anzio beach. On January 1, 1944, Montgomery met the Prime Minister and General Eisenhower, at Marrakesch, and for the first time saw "Cossac," the plan for invading France.

After a few days' study of "Cossac," Montgomery came to the same conclusion Eisenhower arrived at independently: namely, that the plan to deliver a seaborne assault against the German Atlantic front with three divisions in the assault wave was not soundly conceived. He recommended employing five divisions with two divisions in the immediate follow-up plus two or, if possible, three airborne divisions. This was the basis on which "Overlord" was launched.

The period of preparation for invading France found Montgomery immersed in perfecting his command arrangements and raising the fighting morale of the troops. He visited nearly every invasion installation and made countless speeches to officers and men. As for his plan of ground operations, Montgomery wrote:

"Once ashore and firmly established, my plan was to threaten to break out of the initial bridgehead on the eastern flank—that is, in the Caen sector. I intended by means of this threat to draw the main enemy reserves into that sector, to fight them there and keep them there, using the British and Canadian armies for the purpose. Having got the main enemy reserves committed on the eastern flank, my plan was to make the break-out on the western flank, using for this task the American armies under General Bradley, and to pivot the whole front on Caen. The American break-out thrust was to be delivered southwards down to the Loire and then to be developed eastwards in a wide sweep up to the Seine about Paris. This movement was designed to cut off all the enemy forces south of the Seine, over which river the bridges were to be destroyed by air action."

Perhaps no other great strategic plan has been carried out more exactly than Montgomery's plan for destroying the German Seventh Army west of the Seine. His apparent "slowness" in front of Caen gave rise to considerable criticism in both British and American circles, but he drew eight of the ten German armoured divisions in the West to that sector and held them there until the break-out of General Bradley's forces led to the partial encirclement of the German troops in the Mortain–Falaise trap. It is a mighty tribute to the sustained pressure Montgomery's forces maintained on the Caen front that no single massive German counter-offensive occurred during the build-up phase of the invasion. Until his incapacitation through wounds in July, Field Marshal Rommel was reduced to the painful process of "plugging leaks." He was never able to concentrate sufficient forces to really hurt the invader.

It should be said that Hitler's fantastic strategy of not yielding an inch of French territory was a powerful aid to Montgomery in these operations. German losses in the Mortain–Falaise pocket amounted to about 500,000 men, 3,500 guns and 1,000 tanks together with immense captures of trucks, horse transport and equipment. Forty-three German divisions had been destroyed or severely handled. Twenty army, corps, and divisional commanders had been killed or captured. It was a victory of massive proportions which 'sealed the fate of the Third Reich.

Arrangements had been made prior to the invasion that after the activation of the U.S. Twelfth Army Group, General Eisenhower would take direct control of the land battle. This control was assumed on September 1, 1944, leaving Montgomery in command of the Twenty-First Army

Group. On the same day he was raised to the rank of Field Marshal.

At the end of August, Montgomery made a proposal to General Eisenhower which should put at an end all criticisms of his cautiousness and the claim that he delayed operations until his "administrative tail was tidied up." He proposed an immediate single thrust across the Rhine in the north involving the whole logistical resources of the Allied armies. To Montgomery's way of thinking such an advance would prevent the Germans from meeting weakness (in a broad front advance) with weakness and might, by isolating the Ruhr, end the war in three months. This proposal which, interestingly enough, was not supported by Montgomery's Chief-of-Staff, was rejected by General Eisenhower in favour of a broad front advance to the Rhine and the opening of the Port of Antwerp.

It is idle to speculate on what might have happened if Montgomery's proposal had become the basic plan of operations after crossing the Seine. The remnants of the German Seventh and Fifteenth armies soon received a powerful stimulant in the reorganizing ability of Field Marshal Model. Despite losses in France, the Third Reich still had a considerable number of panzer grenadier divisions in process of formation and training. The fate of the Arnhem operation showed what hazards a thin, strong advance might have faced. In the end, Field Marshal Brooke enthusiastically admitted that Eisenhower's plan of destroying the remaining bulk of the German forces west of the Rhine was the correct one.

The autumn of 1944 found Montgomery pressing for a single ground force commander in the West. He wanted, however, to retain command of the Twenty-First Army Group if he were chosen to command the ground forces, but he agreed to serve under Bradley if the latter were selected. For reasons he makes clear in his memoirs, General Eisenhower refused to appoint a single ground commander, but having silenced Montgomery's repeated insistence on this matter after the Ardennes battle, he generously placed the U.S. Ninth Army under Montgomery's command for the approach and crossing of the Rhine.

The German armies in the west were defeated before a single Allied soldier crossed the Rhine. It was poetic justice that when Admiral von Freideburg approached the Allied armies to surrender in May, 1945, he came to Montgomery's caravan camp at Lüneburg heath. Like a training sergeant, Montgomery told the German delegates where to stand and after having read out the terms of surrender, told them where to sign. He had fought the ground forces of nazi Germany longer than any Allied officer in the west. His road of victory had led from Egypt to the Baltic. In this moment of triumph, Montgomery permitted himself a single question of the Germans. Showing Admiral von Freideburg a picture of Rundstedt, he inquired if it were a good likeness of the Field Marshal. The German admiral agreed that it was.

It would be misleading to convey the impression that these mighty Allied military triumphs were achieved without an inevitable amount of discord and controversy between Allied leaders. These disagreements, particularly those involving Montgomery, have been twisted out of their true significance by certain American writers, notably the journalist Ralph Ingersoll and General Eisenhower's aide, Captain Harry Butcher. The result has not been fortunate. No great campaign waged by Allies had ever been conducted with greater unity. War is a passionate, violent affair and men strong enough to wage it successfully are bound to differ on methods. The amazing fact about the campaign in western Europe is *not* that a certain amount of controversy developed between leaders in its conduct, the amazing thing is that this controversy never seriously interfered with the continuous victorious development of agreed upon strategy.

Field Marshal Montgomery admitted more than once that he was a difficult person to get along with. He fought for his ideas to the limit of his power, but, as General Eisenhower has testified, once a decision was made, he carried out his part of the agreement with absolute loyalty. Montgomery resisted pressure of the Prime Minister to begin the Alamein offensive in September, 1942, instead of October. He resisted pressure from Mr. Churchill to reduce the agreed upon number of vehicles to accompany the landing in Normandy. He repeatedly refused to attack until he was certain that every administrative arrangement had been made to ensure maximum chances of victory.

Perhaps his unique success as a soldier was due to his concept that high morale above everything else was essential to victory. After the war, he wrote:

> "I call high morale the greatest single factor in war. A high morale is based on discipline, self-respect and confidence of the soldier in his commanders, in his weapons, and in himself. Without high morale, no success can be achieved—however good may be the strategical or tactical plan, or anything else. High morale is a pearl of very great price. And a sure way to obtain it is by success in battle."

After serving for a term with the occupation forces in Germany, Montgomery became Chief of the Imperial General Staff. Later, as the shadow of communist aggression threatened western Europe, he became the first head of the Franco–British–Belgian–Dutch defence staff. Montgomery's record of uninterrupted success is unique in the annals of modern history. He was never defeated in a single operation which he planned or directed *alone*. Coming to command after defeats in Norway, France and the Mediterranean area, he laid the spiritual foundations for the British Army's role in the defeat of nazi Germany.

Biographical Data

on each

General

CROMWELL

Born	April 25, 1599
Matriculated at Cambridge	April 23, 1616
Married Elizabeth Bourchier	August 22, 1620
M.P. for Huntingdon	1628
"Conversion"	1638
Short Parliament	1640
Created Colonel	February, 1643
Lieutenant-General under Manchester	January, 1644
Battle of Marston Moor	July 3, 1644
Battle of Naseby	June 14, 1645
Collapse of Royalists	June, 1645–July, 1646
Battle of Preston	August 17, 1648
Treaty of Newport	September–October, 1648
Execution of Charles I	January 30, 1649
Irish Campaigns	August, 1649–May, 1650
Commander-in-Chief	June 26, 1650
Battle of Dunbar	September 3, 1650
Battle of Worcester	September 3, 1651
Act of pardon and oblivion	February 24, 1652
Dissolved the Long Parliament	April 20, 1653
Installed as Protector	December 16, 1653
Attempted assassination	May, 1654
Dissolved first Protectorate Parliament	January 22, 1655
Offered the crown	March, 1657
Acceptance of revised "Humble Petition and Advice"	May 25, 1657
Died	September 3, 1658

MARLBOROUGH

JOHN CHURCHILL, 1st Duke of Marlborough (created 1685).

Born	June 6, 1650
Commissioned Ensign	September 14, 1667
Under Turenne in Flanders	1674
Married Sarah Jennings	about 1678
With Duke of York in Brussels and Edinburgh .	1679–1681
Battle of Sedgemoor	July 5, 1685
Glorious Revolution—Churchill at Salisbury.	November, 1688
Created Earl of Marlborough and member of Privy Council	1689(1)
In Flanders under Waldeck	1689
Dismissed from Army	January, 1692
Restored to favour	April, 1698
Accession of Queen Anne	March, 1702
Battle of the Schellenberg	July 2, 1704
Battle of Blenheim	August 13, 1704
Battle of Ramillies	May 23, 1706
Battle of Oudenarde	July 11, 1708
Battle of Malplaquet	September 11, 1709
Marlborough dismissed	December 31, 1711
Retired from England	November, 1712
Death of Queen Anne and return of Marlborough.	August, 1714
Died	June 16, 1722

Earldom awarded by William of Orange.

WELLINGTON

SIR ARTHUR WELLESLEY, 1st Duke of Wellington (created 1814);
1st Marquis of Douro (1814); 1st Marquis of Wellington (1812);
1st Earl of Wellington (1812).

Born in Dublin.	April 29, 1769
Commissioned Ensign	March 7, 1787
Capture of Seringapatane	May 4, 1799
Battle of Assaye	September 23, 1803
Expedition to Copenhagen	August–September, 1807
Passage of Douro	May 12, 1809
Entering of lines of Torres Vedras	October 10, 1810
Taking of Badajoz	April 6, 1812
Capture of Madrid	August 12, 1812
Vitoria and promotion to Field Marshal	June 21, 1813
Invasion of France	November 10, 1813
Toulouse	April 10, 1814
Ambassador at Paris	July 5, 1814
Plenipotentiary at Vienna	January 24, 1815
Battle of Waterloo	June 18, 1815
Congress of Verona	October 22, 1822
Mission to St. Petersburg	February 8, 1826
Commander-in-Chief	January 22, 1827
Prime Minister	February 14, 1828
Cabinet Minister	June 23, 1841
Died	September 14, 1852

KITCHENER

Sir Horatio Herbert Kitchener, 1st Earl (created 1914) Kitchener of Khartoum and of Broome.

Born County Kerry	June 24, 1850
Educated Royal Military College, Woolwich . .	1868–1871
Commissioned Royal Engineers	1871
Palestine Survey	1874–1878
Cyprus Survey	1878–1882
Commanded Egyptian Cavalry	1882–1884
Nile Expedition	1884–1885
Governor of Suakim	1886–1888
Adjutant-General, Egyptian Army	1888–1892
Commanded Dongola Expeditionary Force	1896
Commanded Khartoum Expedition	1898
Chief of Staff, Forces in South Africa	1899–1900
Commander-in-Chief, South Africa	1900–1902
Member of Committee of Imperial Defence	1910
Consul-General in Egypt	1911–1914
Secretary of State for War	1914–1916
Died	June 5, 1916

HAIG

Sir Douglas Haig, 1st Earl, Viscount Dawick, Baron Haig and 29th Laird of Bemersyde.

Born	June 19, 1861
Educated at Clifton	–
Brasenose College, Oxford	1880–1883
Royal Military College, Sandhurst	1883–1884
Joined 7th Hussars	1885
Served in the Soudan	1898
Served in South Africa	1900–1902
Married Hon. Dorothy Vivian	1905
Inspector-General of Cavalry in India	1903–1906
Chief of Staff, India	1909–1912
General Officer Commanding, Aldershot	1912–1914
Commander-in-Chief Expeditionary Forces in France and Flanders	1915–1919
Died	January 29, 1928

ALLENBY

SIR EDMUND HENRY HYNMAN ALLENBY, 1st Viscount (created 1919) of Megiddo and of Felixstowe.

Born . . . . April 23, 1861
Educated Haileybury: Royal Military College, Sandhurst –
Served Bechuanaland Expedition 1884–1885
Served in Zululand 1888
Adjutant Inniskilling Dragoons 1889–1893
Married Adelaide Mabel Chapman 1896
Served in South Africa 1899–1902
Inspector of Cavalry 1910–1914
Commander of Cavalry, British Expeditionary Force, European War 1914
Commander of Fifth Army Corps, British Expeditionary Force 1915
Commander of Third Army, British Expeditionary Force 1915–1917
Commander-in-Chief Egyptian Expeditionary Force, throughout Palestine Campaign 1917–1919
High Commissioner for Egypt 1919–1925
Died . . . . May 14, 1936

WAVELL

SIR ARCHIBALD PERCIVAL WAVELL, 1st Earl (created 1947); Viscount Keren of Eritrea and of Winchester, 1947; Viscount Wavell of Cyrenaica and of Winchester, 1943.

Born	May, 1883
Educated Winchester College: Royal Military College, Sandhurst	—
Appointed to the Black Watch	1901
Served in South African War	1901–1902
Served Indian Frontier	1908
Married Eugenie Marie Quirk, C.I.	1915
Served European War	1914–1918
In France	1914–1916
Military Attache with Russian Army in Caucasus . .	1916–1917
With Egyptian Expeditionary Force	1917–1920
B.G.G.S. XX Corps	1918–1919
B.G.G.S. E.E.F.	1919–1920
Commanded 6th Infantry Brigade, Aldershot . .	1930–1934
Commanded 2nd Division, Aldershot . . .	1935–1937
Commanded troops in Palestine and Transjordan . .	1937–1938
General Officer Commanding Southern Command .	1938–1939
Commander-in-Chief, Middle East . . .	1939–1941
Commander-in-Chief, India	1941–1943
Supreme Commander, South West Pacific .	January–March, 1942
Viceroy and Governor-General, India . . .	1943–1947
Appointed Colonel, The Black Watch (R.H.R.) . .	1946
Appointed High Steward of Colchester . . .	1947
Appointed Constable of the Tower of London . .	1948
Died	May, 1950

ALEXANDER

Sir Harold Rupert Leofric George Alexander, 1st Viscount (created 1946) of Tunis.

Born . . . . December 10, 1891	
Educated Harrow: Royal Military College, Sandhurst .	–
Served European War	1914–1918
General Staff Officer 1st Grade, Northern Command .	1923–1924
Commanded Regiment and Regimental District (Irish Guards)	1928–1930
Married Lady Margaret Bingham	1931
Commanded Nowshera Brigade, Northern Command, India	1934–1938
Loe Agra Operations, North-West	1935
Mohmaud Operations	1935
Commanded 1st Division	1938–1940
General Officer Commanding, Southern Command .	1940–1942
General Officer Commanding, Burma	1942
Commander-in-Chief, Middle East . . .	1942–1943
Deputy Commander-in-Chief, North Africa . . .	1943
Deputy Commander-in-Chief, Allied Forces, Combined Operations, Mediterranean	1943
General Officer Commanding, Allied Forces and Military Governor of Sicily	1943–1944
Commander-in-Chief Allied Armies in Italy . . .	1944
Supreme Commander Allied Armies, Mediterranean Theatre	1944–1945
Governor-General, Canada	1946

MONTGOMERY

SIR BERNARD LAW MONTGOMERY, 1st Viscount (created 1946) of
Alamein and of Hindhead.

Born . . . . November 17, 1887
Educated St. Paul's School . . . . . –
Entered Army 1908
Served European War 1914–1918
Married Mrs. Betty Carver 1927
Commanded 1st Battalion, Royal Warwickshire Regiment 1931–1934
General Staff Officer, 1st Grade: Staff College Quetta . 1934–1937
Commanded 9th Infantry Brigade, Portsmouth . . 1937–1938
Commanded 8th Division 1938–1939
Commanded 3rd Division 1939–1940
Commanded 5th Corps 1940
Commanded 12th Corps 1941
Commanded S.E. Army 1942
Commanded 8th Army during Campaigns in North Africa,
Sicily and Italy 1942
Commander-in-Chief, British Group of Armies and Allied
Armies, Northern France 1944
Commander-in-Chief, 21st Army Group . . . 1944–1945
Commander-in-Chief, British Army of the Rhine . . 1945–1946
Chief of the Imperial General Staff 1946–1948
Permanent Military Chairman, Commander-in-Chief in Com-
mittee, Permanent Defence Organization 1948

Bibliographies arranged

in the same order

as the essays

CROMWELL

Abbot, W. C., *Bibliography of Oliver Cromwell*. 1929.

Baldock, Lieutenant-Colonel T. S., *Cromwell as a Soldier*. 1899.

Bauer, Colonel F. G. B., *Cromwell as a Cavalry Leader*. Vol. 26. 1936.

Belloc, H., *Oliver Cromwell*. 1931.

Buchan, J., *Oliver Cromwell*. 1934.

Carlyle, T., *Oliver Cromwell's Letters and Speeches*. 1845.

Cust, General Sir E., *Oliver Cromwell, a Parliamentary General*. (In "Lives of the Warriors of the Civil Wars of France and England." 1867. Pt. 2.)

Firth, Sir C. H., *Cromwell's Army*. 1902.

——, *Last Years of the Protectorate, 1656–1658*. 1909.

——, *Oliver Cromwell and the Rule of the Puritans in England*. 1935.

Morley, J., Viscount. *Oliver Cromwell*. 1900.

Wedgwood, C. V., *Oliver Cromwell*. 1939.

MARLBOROUGH

Ashley, M., *Marlborough*. 1939.

Atkinson, C. T., *Marlborough and the Rise of the British Army*. 1921.

Belloc, H., *The Tactics and the Strategy of the Great Duke of Marlborough*. 1933.

Broderick, T., *A Complete History of the Late War in the Netherlands*. 1713.

Campbell, J., *The Military History of the Prince Eugene of Savoy and of the late John, Duke of Marlborough*. 2 vols. 1736–7.

Churchill, Rt. Hon. W. S., *Marlborough: His Life and Times*. 1933–8. 4 vols.

Coxe, W., *Memoirs of John, Duke of Marlborough*. 3 vols. 1818–9.

Edwards, H. J. and E. A., *A Short Life of Marlborough*. 1926.

Kane, General R., *Campaigns of King William and the Duke of Marlborough*. 1745.

Maycock, Captain F. W. O., *An Outline of Marlborough's Campaigns*. 1913.

Millner, Sergeant J., *Compendious Journal of all the Marches, Famous Battles and Sieges of the Confederate Allies in their late war*. 1933.

Murray, Sir G., Editor. *The Letters and Despatches of John Churchill, first Duke of Marlborough, from* 1702 *to* 1712. 5 vols. 1845.

WELLINGTON

Aldington, R., *The Duke; being an Account of the Life and Achievements of A. Wellesley, 1st Duke of Wellington.* 1943.

Fortescue, J. W., *Wellington.* 1925.

Guedella, P., *The Duke.* 1931.

Gurwood, Lieutenant-Colonel J., *Despatches of Field Marshal The Duke of Wellington.* 12 vols. 1834–1838.

——, Editor. *Parliamentary Speeches.* 1854.

Maxwell, Rt. Hon. Sir H. E., *The Life of Wellington, etc.* 6th edition. 2 vols. (in 1). 1907.

Oman, Sir C., *The History of the Peninsular War.* 1902. 1930.

——, *Wellington's Army.* 1912.

Roberts, Field Marshal Rt. Hon. F. S., Earl, *The Rise of Wellington.* 1895.

Sherer, Captain M., *Military Memoirs of Field Marshal the Duke of Wellington.* 1830-32.

Tickner, F. W., *Wellington.* 1941.

Despatches, Correspondence and Memoranda (1818–1832), edited by the Second Duke of Wellington. 8 vols. 1867–1880.

The Supplementary Despatches, Correspondence and Memoranda, edited by the Second Duke of Wellington. 15 vols. 1858–1872.

KITCHENER

Arthur, Sir G., *Life of Lord Kitchener.* 1920.

Ballard, C. R., *Kitchener.* 1930.

Burleigh, B., *Sirdah and Khalifa.* 1898.

Cooke, A. O., *Story of Lord Kitchener.* 1936.

Davray, H. D., *Lord Kitchener; his work and prestige.* 1917.

De Watteville, Lieutenant-Colonel H., *Lord Kitchener.* 1939.

De Weerd, H. A., *Kitchener* (in *Great Soldiers of the Two World Wars*). 1941.

Esher, R., 2nd Viscount, *The Tragedy of Lord Kitchener.* 1921.

Germains, V. W., *The Truth about Kitchener.* 1925.

Hodge, A., *Lord Kitchener.* 1936.

Moseley, S. A., *With Kitchener in Cairo.* 1917.

Steevens, G. W., *With Kitchener to Khartoum.* 1898.

HAIG

Arthur, Sir G., *Lord Haig.* 1928.

Boraston, Lieutenant-Colonel J. H., Editor. *Sir Douglas Haig's Despatches, December, 1915–April, 1919.* 2 vols. 1919.

Charteris, Brigadier-General J., *Field Marshal Earl Haig.* 1929.

——, *Haig.* (In *Great Lives.*) 1933.

Churchill, Winston S., *The World Crisis, 1911–1918.* 1931.

Cooper, Rt. Hon. A. D., *Haig.* 2 vols. 1935–1936.

Dewar, G. A. B., and Boraston, Lieutenant-Colonel J. H., *Sir Douglas Haig's Command, December 19, 1915 to November 11, 1918.* 2 vols. (in 1). 1929.

French, Major G., *French Replies to Haig.* 1936.

Hart, Captain B. H. Liddell, *Haig of Bemersyde.* (In *Reputations.*) 1928.

Johnston, C. H. L., *Sir Douglas Haig.* (In *Famous Generals of the Great War.*) 1919.

Simonds, F. H., *Haig.* (In *They Won the War.*) 1931.

ALLENBY

Hart, Captain B. H. Liddell, *History of the World War, 1914–1918.* 1919–1934.

——, *T. E. Lawrence in Arabia and After.* 1934.

H.M. Stationery Office, *The Egyptian Expeditionary Force, July 1917–October, 1918.* Compiled from official sources. 1919.

Lawrence, T. E., *Seven Pillars of Wisdom.* 1935.

Massey, W., *How Jerusalem was Won.* 1930.

Official History of The War: Campaigns in Palestine and Egypt. Vols. I and II. 1928, 1930.

Savage, R., with a preface by David Lloyd George, *Allenby of Armageddon.* 1926.

Wavell, General Sir A. P., *Allenby, A Study in Greatness.* 1940–1944.

WAVELL

Anon., "The Abyssinian Campaigns," the *Fighting Forces*, vol. XIX. December, 1942.

Anon., "The 4th Indian Division," the *Fighting Forces*, vol. XX. June, 1943.

Anon., "Sidi Barrani," the *Fighting Forces*, vol. XX. February, 1944.

British Information Service, *The Abyssinian Campaigns: The Official Story of the Conquest of Italian East Africa.* London, 1942.

——, *The Campaign in Greece and Crete.* London, 1942.

——, *Destruction of an Army: The First Libyan Campaign, September, 1940– February, 1941.* London, 1941.

——, *Making an Army.* London, 1942.

Clifford, Alexander, *The Conquest of North Africa, 1940–1943.* New York, 1943.

Collins, Major-General R. J., *Lord Wavell; a Military Biography.* 1948.

Hill, Russell, *Desert War.* New York, 1942.

Michie, Allan A., *Retreat to Victory.* New York, 1942.

Moorehead, Alan, *Mediterranean Front.* London, 1941.

Rainier, Major P. W., *Pipeline to Battle: An Engineer's Adventures with the British Eighth Army.* New York, 1944.

Rowan-Robinson, Major-General H., *With Wavell in the Middle East.* London, 1941.

Wavell, General A. P., *Allenby, a Study in Greatness.* New York, 1941.

—— Field Marshal, Viscount, *Allenby in Egypt.* London, 1944.

Wyndham, Colonel E. H., "Italy's One Victory," the *Army Quarterly*, vol. XLVI. August, 1943.

ALEXANDER

H.M.S.O. Publications of Lord Alexander: *African Campaign From El Alamein to Tunis, August, 1942–May, 1943.* February 5, 1948.

—— *Conquest of Sicily: July 10–August 17, 1943.* February 12, 1948.

—— *Greece 1944–1945: Report from the Supreme Allied Commander Mediterranean to the Combined Chiefs of Staff in Greece: December 12, 1944–May 9, 1945.* May 5, 1949.

"Illustrated London News": *General Alexander Covers the Middle East.* February 6, 1943.

MONTGOMERY

British Information Service, *The Army at War: Tunisia*.   London, 1944.
——, *The Eighth Army*. London, 1943.
Clifford, Alexander, *The Conquest of North Africa*.   Boston, 1943.
Churchill, Winston S., *The Second World War: The Gathering Storm*. London, 1948.
——, *The Second World War: Their Finest Hour*.   Boston, 1949.
Guingand, Major-Gen. Francis de, *Operation Victory*.   London, 1947.
Eisenhower, General Dwight D., *Crusade in Europe*.   London, 1948.
Freyberg, Lieut.-Gen. Bernard, "Dispatch on the Battle of El Hamma," *Wellington Dominion*.   N.Z., April 14, 1943.
Hart, Capt. B. H. Liddell, *Other Side of the Hill*.   London, 1948.
Montgomery, Field Marshal Viscount, of El Alamein, *El Alamein to the River Sangro*.   London, 1948.
——, *Normandy to the Baltic*.   London, 1946.
Moorehead, Alan, *Don't Blame the Generals*.   New York, 1943.
——, *The End in North Africa*.   New York, 1943.
——, *Montgomery: A Biography*.   New York, 1947.
Rainier, Major Peter W., *Pipeline to Battle: An Engineer's Adventures with the British Eighth Army*.   New York, 1944.
Report by the Supreme Commander to the Combined Chiefs of Staff on the Operations in Europe of the Allied Expeditionary Force, June 6, 1944 to May 8, 1945.   Washington, 1946.
Shulman, Major Milton, *Defeat in the West*.   New York, 1948.
Stacey, Col. C. P., *The Canadian Army, 1939–1945: An Official Historical Summary*.   Ottawa, 1948.

Index

INDEX